the

Featherweight

Patents

Darrel P. Kaiser

Published July 2007
Darrel P. Kaiser

Darrel Kaiser Books
www.DarrelKaiserBooks.com
email:Dar-Bet@att.net

First Edition

ISBN 978-0-6151-5434-3

The Author

Darrel P. Kaiser has been professionally trouble-shooting electrical, electronic, and mechanical components and systems for the US Government for the last 37 years. During those years, he also trained with PFAFF in Germany and Bernina USA in the art of professional sewing machine repair, and continues repair and restoration even today.

He has also been researching the development of the Germanic peoples and his ancestors for over 10 years. While living for over two years in Germany, Darrel "walked the lanes" and did on-site research in the villages of his ancestors.

After all those years of troubleshooting and repair, he turned to teaching at a Government University and writing technical books. Out of his research came his first book on Germanic History and Genealogy, "*Origins and Ancestors Families Karle & Kaiser of the German-Russian Volga Colonies.*"

Darrel has also written and published numerous other books on German and Russian History, Politics, Religion, and Ancestry; a book on the Watercolor quilts of Betty Kaiser, a book on basic electrical troubleshooting, a book on sewing machine troubleshooting, two books on the SINGER 221 *Featherweight*, and two books on the STANDARD *Sewhandy* and GE *MODEL A* sewing machines. This book's final pages show all the titles.

For more on his research into German and Russian History and Genealogy, visit his website at

www.Volga-Germans.com

For more on his books on Troubleshooting, visit his website at

www.BasicTroubleshooting.com

For more on his books about Sewing Machines, visit his website at

www.SewingMachineTech.com

For more on his books about the STANDARD *Sewhandy* and GE *MODEL A* sewing machines, visit his website at

www.SewhandySewingMachines.com

For more information on all of his books, visit his website at

www.DarrelKaiserBooks.com

PREFACE

This book is about the designers of the SINGER Model 221/222 Featherweight sewing machines.

There were many modifications to the SINGER Model 221/222 sewing machines over the years. Most changes did not require patents, and the identity of those designers is lost. The more important changes merited a patent application. Those patent applications identify the inventor and his location, the date of filing and issue, and the specifics design characteristics. There may be more Model 221/222 patents out there; I just have not found them yet.

Lucky for us, the United States Patent Office and the British Patent Office keep meticulous records of all patent applications, and they allow us to look at those records. Without those records, this book would not be possible.

This book has four sections. The first section covers 12 patents involved in the design of the SINGER Model 221/222, and includes historical information on the design and designers. The second section covers four patents related specifically to the SINGER Model 222, along with more historical information. The third section is the Appendix with complete copies of all the patents in the first two sections. The fourth section is the summary.

Enjoy... Email any and all comments or questions to Dar-Bet@att.net.

Table of Contents

the Featherweight Patents

SINGER made the Model 221 Featherweight Sewing Machine. Everyone knows that. But have you ever wondered about who the actual person was that first designed it? Have you ever wondered who thought of all the design changes that became the SINGER Featherweight that we know and enjoy today?

The following pages on the sewing machine patents will answer all of the above. But, before we get in to the actual history, let's look at what a "patent" is, and what it isn't.

A patent for an invention is the grant of a property right to the inventor by the Patent and Trademark Office. The term of a new patent is normally 20 years from the date on which the application for the patent was filed in the United States. US patent grants are effective only within the US, US territories, and US possessions. Other countries also have their own Patent Laws and offices.

The right conferred by the patent grant is "the right to exclude others from making, using, offering for sale, or selling" the invention in the United States or "importing" the invention into the United States. Specifically, this is the right to <u>exclude others</u> from making, using, offering for sale, selling..., <u>but not the right to make, use, offer for sale, sell or import the invention</u>.

The first patents for inventions in America were issued in 1641 by the colonial governments. In 1790, Congress enacted the first U.S. patent laws under the authority of Article 1, Section 8, of the Constitution. These laws are the Patent Act of 1790. Over the decades, these laws have been refined to what we have today.

A utility patent protects the way an article is used and works, while a design patent protects only the ornamental appearance of an invention, not its utilitarian features. US Patent Law says that a design patent is granted to any person who has invented any new and not obvious ornamental design for an article of manufacture. Specifically, the design patent protects only the appearance of an article. It does not address its structural or utility features.

While design and utility patents are meant to provide different protection, the utility and design of an invention are not always easily separated. The same invention may have both functional and ornamental characteristics that would need both utility and design patents.

Most patents fall into the utility patent category with that group subdivided into mechanical, electrical and chemical categories.

A utility patent may be issued to anyone who invents a new and useful method, process, machine, device, manufactured item, or chemical compound - or any new and useful improvement to the same.

As mentioned above, a design patent may be issued to anyone who invents a new, original and ornamental design for an article of manufacture. However, it is only the appearance that is protected.

In the beginning

Many portable sewing machine models were available in the early 1920's from a number of different manufacturers. The Singer Sewing Machine Company filed for a US patent on a portable sewing machine before 1920. They introduced this model as the Singer "portable electric" 99K for sale to the public in 1921.

The idea of a portable sewing machine was not new, however these models were relatively expensive. Even worse, the typical portable of the 1920's was still fairly large and heavy with a carrying weight of over 30 pounds. They were usually made of cast iron, and they may have been called "portable," but you would not be "able to port" them very far.

The machines were really adaptations of table sewing machine designs. A new lighter and less expensive design was needed. Who would design one, and would it sell and make money?

This late 1920's ad shows the typical "portable" (30 pounds) easily carried by a woman down the stairs.

A new lighter and less expensive design finally arrived in late 1927. That was the sewing machine commonly known as the "Standard Sewing Machine Company SEWHANDY". But that is another story... For more information about that sewing machine, see my book "*before the Featherweight - SEWHANDY*"

4

Model 221/222 Patents

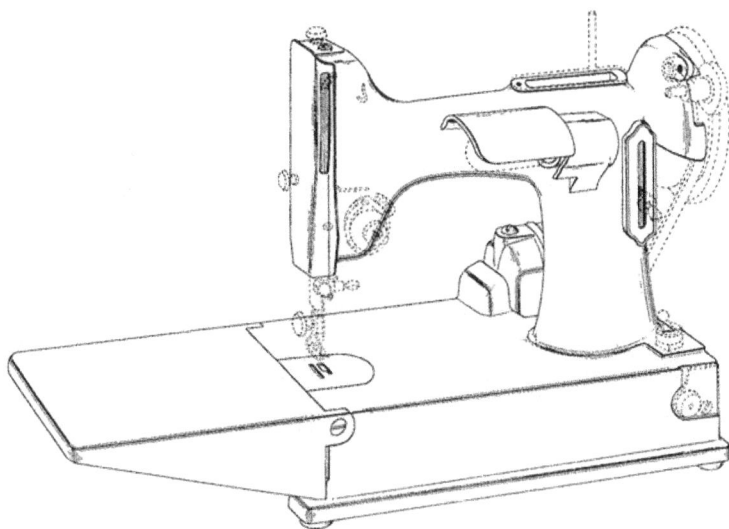

Model 221

Model 221/222 Patents

So when did the Featherweight[1] or Model 221 sewing machine design first come to light? And whose idea was it? The Singer Model 221/222 designs did not just pop out of a designers mind. The design was based on one hundred years of sewing machine development. Three unique features of the Models 221/222 are the hinged shelf, graduated tension regulator, and the inverted metal pan for all the lower mechanicals.

The Hinged Shelf

The most applicable patent that I found for a hinged shelf or foldable end platform was by 21-year-old Chicago resident, insurance office clerk and seamstress Maud Pratt. She filed the application for a "Hand Portable Sewing-Machine" on December 17, 1920. It was granted on October 25, 1921 as US Patent 1,394,396.

Maud writes in her patent application "This forms an ideal support for goods being sewed and makes practical use of the portable machine even on a table... it removes all tendency of the cloth or other goods to drag upon the needle and thus interfere with the free and proper functioning of the stitching mechanism, etc."

---

[1] This sewing machine did not become known as a "featherweight" until described as such in a SINGER newspaper ad in November 1934. SINGER did finally get around to filing for a trademark on "Featherweight" in 1951. In their application, SINGER noted that they had been using the Featherweight name with the SINGER 221 since mid 1933.

Her design is on the following pages. A copy of the full patent is in the appendix at the end of this book.

M. PRATT.
HAND PORTABLE SEWING MACHINE.
APPLICATION FILED DEC. 17, 1920.

1,394,936

Patented Oct. 25, 1921

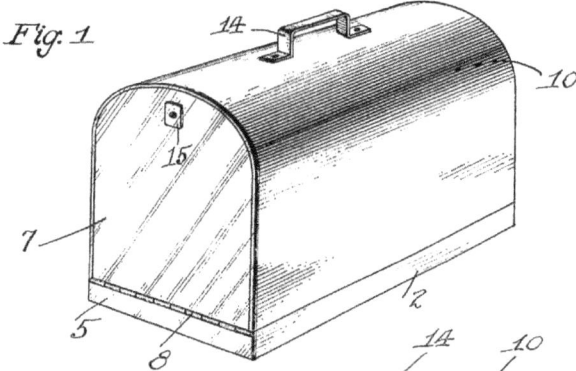

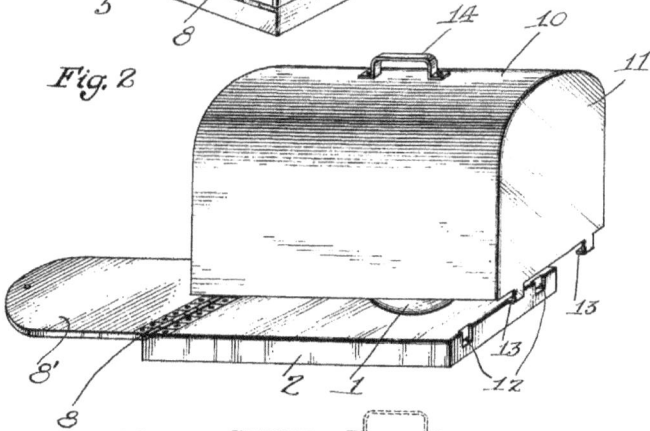

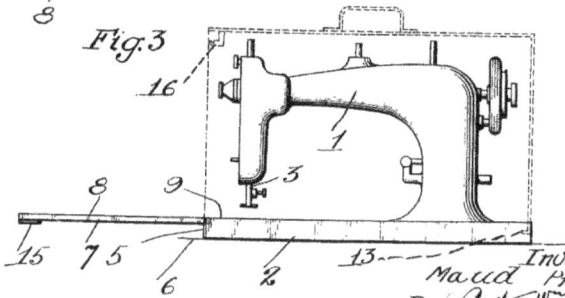

Fig. 1

Fig. 2

Fig. 3

Inventor
Maud Pratt
By *Arthur W. Nelson* Atty.

UNITED STATES PATENT OFFICE.

MAUD PRATT, OF CHICAGO, ILLINOIS.

HAND PORTABLE SEWING-MACHINE.

1,394,936.   Specification of Letters Patent.   **Patented Oct. 25, 1921.**

Application filed December 17, 1920. Serial No. 431,354.

To all whom it may concern:

Be it known that I, MAUD PRATT, a citizen of the United States, and a resident of Chicago, county of Cook, and State of Illinois, have invented certain new and useful Improvements in Hand Portable Sewing-Machines, of which the following is a specification.

My invention relates generally to improvements in a type of sewing machine which is adapted to be carried by the hand from place to place, and which is usually operated by means of an electric motor. Such a machine as heretofore constructed embodies the elements of lightness, compactness and ready portability but has been open to some objections with respect to its use during the sewing operation.

The general object of my invention is to improve the hand portable type of sewing machine so as to make it generally more efficient, and in particular to provide means whereby the goods to be operated upon or sewed shall be held and supported in a position to secure the best results.

It is a further object of my invention to provide means whereby the above result can be attained without increasing the weight or appreciably affecting the cost and without affecting the durability or rigidity of the device.

My invention consists generally in the form, arrangement, construction and coöperation of the parts whereby the above named objects, together with others that will appear hereinafter are attainable; and my invention will be more readily understood by reference to the accompanying drawings which illustrate what I consider, at the present time, to be the preferred embodiment thereof.

In said drawings:

Figure 1 is a perspective view of a hand portable sewing machine embodying my invention, the parts being positioned as in carrying the machine.

Fig. 2 is a perspective illustrative view illustrating a step in the course of preparing the hand portable sewing machine for use; and

Fig. 3 is a side elevation of the machine ready for use.

As here shown, 1, represents what is usually termed the head of the sewing machine and which is mounted or supported upon a base 2. The base 2, as here shown, is of rectangular form and houses certain of the operating parts of the sewing machine (not shown). The size of the base 2 is usually no larger than is necessary properly to support the head 1 and the mechanism within the base 2. 3 represents the presser foot of the machine and is in the plane in which the needle of the sewing machine (not shown) operates and in which the sewing is done. The sewing, therefore, is performed relatively close to the end 5 of the sewing machine base. The base 2 in use is ordinarily placed upon a surface 6 which is representative of a table or some other suitable support.

In using machines of the hand portable type the goods being sewed, in many of the machines heretofore devised, drags over the end of the base corresponding to the end 5 of my base and interferes with the sewing operation. This is particularly objectionable when sewing relatively heavy cloth. Some attempt has been made to obviate this difficulty such for example as by the expedient shown in the Patent to Riddell No. 1344718 of June 29, 1920, but this involves certain objections, such as separate parts which are likely to become misplaced and also involves elements of added cost, weight and multiplicity of parts which are somewhat objectionable.

In my construction I provide a combined cover end and drop shelf or support 7 which is hingedly secured, as indicated at 8, to the end of the base 2 of the machine. The upper surface 8' of the combined cover end and support is in the same plane as the upper surface 9 of the base, and therefore, forms an unbroken continuation thereof when the member 7 is in the horizontal position shown in Figs. 2 and 3. This forms an ideal support for goods being sewed and makes practicable the use of the portable machine even upon a table or other support which is no larger than the base 2 of the sewing machine. It also assists very greatly in the successful use of the machine even when placed upon a relatively large table, as in either event it removes all tendency of the cloth or other goods to drag upon the needle and thus interfere with the free and proper functioning of the stitching mecha-

9

Maud's design was not the only one in the records. Many designers came up with their idea of how the best extension platform would work.

This was a problem for all portables. The earlier ones had a framed wooden base, and their sewing platform was limited by the size of the their sewing machine case.

Some of the other designs used added platforms much like our modern day machines; however, lightweight plastics were not yet in use so the extensions were of metal or wood and were heavy and not very practical.

The Tension Regulator

The tension regulator on the SINGER 221 is from a design by a SINGER Manufacturing Company Developmental Engineer. He was 45 year-old Daniel Henry Chason of Elizabeth, New Jersey.

He filed the application for "Graduated Tension Regulator For Sewing Machines" on May 9, 1930 and was granted US Patent 1,820,119 on August 25, 1931. Chason assigned all rights to this patent to the SINGER Manufacturing Company, Elizabeth, N.J., a corporation of New Jersey.

The Chason design is on the following pages. A copy of the full patent application is in the appendix at the end of this book.

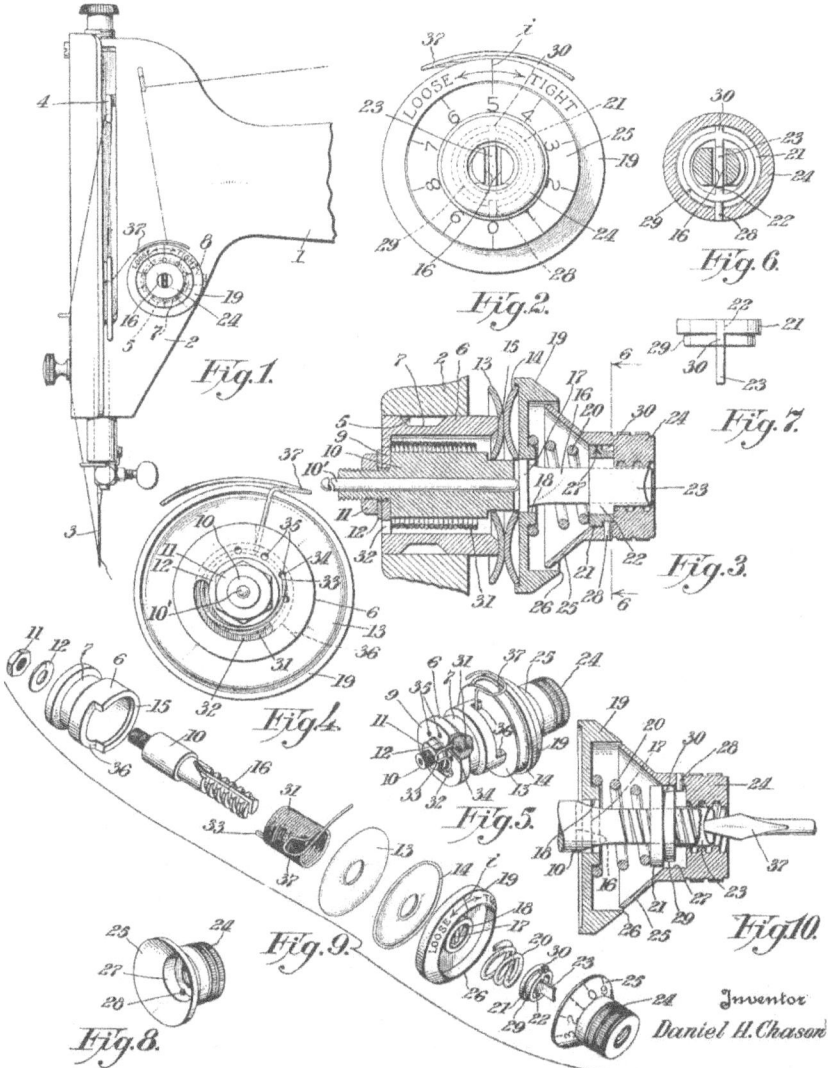

Fig.1.

Fig.2.

Fig.6.

Fig.7.

Fig.3.

Fig.4.

Fig.5.

Fig.8.

Fig.9.

Fig.10.

Inventor

Daniel H. Chason

Witness

Godfry Pecing

By Henry J. Miller

Attorney

11

UNITED STATES PATENT OFFICE

DANIEL H. CHASON, OF ELIZABETH, NEW JERSEY, ASSIGNOR TO THE SINGER MANU-
FACTURING COMPANY, OF ELIZABETH, NEW JERSEY, A CORPORATION OF NEW
JERSEY

GRADUATED TENSION REGULATOR FOR SEWING MACHINES

Application filed May 9, 1930. Serial No. 450,952.

This invention relates to sewing machines and has for an object to provide an improved device for tensioning the sewing thread or threads of such machines.

With the above and other objects in view, as will hereinafter appear, the invention consists in the devices, combinations and arrangements of parts hereinafter set forth and illustrated in the accompanying drawings of a preferred embodiment of the invention, from which the several features of the invention and the advantages attained thereby will be readily understood by those skilled in the art.

In the accompanying drawings Fig. 1 is a side elevation of a portion of a sewing machine bracket-arm fitted with a tension device embodying the invention. Fig. 2 is a front elevation of the tension device. Fig. 3 is a longitudinal vertical section through the tension device. Fig. 4 is a rear elevation and Fig. 5 a perspective view of the tension device. Fig. 6 is a section on the line 6—6, Fig. 3. Fig. 7 is a top plan view of the slidably mounted dial stop member. Fig. 8 is a rearward perspective view of the dial member. Fig. 9 is a disassembled perspective view of the device, and Fig. 10 is a view similar to Fig. 3 but showing how the dial may be removed for disassembly of the device.

1 represents the bracket-arm of a sewing machine terminating in the head 2 for the usual reciprocating needle 3 and take-up 4. The head 2 is formed with an aperture 5 which receives the hollow cylindrical shank 6 of the tension device, which shank is formed with a circumferential groove 7 entered by the set-screw 8 in the head 2 to fix the tension device in working position on the sewing machine.

The shank 6 is of hollow cylindrical form and has an inner end-wall 9 formed with a central aperture through which passes the reduced and threaded inner end of the hollow stem 10 which is tightly fixed to the shank 6 by the nut 11 and washer 12. Surrounding the stem 10 are the opposed tension disks 13, 14, of which the disk 13 rests against the rim 15 of the hollow shank-member 6. The outer end-portion of the stem 10 is

formed with a longitudinal diametrical slot 16 through which passes the diameter-bar 17 crossing the central stem-embracing aperture 18 in the shallow base-cup 19 which is pressed against the tension disk 14 by the bee-hive spring 20.

The spring 20 is engaged at its outer end by the ring-shaped member, preferably in the form of a washer 21, formed with a diameter-bar 22 having a forwardly extending stem-portion 23 disposed in the slot 16 in the stem 10. The washer 21 is engaged or backed by a dial-nut 24 having an outwardly flaring conical skirt 25, the rim of which is slightly smaller than and is received within the rim 26 of the base-cup 19. The skirt 25 is preferably formed integral with and non-adjustable relative to the screw-threaded head of the nut 24. It overhangs and encloses the major portion of the bee-hive spring 20. The nut 24 is preferably screw-threaded onto the split stem 10 and has an inner cylindrically recessed portion 27 which receives the washer 21 and into which cylindrically recessed portion projects the stop-pin 28 fixed in the nut 24. The stop-pin 28 normally works in a clearance groove 29 in the washer 21, and this clearance groove is interrupted at one point in its circumference by the stop-wall 30 which limits the turning movement of the nut 24 to one rotation during which the spring 20 is stressed from minimum to maximum requirements; the strength and stiffness of the spring 20 and the pitch of the screw-threads on the stem 10 for the nut 24 being proportioned to attain this result. The washer 21 thus constitutes a stop between the nut 24 and spring 20, which stop is engaged by the stop 28 on the nut 24.

There is disposed within the hollow stem 10 the usual presser-controlled tension-release pin 10' which engages the diameter-bar 17 of the base-cup 19 and relieves the tension-disks of the pressure of the spring 20 when the usual presser-foot (not shown) is lifted.

Surrounding the stem 10 within the shank 6 is the check-spring 31 one end of which extends through the arcuate slot 32 in the end wall 9 of the shank member 6 and is formed with a loop 33 and inturned end 34 which

The Inverted Metal pan

The inverted metal pan bed design was patent applied for in December 1927 for the SEWHANDY sewing machine. For more information about that patent and the SEWHANDY sewing machine, see my book *"before the Featherweight - SEWHANDY"*. Even though it was patented, Singer adapted the concept for use in their new Model 221.

The Model 221 Inventor

We now know where some of the unique parts came from, but who pulled it all together to become the SINGER Featherweight?

This original new portable electric sewing machine design was the brainstorm of inventor and designer Herbert John Goosman.

Herbert John Goosman was born in Cincinnati, Ohio on November 22, 1891. His parents were Richard and Josephine Goosman. His father Richard emigrated from Germany to America in 1873 and was employed as a baker.

From census records, we know that in 1901 Herbert was still a student living at home in Cincinnati. He attended and graduated from the University of Cincinnati with a degree in Mechanical Engineering in 1916. He did so well during his lifetime that in 1969 he was awarded Distinguished Alumni status by the University of Cincinnati.

By 1930, Herbert Goosman was married to his wife Anna and was living in Elizabeth, Union County, New Jersey. He was working as a Mechanical Engineer for the SINGER Manufacturing Company at the Elizabethport plant in New Jersey.

As of 1946, he was the Works Manager for SINGER at Elizabethport. He continued designing for SINGER until sometime after March 1965.

The Goosman Patent

On July 13, 1933, Herbert J. Goosman filed for a patent on "Electrically Lighted Sewing Machine" His application became US Patent 2,031,562 and was granted February 18, 1936. The application assigned all rights to this patent to The Singer Manufacturing Company, Elizabeth, N.J.

This was not actually the patent application for the Model 221, but was for the electrical lighting of what would soon be the Model 221. For some unknown reason, the utility patent application for the Model 221 was not filed until 9 months later in April 1934.

What is unique about this patent application is that it shows the Model 221 sewing machine design before the start of production.

His design is on the following pages. A copy of the full patent application is in the appendix at the end of this book.

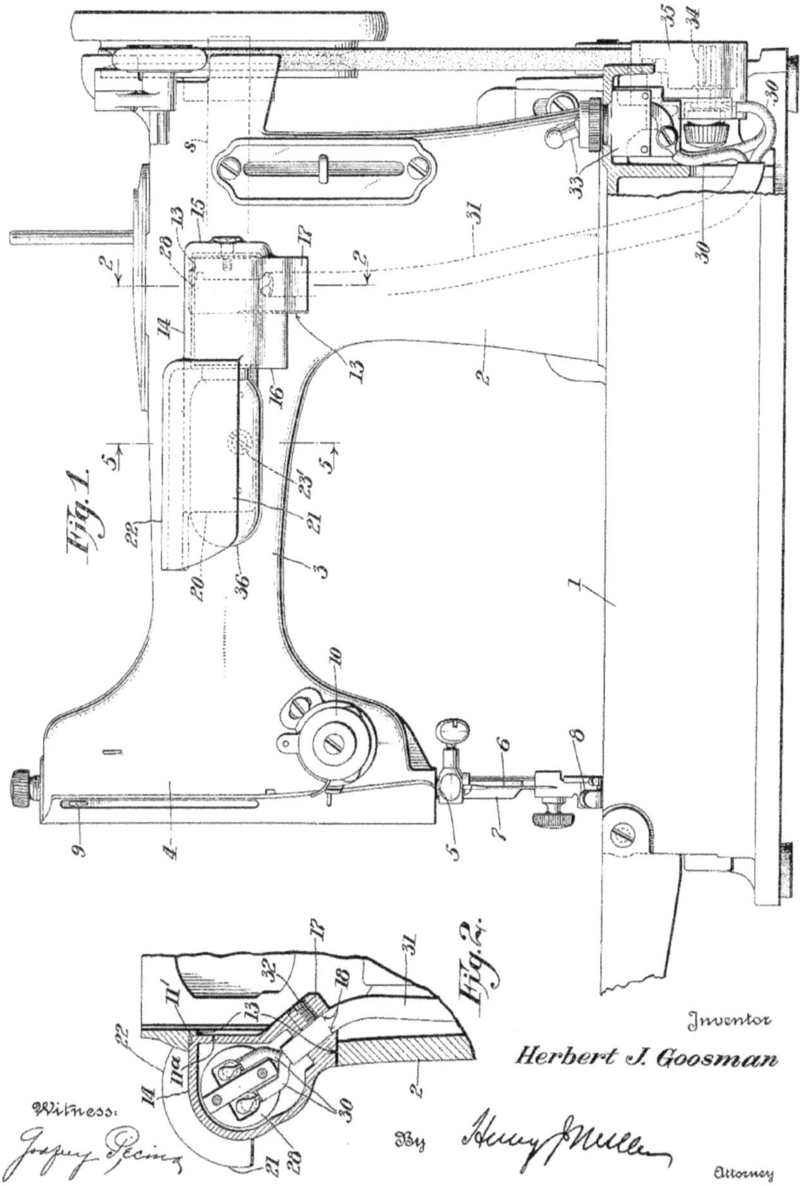

Fig. 1

Fig. 2

Inventor

Herbert J. Goosman

By Henry J. Miller

Witness:

Joseph Pering

Attorney

15

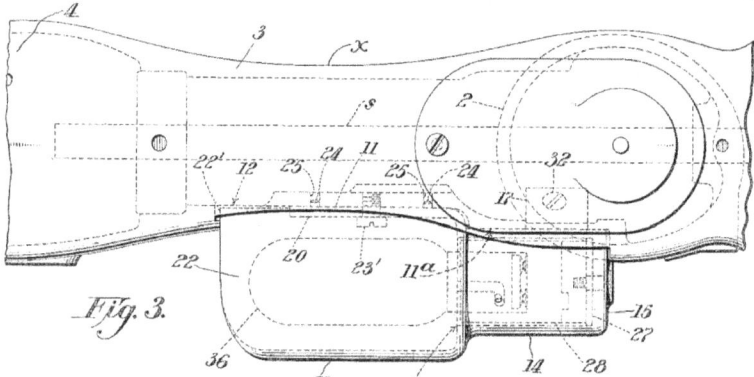

Fig. 3.

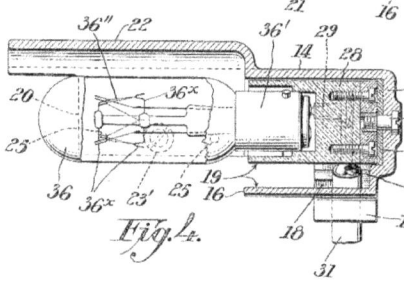

Fig. 4.

Fig. 4ª.

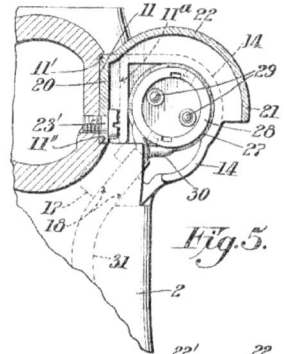

Fig. 5.

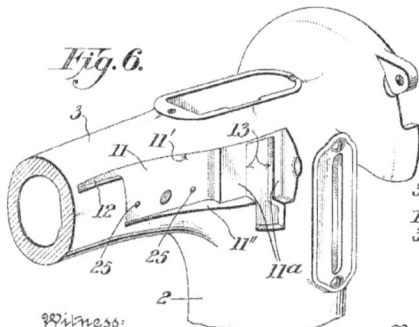

Fig. 6.

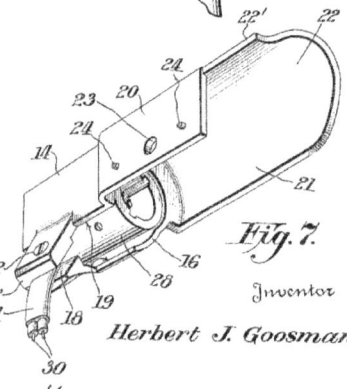

Fig. 7.

Inventor

Herbert J. Goosman

By Henry J. Miller

Attorney

16

UNITED STATES PATENT OFFICE

2,031,562

ELECTRICALLY LIGHTED SEWING MACHINE

Herbert J. Goosman, Elizabeth, N. J., assignor to The Singer Manufacturing Company, Elizabeth, N. J., a corporation of New Jersey

Application July 13, 1933, Serial No. 680,219

10 Claims. (Cl. 240—2.14)

Electric sewing machine lighting devices as heretofore constructed and applied to the sewing machine, when of ample illuminating capacity, have been objected to in some cases because of their inordinate size relative to the sewing machine frame and in general because of the high temperature to which the lamp-shade is raised by the heat from the lamp; such high temperature making the lamp-shade a radiator of a discomforting amount of heat into the operator's face and further making it necessary for the operator to use great care not to touch the hot lamp-shade.

It has heretofore been proposed to overcome the objection of discomforting heat radiation by placing the lighting device horizontally directly in rear of the overhanging member of the sewing machine gooseneck, which member functioned as a barrier to radiant heat between the lighting device and the operator's face. In cases where, for any reason, it is desired to position the lighting device in front of the gooseneck, the desirable heat-barrier function of the gooseneck is lost.

It has also been proposed to prevent overheating of the lamp-shade by interposing between it and the lamp-bulb a thin sheet-metal liner separated from the shade by an air-gap through which cooling currents of air may freely flow by convection.

The present invention has for an object to provide simple, sturdy, inexpensive, unobtrusive, easily constructed, and readily assembled means for the electric illumination of a sewing machine, which will adequately illuminate the work being stitched without danger or discomfort to the operator, and which does not depend upon an additional liner or upon the heat barrier function of the sewing machine gooseneck to shield the operator from discomforting heat radiation from the lighting device.

Another object of the invention is to provide an electrically lighted sewing machine, the lighting device of which, while of relatively small physical size and relatively high wattage, is so contrived and combined with the sewing machine as to afford generous illumination of the work without discomforting radiation of heat.

A further object of the invention is to provide a sewing machine with a built-in lighting device which is simple in construction, inexpensive to manufacture, easy to assemble and apply to the sewing machine, and which does not interfere in any manner with the normal operation and use of the sewing machine or with the assembling or disassembling of the parts of the machine.

With the above and other objects in view, as will hereinafter appear, the invention comprises the devices, combinations, and arrangements of parts hereinafter set forth and illustrated in the accompanying drawings of a preferred embodiment of the invention, from which the several features of the invention and the advantages attained thereby will be readily understood by those skilled in the art.

In the accompanying drawings Fig. 1 is a front side elevation of a sewing machine embodying the invention. Fig. 2 is a section on the line 2—2, Fig. 1. Fig. 3 is a fragmentary top plan view of the machine. Fig. 4 is a vertical longitudinal section through the electric lighting device of the machine. Fig. 4a is a detail view of a portion of the lamp filament used in this device. Fig. 5 is a section on the line 5—5, Fig. 1. Fig. 6 is a fragmentary perspective view of the sewing machine gooseneck from which the lighting device has been removed and Fig. 7 is a perspective view of the lighting device removed from the machine.

For the purposes of the present disclosure the invention is described as embodied in a preferred form in a sewing machine having a hollow bed 1 from which rises the standard 2 of the hollow inverted L-shaped gooseneck 3 terminating in the head 4 carrying the usual reciprocatory needle-bar 5, needle 6, presser-bar 7, presser-foot 8, take-up 9 and tension device 10. Disposed within and lengthwise of the overhanging member 3 of the gooseneck is the sewing machine main shaft s which is connected in the usual manner to drive the needle-bar 5, take-up 9 and the usual loop-taking and feeding devices (not shown) customarily located below or within the bed 1. The overhanging member 3 of the gooseneck is preferably of curved contour and is tapered inwardly, Fig. 3, from the standard 2, or gradually reduced in section, to a point x intermediate the standard 2 and head 4, from which intermediate point x the gooseneck is tapered outwardly or enlarged in section toward the head 4. The gooseneck is preferably formed in its curved and tapered front side wall, Fig. 6, with a flat vertical seat 11 which may be sunk somewhat below the normal curved and tapering surface of the gooseneck and made parallel to the main shaft s. The gooseneck 3 may be formed in its side wall at one end of the seat 11 with a slot 12 and is preferably formed adjacent the other end of the seat 11 with a step or auxiliary seat 11ᵃ in which there is an aperture 13 opening into the hollow interior of the gooseneck 3.

The electric lighting device preferably comprises an electric lamp-socket shell 14 of hollow tubular form closed at one end 15 and open at its other end 16. Projecting rearwardly from the socket-shell 14 is a lug 17 formed with a lateral slot 18. The socket-shell 14 has a slot 19 in its lower wall opening into the lateral slot 18 in the lug 17.

Preferably, cast integral with the lamp-socket

The Goosman Design Patent

Herbert J. Goosman filed for a design patent on January 25, 1934. The design patent only covered the ornamental design or the "looks" of the Model 221 sewing machine. The utility patent on how the sewing machine worked was still a few months away.

His Design patent was issued by the Patent Office about two months later as US Design Patent 91,816. The application assigned all rights to The SINGER Manufacturing Company, Elizabeth, N.J.

The Goosman Model 221 design is below and on the following page. A copy of the full patent application is in the appendix at the end of this book.

Patented Mar. 27, 1934

Des. 91,816

UNITED STATES PATENT OFFICE

91,816

DESIGN FOR AN ELECTRIC SEWING MACHINE

Herbert J. Goosman, Elizabeth, N. J., assignor to The Singer Manufacturing Company, Elizabeth, N. J., a corporation of New Jersey

Application January 25, 1934, Serial No. 50,502

Term of patent 14 years

To all whom it may concern:

Be it known that I, HERBERT J. GOOSMAN, a citizen of the United States, residing at Elizabeth, in the county of Union and State of New Jersey, have invented a new, original, and ornamental Design for an Electric Sewing Machine, of which the following is a specification, reference being had to the accompanying drawing, forming a part thereof.

Figures 1 and 2 are perspective views of an electric sewing machine showing my new design; the parts shown in dotted lines being conventional.

I claim:

The ornamental design for an electric sewing machine, as shown and described.

In testimony whereof I have signed my name to this specification.

HERBERT J. GOOSMAN

H. J. GOOSMAN

Des. 91,816

ELECTRIC SEWING MACHINE

Filed Jan. 25, 1934

Fig.1.

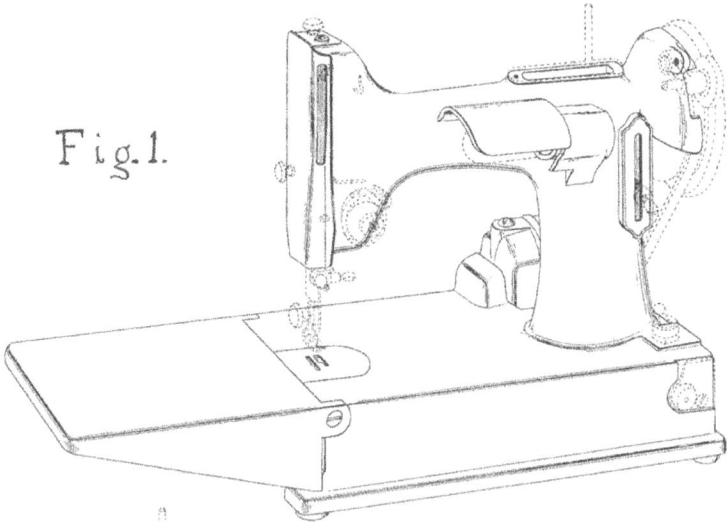

Fig. 2.

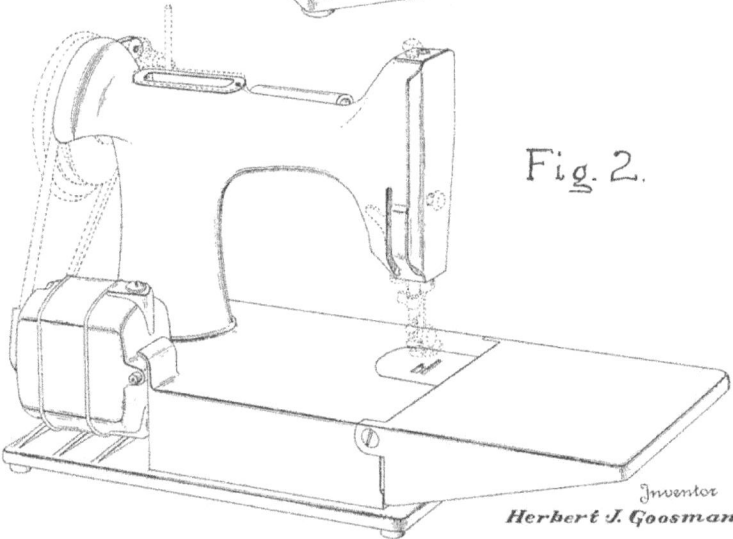

Inventor

Herbert J. Goosman

Witness:

John H. Cave

By Henry J. Miller

Attorney

The Goosman Utility Patent
Herbert Goosman filed the application for "Sewing Machine Frame" on April 11, 1934 (issued as Patent 2,063,841 on December 8, 1936.

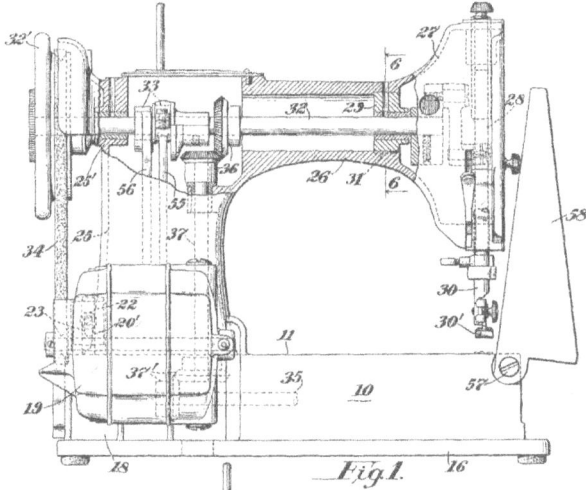

Dec. 8, 1936.   H. J. GOOSMAN   2,063,841
                              SEWING MACHINE FRAME
                              Filed April 11, 1934   3 Sheets—Sheet 1

Fig.1.

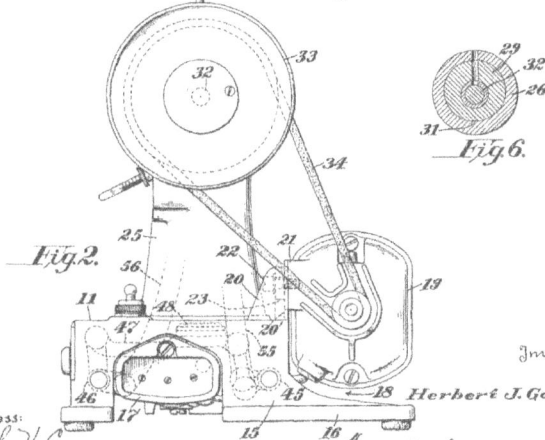

Fig.2.   *Fig.6.*

Inventor

Witness: Herbert J. Goosman
John N. Cave   By   Harry J. Miller
                                                   Attorney

20

Goosman assigned all rights to The SINGER Manufacturing Company, Elizabeth, N.J.

Dec. 8, 1936.   H. J. GOOSMAN   2,063,841

SEWING MACHINE FRAME

Filed April 11, 1934   3 Sheets—Sheet 2

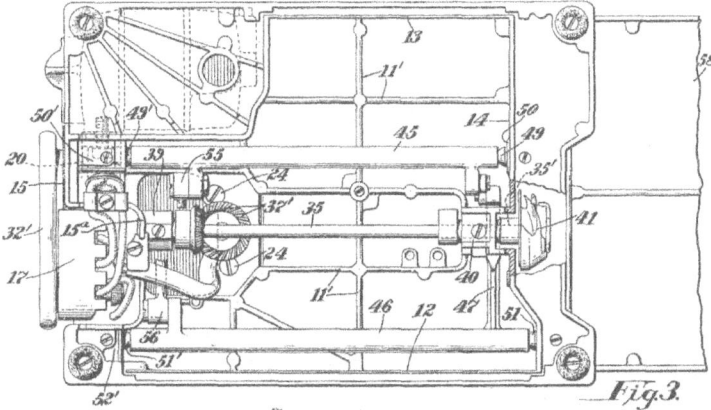

Fig.3.

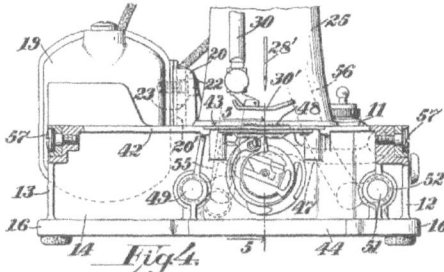

Fig.4.

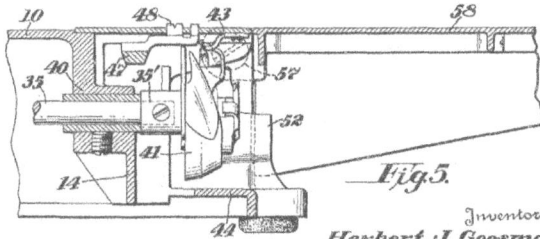

Fig.5.

Inventor
Herbert J. Goosman

Witness:
John N. Cave

By   Henry J. Miller

Attorney

21

A copy of the full patent application is in the appendix at the end of this book.

Dec. 8, 1936.   H. J. GOOSMAN   2,063,841

SEWING MACHINE FRAME

Filed April 11, 1934   3 Sheets—Sheet 3

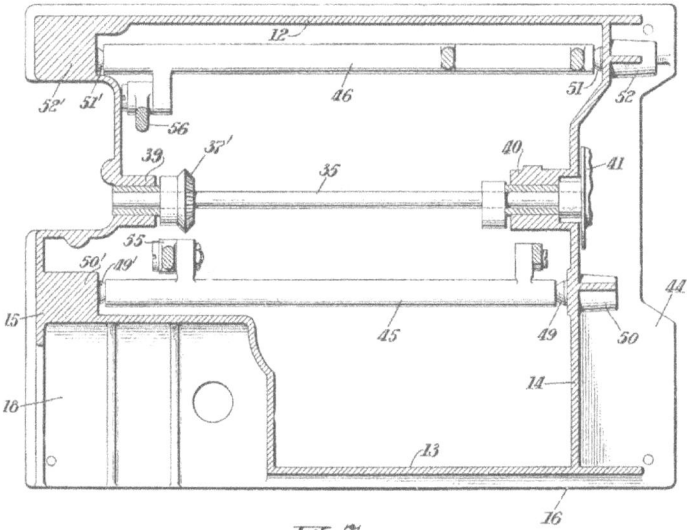

Fig. 7.

Inventor
Herbert J. Goosman

Witness:
Godfrey Pecing   By *Henry J. Miller*
     Attorney

22

UNITED STATES PATENT OFFICE

2,063,841

SEWING MACHINE FRAME

Herbert J. Goosman, Elizabeth, N. J., assignor to
The Singer Manufacturing Company, Elizabeth, N. J., a corporation of New Jersey

Application April 11, 1934, Serial No. 719,996

8 Claims. (Cl. 112—258)

This invention relates to sewing machines and more particularly to sewing machines of the domestic portable type and has for its object to produce a sewing machine which is compact and exceedingly light in weight.

Another object of the present invention is to provide a frame for such machine having the bearing supports for the operating parts die-cast with the frame and to provide a die-cast frame which requires a minimum of machining.

Another object of the invention is to provide a sewing machine bed having an enclosure in which the loop-taker and feed-actuating mechanism are housed and the loop-taker disposed outside of the housing in a position where the bobbin may be removed and the loop-taker inspected, cleaned and repaired.

With the above and other objects in view, as will hereinafter appear, the invention comprises the devices, combinations, and arrangements of parts hereinafter set forth and illustrated in the accompanying drawings of a preferred embodiment of the invention, from which the several features of the invention and the advantages attained thereby will be readily understood by those skilled in the art.

The several features of the present invention will be clearly understood from the following description and accompanying drawings:—

Figure 1 is a rear elevation of my improved sewing machine, a portion of the bracket-arm being broken away to show the operating parts and their supports.

Figure 2 is an end elevation looking from the left of Figure 1.

Figure 3 is a bottom plan view.

Figure 4 is an end elevation of the bed and upper and lower stitch-forming mechanisms.

Figure 5 is a sectional view taken substantially along the line 5—5 of Figure 4, the loop-taker and its actuating shaft being shown in elevation.

Figure 6 is a section taken along the line 6—6 of Figure 1.

Figure 7 is a horizontal sectional view of the bed taken in a plane passing substantially through the shaft 35.

The frame of the machine is die-cast in metal of aluminum alloy of high aluminum content. Such an alloy may contain, for instance, from 6 to 8 percent of copper and from 2 to 3 percent of silicon with the balance of commercially pure aluminum. Due to the precision with which a frame may be die-cast only a minimum amount of machining, reaming and drilling are necessary.

As illustrated in the drawings the frame of the machine comprises a substantially rectangular shaped bed or base, indicated generally as 10, having a work-supporting plate 11 provided on its under face with transversely arranged strengthening ribs 11', downwardly extending side-walls 12 and 13 and end-walls 14 and 15 forming an enclosure. The side-walls and end-walls terminate in a flange portion 16. The end-wall 15 is recessed to receive an electrical terminal 17 and the side-wall 13 and end-wall 15 are inwardly offset to form a recess 18 for the reception of an electric motor 19. Fixed to the work-supporting plate 11 is a motor-supporting bracket 20 formed with a channel 20' which slidably receives the rectangular shaped lug 21 carried by the frame of the motor 19. The lug 21 is adjustably fixed to the bracket 20 by means of a screw 22 which extends through a slot 23 in the bracket 20 and is threaded into the lug 21. From the above it will be obvious that the motor 19 may be raised or lowered on its support.

Fixed to the hollow bed 10 by the screws 24 is the standard 25 which carries the overhanging bracket-arm 26 terminating in a hollow head 27 carrying the usual reciprocatory needle-bar 28, needle 28', presser-bar 30 and presser-foot 30'. Disposed within and lengthwise of the overhanging bracket-arm 26 is the sewing machine main shaft 32 having a balance-wheel 32' fixed thereto and driven from the motor 19 by the belt 34. The shaft 32 is connected in the usual manner to drive the needle-bar 28 and the loop-taker actuating shaft 35 is driven through the gears 36, vertical shaft 37 and gears 37'.

The main shaft 32 adjacent the balance-wheel 32' is carried by the bearing support 25' die-cast with the standard 25. The standard 25, bracket-arm 26 and head 27 are die-cast in a single piece and the interior diameter of the bracket-arm 26 is made greater at the end of the arm adjacent the head 27 to facilitate the removal of the core after the casting operation. To support the shaft 32 in the bracket-arm there is provided a bearing support 29 which is fixed in the interior of the arm by a driving fit or by spinning a portion of the metal in the bracket-arm over the bearing support 29 to securely hold it against endwise displacement. As shown in Figures 1 and 6, the aperture in the support 29 through which the shaft 32 extends is off center, the purpose being to align this aperture with the aper-

More Patents – A month later on May 12, he filed an application for "Thread Case Rotation Restriction Means" for the sewing Machine. It was issued on July 9, 1935 as Patent 2,007,894.

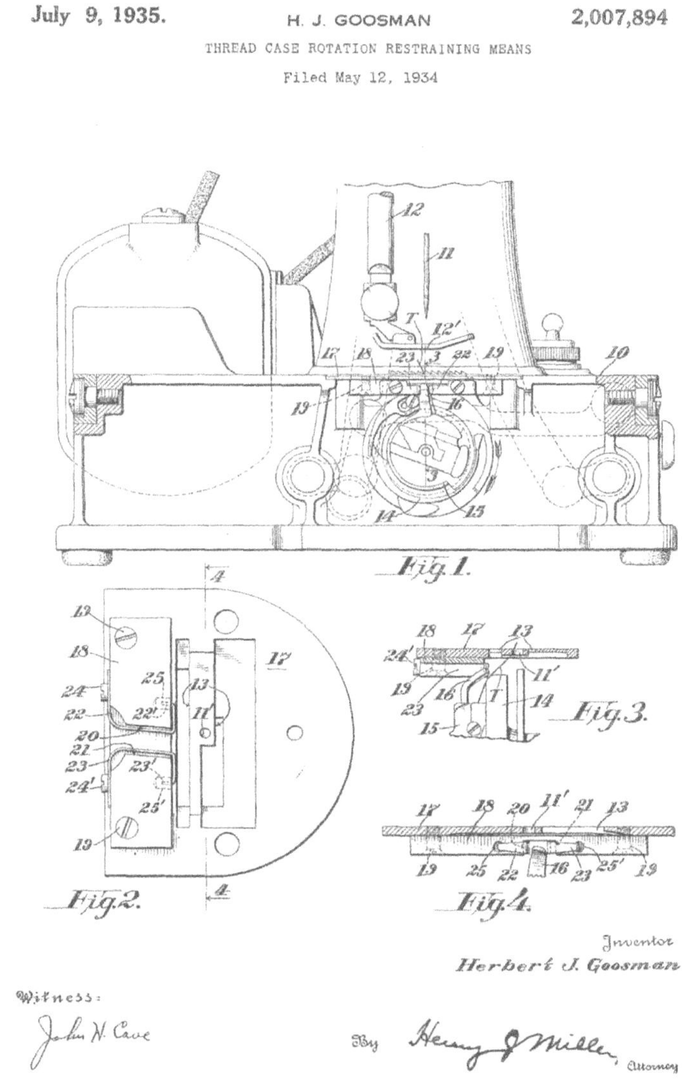

July 9, 1935. H. J. GOOSMAN 2,007,894

THREAD CASE ROTATION RESTRAINING MEANS

Filed May 12, 1934

Fig.1.

Fig.2.

Fig.3.

Fig.4.

Inventor
Herbert J. Goosman

By Henry J. Miller, Attorney

Witness:
John N. Cave

24

And Goosman assigned all rights to The SINGER Manufacturing Company, Elizabeth, N.J. A copy of the full patent application is in the appendix.

Patented July 9, 1935

2,007,894

UNITED STATES PATENT OFFICE

2,007,894

THREAD-CASE ROTATION-RESTRAINING MEANS

Herbert J. Goosman, Elizabeth, N. J., assignor to The Singer Manufacturing Company, Elizabeth, N. J., a corporation of New Jersey

Application May 12, 1934, Serial No. 725,291

5 Claims. (Cl. 112—181)

This invention relates to sewing machines and more particularly to sewing machines of the lockstitch type and has for its objective the provision of sound and vibration absorbing elements which will absorb the impact of the thread-case rotation restraining finger during the operation of the stitch-forming mechanism.

With the above and other objects in view, as will hereinafter appear, the invention comprises the devices, combinations, and arrangements of parts hereinafter set forth and illustrated in the accompanying drawing of a preferred embodiment of the invention, from which the several features of the invention and the advantages attained thereby will be readily understood by those skilled in the art.

The several features of the present invention will be clearly understood from the following description and accompanying drawing in which—

Figure 1 is an end elevation representing the stitch-forming mechanism of a sewing machine with my improved thread-case rotation-restraining elements embodied therein.

Figure 2 is a bottom plan view of the throat-plate.

Figure 3 is a fragmentary sectional view taken substantially along the line 3—3 of Figure 1, the loop-taker and thread-case being shown in elevation.

Figure 4 is a section of the throat-plate taken along the line 4—4 of Figure 2.

The present invention is shown embodied in a sewing machine such as that disclosed in my copending application, Serial No. 719,996, filed April 11, 1934. This machine comprises the usual bed 10, reciprocatory needle 11, presser-bar 12 and presser-foot 12'. Mounted for rotary movement on the bed 10 is a loop-taker 14 having journaled therein a thread-case 15 formed with a rotation-restraining finger 16. The loop-taker and thread-case are shown and described in detail in my copending application, Serial No. 692,934, filed October 10, 1933.

Fixed to and carried by the bed of the machine is a throat-plate 17 formed with the usual needle-aperture 11' and feed-dog slots 13 and having a rotation-restraining bar 18 fixed by the screws 19 to the lower face thereof. The throat-plate and rotation-restraining bar, for the purpose of this improvement, are parts of the sewing machine bed. The bar 18 is provided with a groove defined by the walls 20 and 21 and fixed to the bar are two U-shaped cushioning flat-springs 22 and 23. The springs 22 and 23 each have one of their limbs fixed to one edge of the bar 18 by the screws 24

and 24' and the bends are spaced from and substantially parallel to the walls 20 and 21. The other limbs, which are free, extend along the other edge of the bar and terminate in portions 22' and 23', respectively, which extend into apertures 25 and 25' of larger diameter than the width of the springs 22 and 23.

The cushion springs 22 and 23 are spaced from each other to provide an opening for the finger 16 on the thread-case, the space between the springs being slightly greater than the width of the finger 16. As is well known in sewing machines of this type, the loop of needle-thread is seized by the loop-taker beak, which moves in the direction of the arrow in Figure 1, and casts it around the thread-case 15 and, as the needle-thread loop is drawn up by the take-up, the thread must pass between the spring 22 and finger 16. It will be understood that the friction between the thread-case and loop-taker causes the finger 16 to press against the spring 22, and when the machine is operated the passage of the thread between the spring and finger occurs very quickly and with a snap-like action with the result that the finger 16, in some instances, is thrown against the bend of the spring 23 which absorbs the impact and reduces the noise. The friction between the thread-case and loop-taker then causes the thread-case to move in the direction of movement of the thread-case as indicated by the arrow in Figure 1 and this movement of the thread-case throws the finger 16 against the bend of the spring 22 which deadens this blow. Also, due to the fact that the lead of the lower thread T is at one side of a vertical plane passing through the center of the thread-case when the stitch is set, the lower thread T, which is under tension at this time, moves the thread-case in a counter-clockwise direction, as viewed in Figure 1, thereby causing the finger 16 to strike the spring 23 which absorbs the blow.

It will be obvious from the above description that the springs 22 and 23 will absorb the blow of the thread-case rotation-restraining finger as it vibrates back and forth in the space between the springs thereby reducing noise and vibration.

Having thus set forth the nature of the invention, what I claim herein is:—

1. A sewing machine having in combination, stitch-forming mechanism including a reciprocatory needle, a circularly moving loop-taker cooperating with said needle, a thread-case carried by said loop-taker and having a rotation-restraining finger, a throat-plate, a bar located beneath said throat-plate, said bar having a groove which re-

The Scotland Connection

On May 18, 1934, Glasgow Scotland Denis Shaw Craddock applied for a British patent with the London Patent Office. The design was almost identical to the Goosman design.

PATENT SPECIFICATION

Application Date: *May 18, 1934. No. 15012/34.*

Complete Specification Left: *May 20, 1935.*

Complete Specification Accepted: *Sept. 24, 1935.*

435,578

PROVISIONAL SPECIFICATION

Improvements in Sewing Machines

We, THE SINGER MANUFACTURING COMPANY LIMITED, a British Company of Singer, Clydebank, Dumbartonshire, and DENIS SHAW CRADDOCK, of British Nationality, of 3, Gray Street, Glasgow, do hereby declare the nature of this invention to be as follows:—

This invention relates to improvements in sewing machines.

In a sewing machine constructed in accordance with the present invention the mechanism below the bed-plate is enclosed within a sheet metal box structure attached to the bed-plate and provided with a hinged bottom wall openable to afford access to the lower mechanism.

Hinged on a horizontal axis to the box structure at the forward end of the bed-plate is a sheet metal flap adapted, when the machine is in use, to form an extension of the bed-plate. In order to permit the machine to be accommodated within a travelling case of minimum capacity, the extension plate is foldable into a position above and perpendicular to the bed-plate adjacent to the head of the arm of the machine.

According to a preferred arrangement the bed-plate rests at each corner on a resilient pad supported by a strut member within and unitary with the box structure and extending the full depth of said box structure so that its lower end engages the bottom wall of the box structure at a point in vertical register with a resilient supporting foot on the exterior of said bottom wall for engagement with a table or other machine-supporting surface. As will be understood, the construction is such that the weight of the machine is transmitted through the strut members to the resilient feet.

The box structure is conveniently pivotally attached to the bed-plate on an axis transverse to and located about midway of the length of the bed-plate, by means of two short pivot-forming bolts each of which penetrates an aperture in one longitudinal wall of the box structure and a registering aperture in a longitudinal rib depending from the adjacent edge of the bed-plate. It will thus be seen that, by virtue of its pivotal connection with the box structure, the machine is permitted readily to accommodate itself to its resilient supports.

The bottom wall of the box structure is hinged along its rear longitudinal edge to the rear wall of said structure so that, to gain access to the mechanism below the bed-plate, it is necessary only to tip the machine backwardly on to its side, whereupon the bottom wall may be opened forwardly and downwardly.

Dated this 17th day of May, 1934.
CRUIKSHANK & FAIRWEATHER,
86, St. Vincent Street, Glasgow, and
65/66, Chancery Lane, London, W.C.2,
Agents for the Applicants.

COMPLETE SPECIFICATION

Improvements in Sewing Machines

We, THE SINGER MANUFACTURING COMPANY LIMITED, a British Company of Singer, Clydebank, Dumbartonshire, and DENIS SHAW CRADDOCK, of British Nationality, of 3, Gray Street, Glasgow, do hereby declare the nature of this invention and in what manner the same is to be performed, to be particularly described and ascertained in and by the following statement:—

This invention relates to improvements in sewing machines.

[*Price 1/-*]

In a sewing machine constructed in accordance with the present invention the mechanism below the bed-plate is enclosed within a box structure attached to the bed-plate and provided with a hinged bottom wall openable to afford access to the lower mechanism.

A sewing machine constructed in accordance with the present invention is illustrated in the accompanying drawings in which Fig. 1 is a front elevation, Fig. 2 an inverted plan view, the bottom wall

A copy of the full patent application is in the appendix at the end of this book.

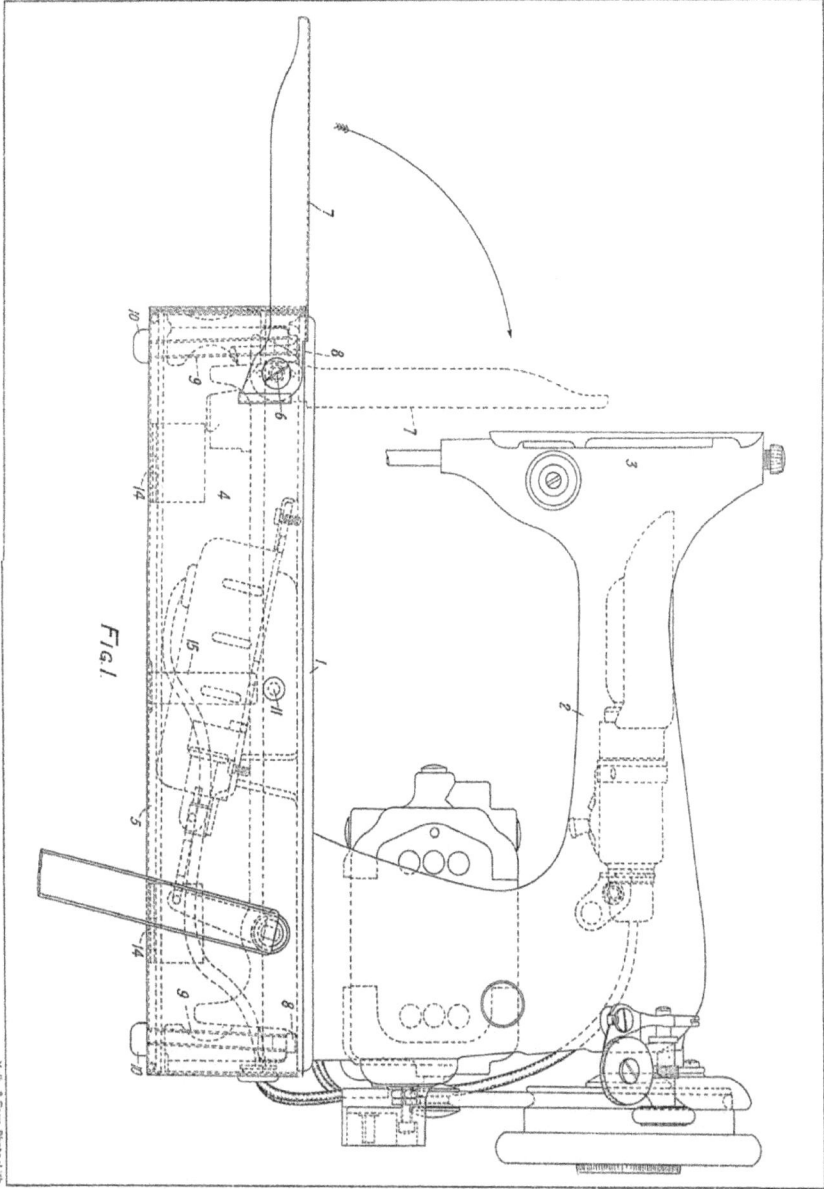

[This Drawing is a reproduction of the Original on a reduced scale.]

435,578 COMPLETE SPECIFICATION

Fig.I.

Malby & Sons, Photo-Lith.

3 SHEETS
SHEET 1

On November 12, 1941, SINGER Mfg Co. of Clydebank mechanic James Heggie filed a British patent application for "Feeding Mechanism..." (GB Patent 545,156 issued on May 13, 1942).

PATENT SPECIFICATION

Application Date: Nov. 11, 1940. No. 16326/40.

545,156

Complete Specification Left: Nov. 5, 1941.

Complete Specification Accepted: May 13, 1942.

PROVISIONAL SPECIFICATION

Feeding Mechanism for Sewing Machines

We, The Singer Manufacturing Company Limited, a British Company, of Singer, Clydebank, Dumbartonshire, and James Heggie, of British Nationality, of 7, Drumry Road, Clydebank, Dumbartonshire, do hereby declare the nature of this invention to be as follows:—

This invention relates to feeding mechanism for sewing machines, more particularly applicable to sewing machines of the type formed with a cylindrical work-arm as used, for example, in the stitching and trimming of footwear.

An object of the invention is to produce a construction in which the free end or head of the work-arm is rendered compact by reason that certain elements of the feeding mechanism, in lieu of being located in the work-arm head, are located within the contour of the arm but spaced from said head.

In a construction of cylinder arm machine according to the invention a bifurcated feed-dog-carrier mounted within the head of the work-arm in front of a rotary loop-taker derives its rising and falling movements from a feed-lift shaft journalled within the work-arm and actuated by pitman mechanism from the main shaft journalled in the usual overhanging bracket arm. The feed-lift-rock shaft carries, within the work-arm, a bracket in which is journalled a feed shaft carrying, at its forward end, the feed-dog-carrier. Mounted on the rear end of said feed-shaft within a laterally exposed part of the work-arm is a forked lever which struddles a sleeve journalled on a boss carried by a lever secured on one end of a short feed-rock-shaft journalled within the work-arm and operatively connected at its other end by means of pitman mechanism with the main shaft. The boss loosely surrounds a shaft which drives the lower stitch-forming mechanism and which is operatively connected at its rear end by gearing with the lower end of a vertical shaft of which the upper end is geared to the main-shaft.

Lateral cut-aways in the work-arm permit ready access to the feed actuating shafts.

Dated this 9th day of November, 1940.
CRUIKSHANK & FAIRWEATHER,
29, St. Vincent Place, Glasgow, C.1,
Agents for the Applicants.

COMPLETE SPECIFICATION

Feeding Mechanism for Sewing Machines

We, The Singer Manufacturing Company Limited, a British Company, of Singer, Clydebank, Dumbartonshire, and James Heggie, of British Nationality, of 7, Drumry Road, Clydebank, Dumbartonshire, do hereby declare the nature of this invention and in what manner the same is to be performed, to be particularly described and ascertained in and by the following statement:—

This invention relates to feeding mechanism for sewing machines, more particularly applicable to sewing machines of the type formed with a cylindrical work-arm as used, for example, in the stitching and trimming of footwear.

An object of the invention is to produce a construction in which the free end or head of the work-arm is rendered compact by reason that certain elements of the feeding mechanism, in lieu of being located in the head of the work-arm, are located within the contour of the arm but spaced from said head.

The invention consists of feeding mechanism for a sewing machine of the type equipped with a work-arm, including a feed-shaft located within the work-arm, a feed-dog-carrier secured on the forward end of said feed-shaft, a feed-lift-shaft journalled within the work-arm and carrying a bracket in which the feed-shaft is journalled eccentrically to said feed-lift-shaft, whereby the feed-shaft and the feed-dog-carrier derive rising and falling movements from oscillatory movements of the feed-lift-shaft, a feed-

[Price 1/-]

A copy of the full patent application is in the appendix at the end of this book.

545,156 COMPLETE SPECIFICATION

1 SHEET

Malby & Sons, Photo-Lith.

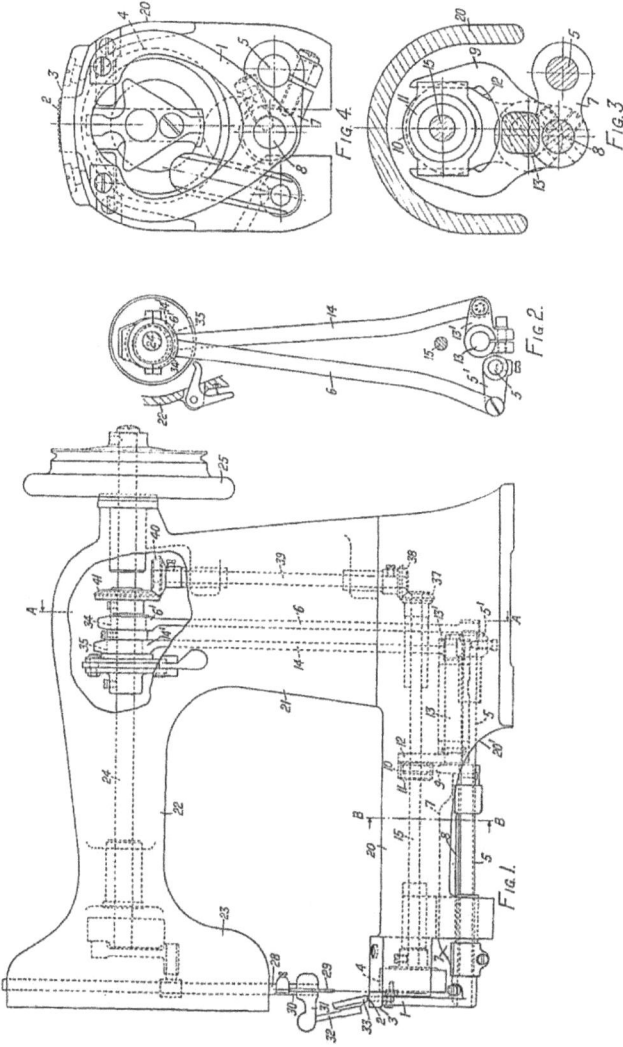

Fig. 1.

Fig. 2.

Fig. 3.

Fig. 4.

On November 12, 1941, James Heggie filed a US patent application for "Feeding Mechanism..." (US Patent 2,325,510 issued on July 27, 1943).

July 27, 1943.   J. HEGGIE   2,325,510

FEEDING MECHANISM FOR SEWING MACHINES

Filed Nov. 12, 1941   2 Sheets—Sheet 1

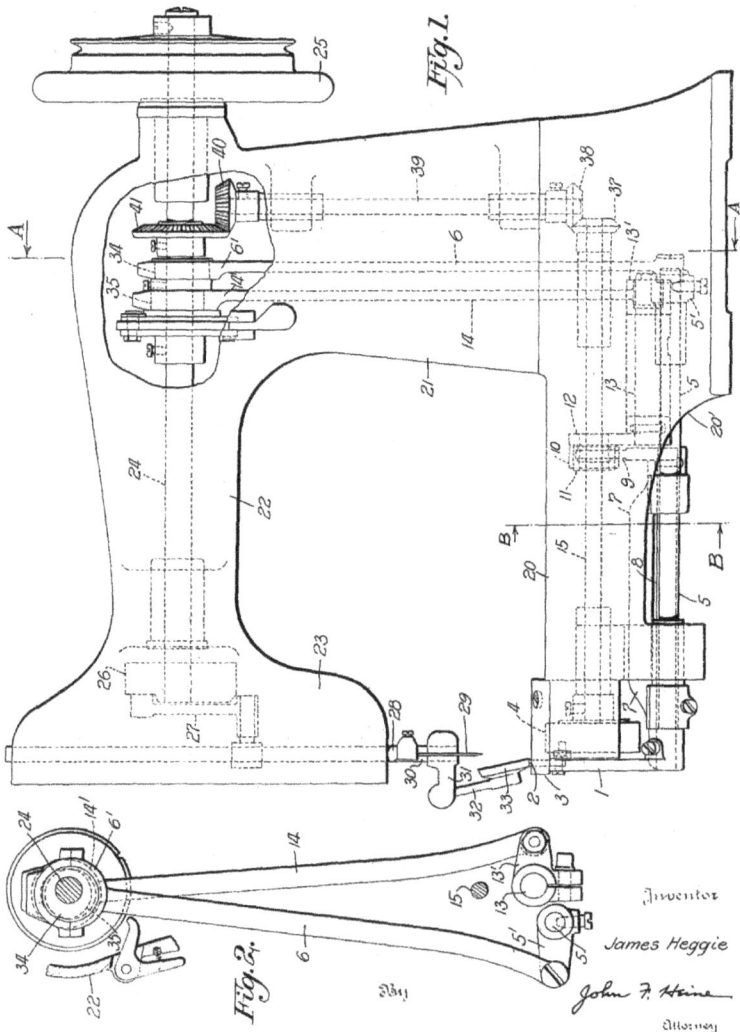

Heggie assigned all rights to The SINGER Manufacturing Company, Elizabeth, N.J.

July 27, 1943.   J. HEGGIE   2,325,510

FEEDING MECHANISM FOR SEWING MACHINES

Filed Nov. 12, 1941   2 Sheets—Sheet 2

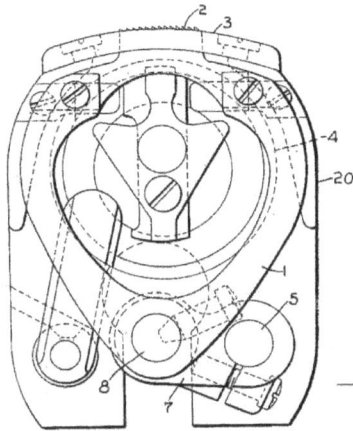

Fig. 4.

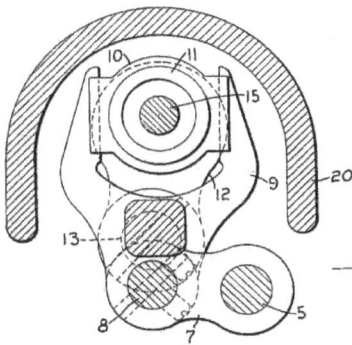

Fig. 3.

Inventor
James Heggie

Witness:

John N. Cave

By John F. Heine

Attorney

31

A copy of the full patent application is in the appendix at the end of this book.

Patented July 27, 1943

2,325,510

UNITED STATES PATENT OFFICE

2,325,510

FEEDING MECHANISM FOR SEWING MACHINES

James Heggie, Clydebank, Scotland, assignor to
The Singer Manufacturing Company, Elizabeth, N. J., a corporation of New Jersey

Application November 12, 1941, Serial No. 418,821
In Great Britain November 11, 1940

5 Claims. (Cl. 112—215)

(Granted under the provisions of sec. 14, act of
March 2, 1927; 357 O. G. 5)

This invention relates to feeding mechanism for sewing machines, more particularly applicable to sewing machines of the type formed with a cylindrical work-arm as used, for example, in the stitching and trimming of footwear.

An object of the invention is to produce a construction in which the free end or head of the work-arm is rendered compact by reason that certain elements of the feeding mechanism, in lieu of being located in the work-arm head, are located within the contour of the arm but spaced from, i. e., rearward of, said head.

Feeding mechanism according to the invention includes a feed-dog-carrier mounted within the work-arm head on the forward end of a feed-shaft which is operatively connected within the body of the work-arm to a feed-rock-shaft, and a feed-lift-shaft journalled within the work-arm and carrying a bracket fixed thereto in which said feed-shaft is journalled, said feed-rock-shaft and said feed-lift-shaft deriving actuation from the main or upper shaft of the sewing machine.

The invention is illustrated in the accompanying drawings in which Fig. 1 is a side elevation of a sewing machine incorporating the improved feeding mechanism. Fig. 2 is a fragmentary transverse vertical section mainly on the line A—A of Fig. 1. Fig. 3 is a vertical transverse section on the line B—B of Fig. 1. Fig. 4 is an end elevation looking on the front of the work-arm. Figs. 3 and 4 are drawn to a larger scale than Figs. 1 and 2.

Referring to the drawings, 20 denotes a cylindrical work-arm, 21 a standard uprising from the rear end of the work-arm 20, and 22 an overhanging bracket-arm terminating in a head 23, constituting the frame of the sewing machine.

Journalled in the bracket-arm 22 is a main shaft 24 provided at its rear end with a driving pulley and flywheel 25 and at its front end with a crank disc 26 which drives, through the medium of a connecting rod 27, a reciprocatory needle-bar 28 which is journalled in the head 23 and is equipped at its lower end with a needle 29. 30 denotes a presser-bar also mounted in the head 23 and equipped at its lower end with a bracket 31 to which is connected an arm 32 carrying a presser-wheel 33 which co-operates with a feed-dog 2 projecting upwardly through a throat-plate 3 attached to the head of the work-arm 20.

Mounted within the head of the work-arm 20, in front of a rotary loop-taker 4 which co-operates with the needle 29, is a bifurcated feed-dog-carrier 1 secured on the forward end of a feed-shaft 8. The feed-shaft 8 and therewith

the feed-dog-carrier derive rising and falling movements from a feed-lift-shaft 5 journalled within the work-arm 20 and having fixed on its rear end a crank-arm 5' which is operatively connected to the lower end of a pitman 6 of which the upper end is formed as a strap 6' embracing an eccentric 34 secured on the main shaft 24. Fixed to the shaft 5, within the work-arm 20, is a bracket 7 in which is journalled, eccentrically of the shaft 5, the feed-shaft 8. Mounted on the rear end of the feed-shaft 8, within a laterally exposed body part of the work-arm 20, is a forked lever 9 which slidably straddles a bush 10 journalled on a boss 11 carried by a lever 12 secured on the forward end of a short feed-rock-shaft 13 journalled within the work-arm 20, the construction being such that the feed-shaft 8 rises and falls under the action of the shaft 5 and is also oscillated, i. e., performs feeding movements, about its own axis under the action of the feed-rock-shaft 13. Fixed on the rear end of the feed-rock-shaft 13 is a crank-arm 13' to which is operatively connected the lower end of a pitman 14 provided at its upper end with a strap 14' embracing an eccentric 35 secured on the main shaft 24.

The loop-taker 4 is secured on the forward end of a shaft 15 journalled within the work-arm 20 and loosely surrounded by the boss 11. At its rear end the shaft 15 is connected by bevel gear wheels 37, 38 with the lower end of an upright shaft 39 connected at its upper end by bevel gear wheels 40, 41 with the shaft 24.

Lateral cut-aways 20' in the work-arm 20 permit ready access to the feed-actuating mechanism.

What is claimed is:

1. In a sewing machine having a frame including a bracket-arm and a work-arm formed with a head, in combination, a main shaft journalled in said bracket-arm, a feed-rock-shaft journalled within said work-arm, a feed-lift-shaft journalled within said work-arm, a bracket fixed to said feed-lift-shaft within said work-arm, a feed-shaft journalled in said bracket and eccentric to said feed-lift-shaft, operative connections within the body of said work-arm for communicating oscillatory movements to said feed-shaft from said feed-rock-shaft, a feed-dog carrier mounted within the head of said work-arm on the forward end of said feed-shaft, and operative connections between said feed-rock-shaft and feed-lift-shaft and said main shaft.

2. In a sewing machine having a frame including a bracket-arm and a work-arm formed with

a head, in combination, a main shaft journalled in said bracket-arm, a feed-rock-shaft journalled within said work-arm, a lever secured on the forward end of said feed-rock-shaft, a bush mounted on said lever, a feed-lift-shaft jour- 5 nalled within said work-arm, a bracket fixed to said feed-lift-shaft, a feed-shaft journalled in said bracket and eccentric to said feed-lift-shaft, a forked lever mounted on the rear end of said feed-shaft within the body of said work-arm and 10 slidably engaging said bush whereby oscillatory movements are imparted to said feed-shaft by said feed-rock-shaft, a feed-dog carrier mounted within the head of said work-arm on the forward end of said feed-shaft, and operative con- 15 nections between said feed-rock-shaft and feed-lift-shaft and said main shaft.

3. In a sewing machine having a frame including a bracket-arm and a work-arm formed with a head, in combination, a main shaft journalled 20 in said bracket-arm, a loop-taker shaft journalled within said work-arm, a lever secured on the forward end of said feed-rock-shaft, a boss carried by said lever and loosely surround- 25 ing said loop-taker-shaft, a bush journalled on said boss, a feed-lift-shaft journalled within said work-arm, a bracket fixed to said feed-lift-shaft within said work-arm, a feed-shaft journalled in said bracket and eccentric to said feed-lift-shaft 30 whereby to rise and fall with rocking movements of said feed-lift-shaft, a forked lever mounted on the rear end of said feed-shaft within the body of said work-arm and slidably engaging said bush, whereby oscillatory movements are im- 35 parted to said feed-shaft by said feed-rock-shaft, a feed-dog carrier mounted within the head of

said work-arm on the forward end of said feed-shaft, and operative connections between said feed-rock-shaft and feed-lift-shaft and said main shaft.

4. In a sewing machine having a frame including a bracket-arm and a work-arm formed with a head, in combination, a main shaft journalled in said bracket-arm, a feed-rock-shaft journalled within said work-arm, a feed-lift-shaft journalled within said work-arm, a bracket fixed to said feed-lift-shaft within said work-arm, a feed-shaft journalled in said bracket, a pair of inter-connected levers within the body of said work-arm carried, respectively, by said feed-shaft and said feed-rock-shaft, a feed-dog carrier mounted within the head of said work-arm on the forward end of said feed-shaft, and operative connections including cranks and pitmans between said feed-rock-shaft and feed-lift-shaft and said main shaft.

5. In a sewing machine having a frame including a bracket-arm and a work-arm formed with a head, in combination, a main shaft journalled in said bracket-arm, a feed-rock-shaft journalled within said work-arm, a bracket fixed to said feed-lift-shaft within said work-arm, a feed-shaft journalled in said bracket and eccentric to said feed-lift-shaft, connections within the body of said work-arm for communicating feeding movements from said feed-rock-shaft to said feed-shaft, a feed-dog carrier mounted within the head of said work-arm on the forward end of said feed-shaft, and operative connections between said feed-rock-shaft and feed-lift-shaft and said main shaft.

JAMES HEGGIE.

The 221K Design

The SINGER Model 221K with its inner-toothed belt drive was introduced around 1964. These K7 machines were all manufactured at the Kilbowie Clydebank Factory in Scotland.

Connecting the upper and lower sewing machine drives by flexible belt drew the attention of numerous inventors over the years. The problem is that the upper and lower drives MUST stay exactly in time in relation to each other.

On October 24, 1939, SINGER Bridgeport Connecticut Chief Experimental Engineer George A. Fleckenstein filed an application "Sewing Machine." It became US Patent 2,276,246 on March 10, 1942. All rights were assigned to The

SINGER Mfg Company, Elizabeth, N.J. This is one of the first workable designs that later led to the 221 K7. Note that the SEWHANDY machine was used in the patent application illustration.

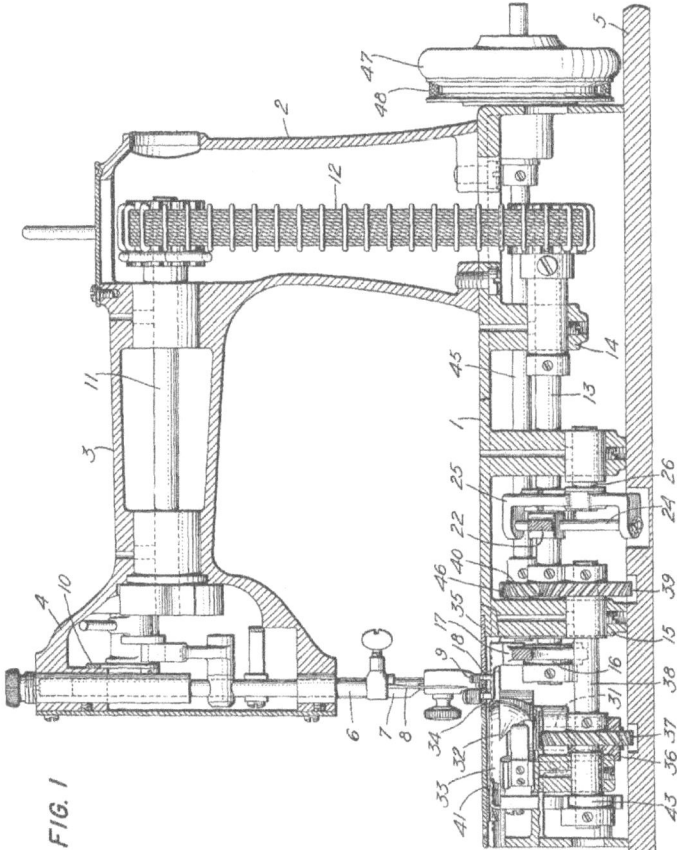

March 10, 1942.   G. A. FLECKENSTEIN   2,276,246

SEWING MACHINE

Filed Oct. 24, 1939   4 Sheets—Sheet 1

FIG. I

Inventor

GEORGE A. FLECKENSTEIN

By Henry J Miller

Attorney

The full patent application is in the appendix.

March 10, 1942.   G. A. FLECKENSTEIN   2,276,246

SEWING MACHINE

Filed Oct. 24, 1939   4 Sheets—Sheet 4

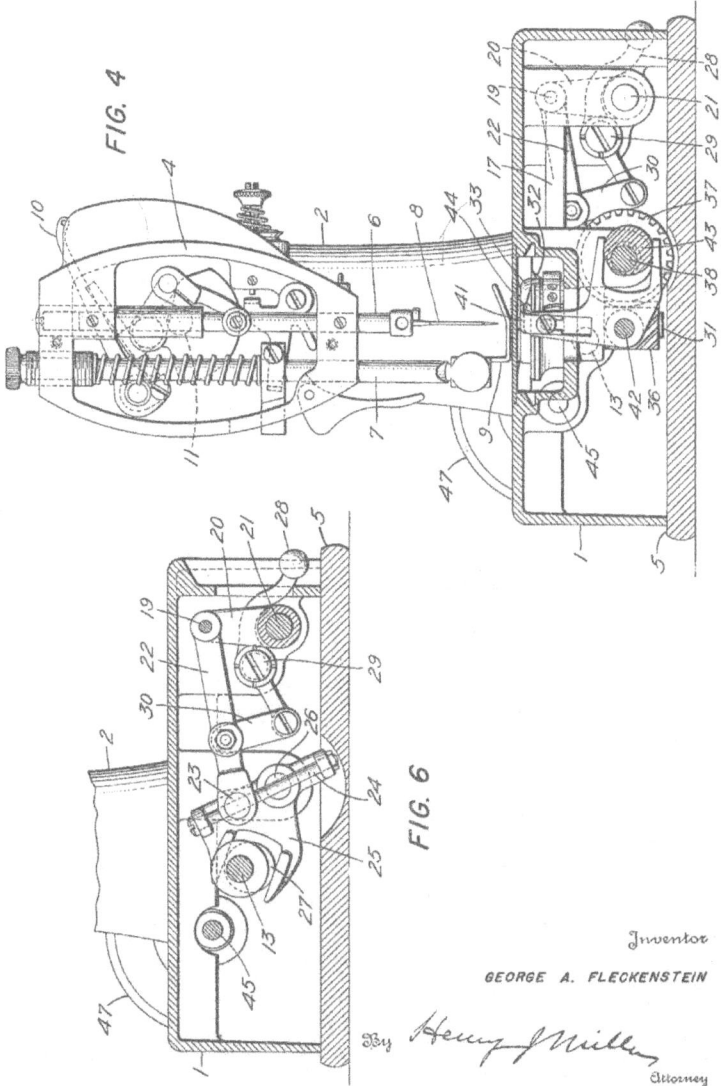

FIG. 4

FIG. 6

Inventor

GEORGE A. FLECKENSTEIN

By Henry J. Miller

Attorney

35

Patented Mar. 10, 1942

2,276,246

UNITED STATES PATENT OFFICE

2,276,246

SEWING MACHINE

George A. Fleckenstein, Stratford, Conn., assignor
to The Singer Manufacturing Company, Elizabeth, N. J., a corporation of New Jersey

Application October 24, 1939, Serial No. 300,903

8 Claims.   (Cl. 112—220)

This invention relates to sewing machines more particularly of the small portable family type machines having a box bed and overhanging bracket-arm containing the stitch-forming and work-feeding mechanisms of the machine. The bed of the machine houses the work-feeding mechanism and vertical axis rotary loop-taker, which require to be driven at different speeds. The bed also houses the main-shaft of the machine and the electric motor for driving it by means of the usual belt and balance-wheel or belt-pulley, the latter being carried by an outboard projection of the main-shaft.

An object of the present invention is to provide a simplified arrangement of shafting and gearing for such a machine within the limited space available in the machine frame, using a small high speed motor with a small driving pulley belted to a balance-wheel on a main-shaft so located as to afford a belt drive of adequate length while keeping the rim of the balance-wheel above the base-plate of the machine upon which the bed is fastened.

With the above and other objects in view, as will hereinafter appear, the invention comprises the devices, combinations and arrangements of parts hereinafter set forth and illustrated in the accompanying drawings of a preferred embodiment of the invention, from which the several features of the invention and the advantages attained thereby will be readily understood by those skilled in the art.

Of the accompanying drawings, Fig. 1 is a longitudinal vertical section through a sewing machine embodying the invention. Fig. 2 is a bottom plan view of the machine with the bottom or base-plate removed from the machine bed. Fig. 3 is a transverse vertical section through the bed and bracket-arm standard. Fig. 4 is a transverse vertical section through the machine bed, showing the bracket-arm head and needle-mechanism therein in elevation. Fig. 5 is a transverse vertical section substantially on the line 5—5, Fig. 2, and Fig. 6 is a transverse vertical section substantially on the line 6—6, Fig. 2.

The machine is formed with a frame including the box bed 1 and overhanging bracket-arm with a vertical standard 2 and horizontal portion 3 terminating in the head 4. The open bottom of the bed 1 is closed by the bottom or base-plate 5.

The bracket-arm head 4 carries the usual reciprocatory needle-bar 6 and spring-pressed presser-bar 7 fitted, respectively, with the needle 8 and presser-foot 9. The head 4 also carries the needle-thread take-up lever 10. The needle-bar 6 and take-up lever 10 are actuated in the usual manner by the top rotary shaft 11 which is journaled in the horizontal member 3 of the bracket-arm and is connected at its rear end by the clip-belt 12 to the bottom free-ended rotary shaft 13 which is disposed directly below the bracket-arm and is journaled in bearing lugs 14, 15 between the ends of the shaft 13 in the bed 1.

Mounted on the free end of the bottom rotary shaft 13, remote from the clip-belt 12, is at least one of the feed-eccentrics, preferably the feed-lift eccentric 16, which is embraced by the feed-bar 17 carrying the feed-dog 18. The feed-bar 17 is fulcrumed at its rearward end upon the pin 19 carried by the feed-rocker 20 which is journaled on the pivot-shaft 21 fixed in lugs in the bed

Connected to the pin 19, Fig. 6, is one end of the link 22 the opposite forked end of which pivotally carries a cross-pin 23 which is free to slide on the pin 24 carried by the rocking yoke 25 fulcrumed at 26 in the bed 1 and rocked by the feed-advance eccentric 27 on the bottom shaft 13. The stitch-length may be regulated, or even reversed, by shifting the link 22 to carry the cross-pin 23 toward or across a position of axial coincidence with the yoke-fulcrum 26. Such regulation may be effected by movement of the feed-regulator lever 28 which is frictionally fulcrumed at 29 in the bed 1 and connected by the link 30 to the link 22.

Complemental to the needle 8 in the formation of stitches is the loop-taker or rotary hook which is a cup-shaped body carried by the vertical hook-shaft 31 and formed with a loop-taking beak 32. Within the hook-cup is disposed the usual stationary bobbin-case 33 which carries the usual bobbin or under thread mass, not shown. This bobbin-case is restrained against rotation with the hook by means of the usual rotation-restraining tongue 34, Fig. 1, which freely enters a notch in the under side of the throat-plate 35.

The vertical hook-shaft 31 carries the spiral gear 36 which meshes with the spiral gear 37 on the countershaft 38 journaled parallel to and in front of the bottom rotary shaft 13. The countershaft 38 carries a gear 39 which meshes with a gear 40 of equal size on the bottom rotary shaft 13. The rotary hook preferably makes two revolutions to one revolution of the bottom shaft 13.

The machine is preferably provided with a bobbin-case opener or kicker 41, Fig. 4, which is pivoted at 42 in the bed 1 and actuated by the eccentric 43 on the countershaft 38. At the time when the needle-loop which has been cast about the bobbin-case 33 is being drawn up by the take-up 10 and is about to be drawn between the rotation-restraining tongue 34 and the engaged wall of the notch in the under side of the throat-plate 35, the kicker 41 engages the shoulder 44, Fig. 4, on the bobbin-case and turns the bobbin-case slightly or enough to open a gap or

The *Rejected* Design

The next patent related to the SINGER Model 221/222 is one that was never put in to production. On February 9, 1941, SINGER Mfg. Co. Bridgeport Connecticut factory engineers Leonard C. Marsac and David A. Graesser filed an application "Sewing Machine Drive." It was issued by the US Patent Office as Patent 2,282,071 on May 5, 1942. As usual, all rights were assigned to The SINGER Mfg Company, Elizabeth, N.J.

Apparently, SINGER had heard of problems from consumers that they were not happy with the Model 221 Featherweight motor operation when it was running at low speeds. The inventors wrote in their patent application "Unfortunately this type of machine has had the undesirable characteristic of running unevenly in the low speed range."

Marsac and Graesser actually identified the problem sewing machine as "The machine herein illustrated is a Singer No. 221 class machine of the light-weight portable type weighing about 11 pounds.." While the new design of Marsac and Graesser would have fixed the problem, SINGER apparently felt it was not serious enough to warrant this fix. It was never put in to production.

This "rejected" design is on the following pages. A copy of the full patent application is in the appendix at the end of this book.

Fig. 1.

Fig. 2.

Fig. 4.

Fig. 3.

BY

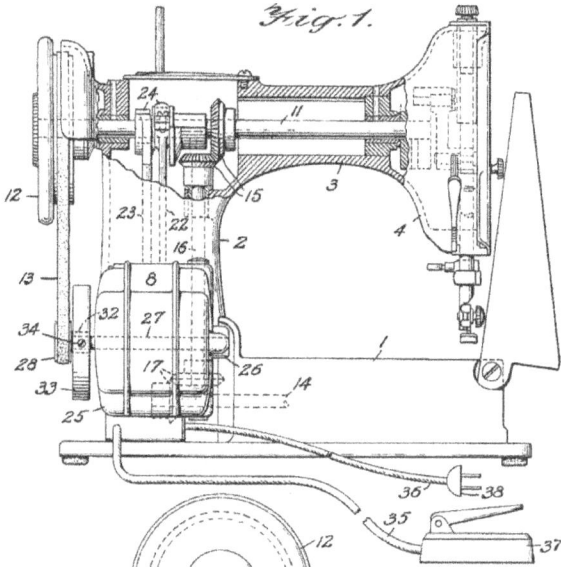

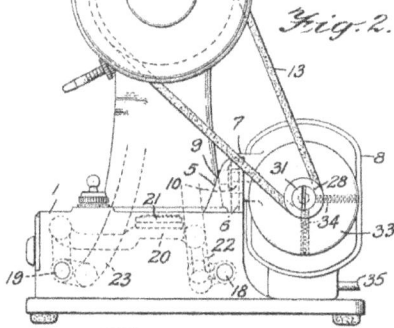

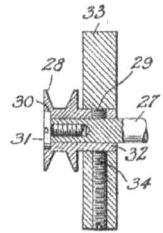

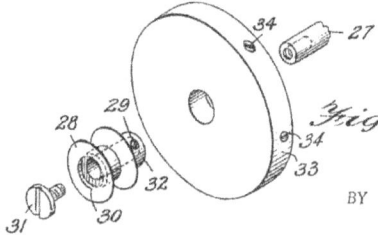

INVENTORS
LEONARD C. MARSAC
DAVID A. GRAESSER

John F. Heine

ATTORNEY

38

UNITED STATES PATENT OFFICE

2,282,071

SEWING MACHINE DRIVE

Leonard C. Marsac, Cranford, and David A. Graesser, Elizabeth, N. J., assignors to The Singer Manufacturing Company, Elizabeth, N. J., a corporation of New Jersey

Application February 19, 1941, Serial No. 379,588

2 Claims. (Cl. 112—220)

This invention relates to motor-driven sewing machines, and more particularly to variable speed sewing machines which are driven by small individual motors permanently connected in driving relation therewith. These driving motors are usually of the high-speed series wound type and their speed is controlled by a manually actuated rheostat connected in series therewith.

This type of sewing machine is most commonly used in the home where a light compact sewing outfit having a moderate operating speed is required. Such a high-speed motor is therefore usually provided with a small driving pulley which is at all times operatively connected, by means of a belt, to a larger driven pulley mounted on the sewing machine. Thus a proper speed reduction is effected between the motor and the sewing machine.

Unfortunately this type of machine has had the undesirable characteristic of running unevenly in the low-speed range. This characteristic is highly objectionable as it is within the low-speed range that this type machine is often used in order to perform such work as embroidering, darning and hemstitching. This type of work is best accomplished with a sewing machine producing about fifty to seventy-five stitches per minute as compared to a regular sewing speed of about twelve hundred stitches per minute.

Some prior motor-driven sewing machines have been proposed, with little or no success, to overcome the above noted objectionable characteristic by the use of a heavier balance-wheel on the main shaft, or by the use of gears in lieu of the driving belt, or by generally strengthening the machine itself. Such expedients make for a heavy, slow running and costly machine.

It is therefore, an object of the present invention to provide an inexpensive, practical and light-weight family sewing machine including a motor-drive that will deliver a steady flow of power to the machine at all speeds and, particularly, in the low speed range used, for example, in embroidering and darning operations.

It is known that a machine of the above described type will operate smoothly at low speeds if a balance-wheel of relatively heavy weight is applied to the sewing machine main-shaft. However, such a machine is found to be sluggish in operation and too great a starting load is thereby applied to the small driving motor. The present applicants have drastically reduced the weight of the main shaft balance-wheel and have mounted a relatively small, light-weight balance-wheel upon the motor shaft. The weight of the motor balance-wheel is much less than the weight which was removed from the above mentioned machine balance-wheel.

The applicants have found that by providing a small balance-wheel on the motor-shaft and by reducing the weight of the main-shaft balance-wheel, a steady flow of power will be available at all speeds, thus permitting a fine speed control at all times and particularly while in the low-speed range. In addition, it has been found that by removing weight from the main-shaft balance-wheel, slippage between the motor-driving pulley and the sewing machine driving belt is reduced to a marked extent. In the present machine the weight of the combined main shaft balance-wheel and driven pulley is reduced to a minimum by constructing the same of cast aluminum, light gauge sheet-metal or some similar material. This unit in the present machine now functions primarily, not as a balance-wheel, but as a hand-wheel, it being understood that hand-wheels on family sewing machines are required by their operators so that the machine may be turned over by hand, as in raising the needle for removal of work.

To more concretely illustrate the results of the present invention, the following figures are cited. It must be understood however that the invention is not limited in any manner by these figures and that they merely illustrate one specific form in which the invention may be applied.

The sewing machine herein illustrated is a Singer No. 221 class machine of the light-weight portable type weighing about eleven pounds and utilizing, prior to the application of the present invention, a main-shaft balance- and pulley-wheel weighing one pound and a half. Upon the application of the present invention, this old balance- and pulley-wheel was replaced by a combined hand-wheel and belt-pulley weighing ten ounces, and a seven ounce fly-wheel was mounted upon the motor-shaft. Thus it was found that not only were the slow-speed running qualities of the machine improved but an overall weight saving of seven ounces was made, such a saving representing four percent of the total weight of the prior machine.

The invention both in structure and in operation, as well as additional objects thereof, will be best understood from the following description taken in conjunction with the accompanying drawing in which:

Fig. 1 is a rear elevation of the improved sewing machine, a portion of the bracket-arm being

The World War II Design

The last of the SINGER Model 221 patents that I have included is also one that never did get into production. Remember the "Graduated Tension Regulator..." Patent 1,820,119 from 1931 (Page 8). SINGER Engineer Daniel Chason was now 55 years old, and was still working on Model 221 designs.

Chason came up with a radical design to improve the Model 221. It would make it even lighter, more rigid, and cheaper to manufacture. His design was a "sure thing." On June 8, 1942, Chason filed a patent application for "Sewing Machine Bed." The patent was issued on February 15, 1944 as US Patent 2,341,975. He assigned all rights to this patent to The SINGER Manufacturing Company, Elizabeth, N.J.

His new design used pressed and bent sheet metal in place of the die cast bed. While it is certain that the design would have done all it claimed, SINGER never put the design into production. Maybe they were satisfied with the money they were making on the current design. Maybe the tooling costs for the new design were not in the budget. The most likely reason was that World War II was on, and that the WAR PRODUCTION BOARD had stopped all production of family sewing machines. Their order, Limitation Order L-98, became effective on June 15, 1942. Chason filed this patent application seven days earlier....

Limitation Order L-98 also ordered the majority of existing back stock of finished family sewing machines frozen and designated for use only by government agencies.

From June 15, 1942 to July 1945, SINGER was involved with the design and manufacturing of a variety of items for the war effort. These items included .45 caliber automatic pistols, Fire Control for 37mm and 40mm anti-aircraft guns, B-29 gunfire control computers, Hydraulic servo assemblies, gun turret castings for the B-29 bomber, gun sights for Naval Mark XV 3-inch, 5-inch, and 40mm anti-aircraft guns, Caliber .30 M1 carbine receiver, and many more.

With all that World War II work going on at the SINGER Manufacturing Company, the Chason Model 221 design change was probably not a priority in anyone's foreseeable future. Not with a WAR to win!

After July 1945, the War was over and everything had to be "new." The Featherweight Model 221 was 12 years old. SINGER had new models that they probably felt would be more profitable. Whatever the reason, SINGER never put his design into production. Too bad, his design was a major improvement on the base, and would have created a 9 pound machine

This Chason design is on the following pages. A copy of the full patent application is in the appendix at the end of this book.

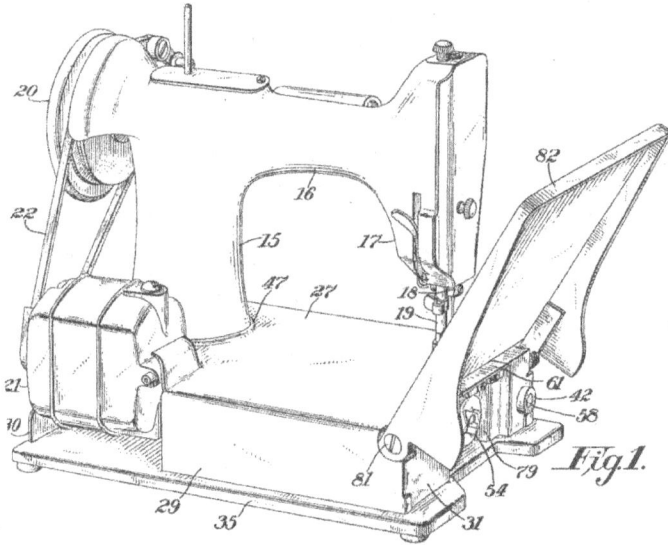

Fig.1.

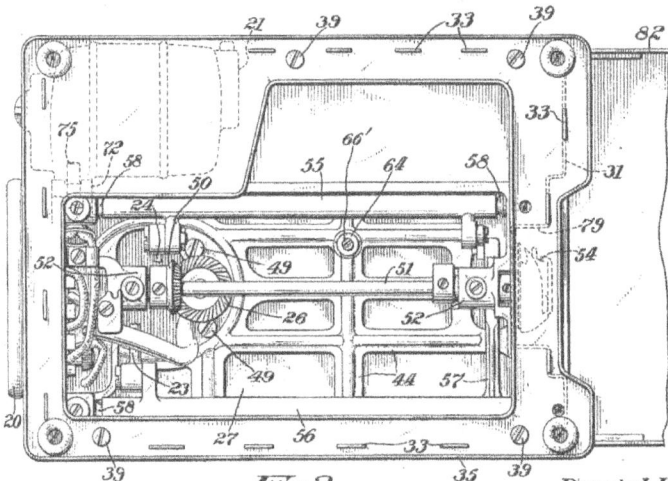

Fig.2.

Inventor

Daniel H. Chason

Witness:

John H. Cave

By *William F. Stewart*

Attorney

42

Fig.3.

Fig.4.

Fig.8.

Fig.5.

Fig.6.

Fig.7.

Fig.9.

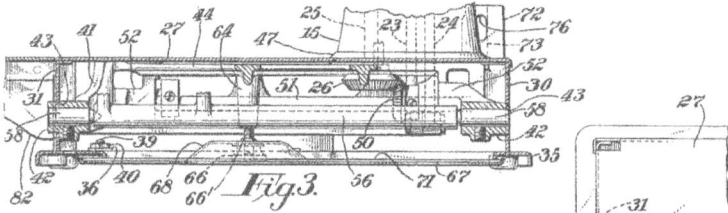

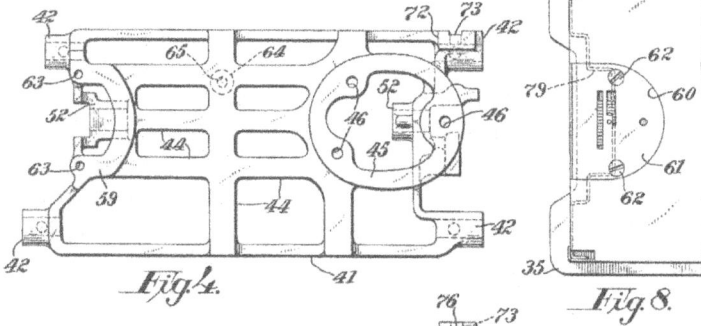

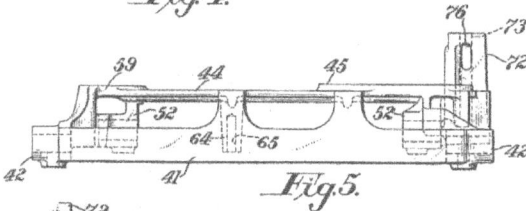

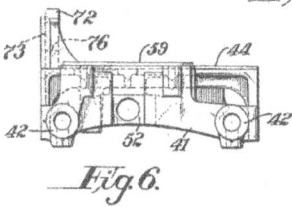

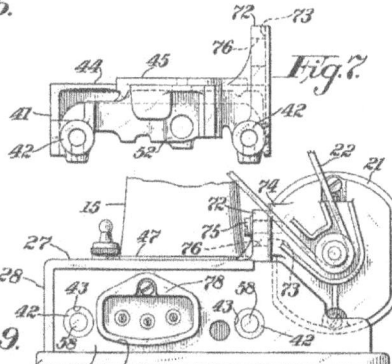

Witness:

John H. Cave

Inventor

Daniel H. Chason

By

William P. Stewart

Attorney

43

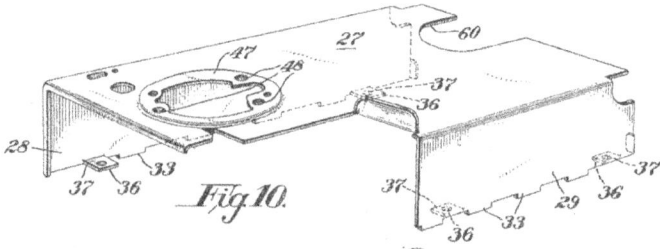

Fig 10.

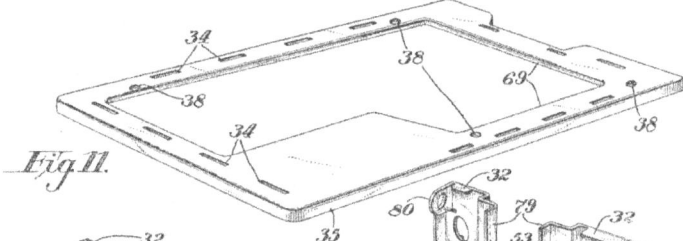

Fig 11.

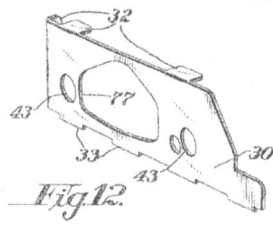

Fig 12.

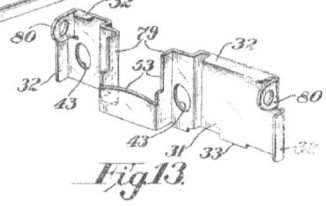

Fig 13.

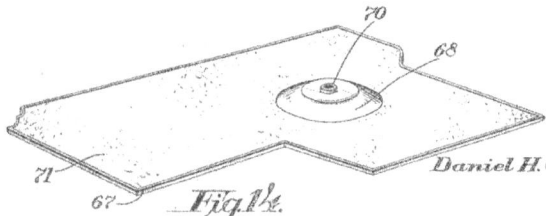

Fig 14.

Inventor

Daniel H. Chason

Witness:

John H. Cave

By

William P. Stewart

Attorney

44

UNITED STATES PATENT OFFICE

2,341,975

SEWING MACHINE BED

Daniel H. Chason, Elizabeth, N. J., assignor to
The Singer Manufacturing Company, Elizabeth, N. J., a corporation of New Jersey

Application June 8, 1942, Serial No. 446,179

8 Claims.   (Cl. 112—258)

This invention relates to sewing machines and more particularly to sewing machines of the portable type and has for its primary object to produce a sewing machine which is light in weight.

Another object of the present invention is to provide such a machine with a bed which will be not only light in weight but exceedingly rigid and inexpensive to manufacture.

A further object of the invention is to provide a sewing machine bed having a receptacle portion which may be constructed of sheet-metal, plastic or equivalent light weight materials.

With the above and other objects in view, as will hereinafter appear, the invention comprises the devices, combinations and arrangements of parts hereinafter set forth and illustrated in the accompanying drawings of a preferred embodiment of the invention, from which the several features of the invention and the advantages attained thereby will be readily understood by those skilled in the art.

The invention, both in structure and in operation, as well as additional objects thereof, will be best understood from the following description taken in conjunction with the accompanying drawings, in which:

Fig. 1 is a perspective view from the back side of a sewing machine incorporating the present invention.

Fig. 2 is a bottom plan view of the machine with the bottom closure-plate removed.

Fig. 3 is a vertical section taken longitudinally through the bed portion of the machine.

Fig. 4 is a top plan view of the bed-frame.

Fig. 5 is a side elevation of the bed-frame shown in Fig. 4.

Fig. 6 is a left-hand end elevation of the bed-frame shown in Fig. 5.

Fig. 7 is a right-hand end elevation of the bed-frame shown in Fig. 5.

Fig. 8 is a top plan view of a portion of the machine cloth-plate at the work-feeding end thereof.

Fig. 9 is a right-hand end elevation of the machine shown in Fig. 3.

Fig. 10 is a perspective view of the cloth-plate of the machine.

Fig. 11 is a perspective view of the platform member of the machine.

Fig. 12 is a perspective view of the right-hand end-wall shown in Fig. 3.

Fig. 13 is a perspective view of the left-hand end-wall shown in Fig. 3.

Fig. 14 is a perspective view of the bottom closure-plate shown in Fig. 3.

For the purposes of the present disclosure the invention is described as embodied in a preferred form in a sewing machine having an upright standard 15 which carries the overhanging bracket-arm 16 terminating in a hollow head 17. Journaled for endwise movement in the head 17 are the usual reciprocatory needle-bar 18 and presser-bar 19. Suitably mounted upon one end of the bracket-arm is the usual balance-wheel 20 driven from a motor 21 by a belt 22. Disposed within the standard 15 is the usual actuating mechanism comprising the feed-actuating pitmans 23 and 24, and the rotary shaft 25 carrying the bevel gear 26 at its lower end.

For a more detailed description of the actuating mechanism disposed within the standard and the bracket-arm, reference may be had to the U. S. patent to H. J. Goosman, No. 2,063,841, dated Dec. 8, 1936.

Supporting the upright standard 15 is a chambered bed portion comprising a cloth-plate 27 having side-walls 28 and 29 depending therefrom. End-walls 30 and 31, having lips 32, are secured to the end portions of the cloth-plate and the side-walls by welding or suitably fastening the lips 32 to the inner portions of the cloth-plate and side-walls. The depending side-walls 28 and 29 and the depending end-walls 30 and 31 form with the cloth-plate 27 a substantially rectangular shaped receptacle or enclosure.

Tongues 33 are formed on the bottom edges of the side- and end-walls of the cloth-plate; said tongues entering slots 34 provided in a platform member 35. Also formed on the side walls 28 and 29 are vertically apertured brackets 36, of which the apertures 37 are aligned with vertical apertures 38 provided in the platform member 35. Bolts 39 are received in these apertures, and nuts 40 are threaded on the bolts for the purpose of securing the platform member 35 to the chambered bed or receptacle portion comprising the above described cloth-plate.

In the preferred form of this bed portion, the cloth-plate and its depending walls are constructed from a thin sheet-metal, but it is obvious that it could be constructed from divers other materials including a molded plastic substance.

In order to give the bed portion the proper degree of rigidity, a substantially rectangular shaped skeleton-frame member 41 is provided within the chambered bed portion. Upon each of the two end portions of this frame member 41 are formed bearing-elements in the form of bosses 42 which snugly enter apertures 43 pro-

Model 222 Patents

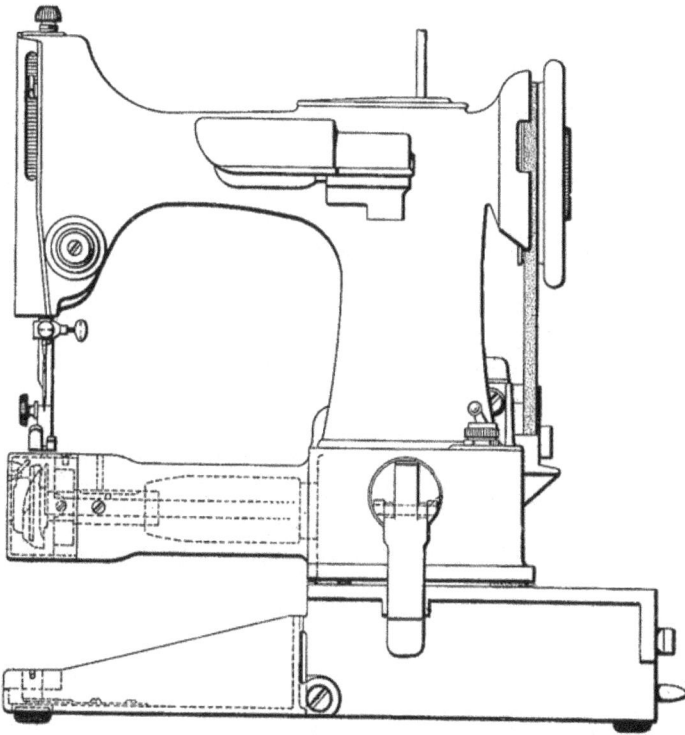

Model 222

Model 222 Patents

The SINGER Model 222 was the top line of the Featherweight design. It had all of the standard Model 221 features, plus it allowed you to lower the feed dogs for freehand embroidery. However, the real difference between the Model 221 and 222 was that it could easily change from a standard bed machine to a free arm machine. It was designed to be both.

The convertible design of the Model 222 presented a whole range of new technical problems for the SINGER designers. The method of converting from one to the other had to be simple, quick, and easy for the everyday woman. Making the design even more challenging was how to eliminate most all of the raised bed, and still have room to put all the linkages, shafts, and gears needed so that it would still sew.

The Canadian Design

The first patent relating to those design problems actually pre-dates the SINGER Model 221. Bertram Eaton, a resident of Toronto, Canada, filed an application on June 7, 1928 for a "Sewing Machine." It was issued by the United States Patent Office on October 14, 1930 as Patent 1,778,107.

His design is shown on the following pages. A copy of the full patent application is in the appendix at the end of this book.

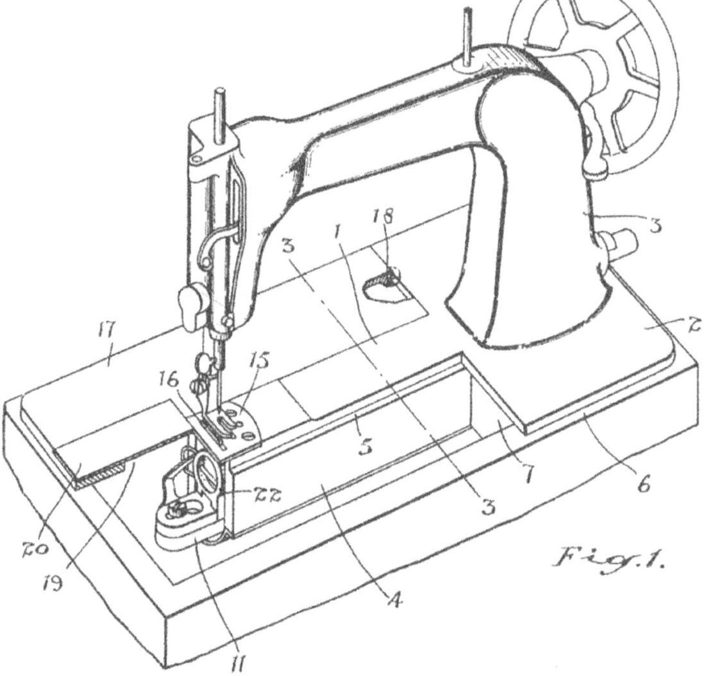

Fig.1.

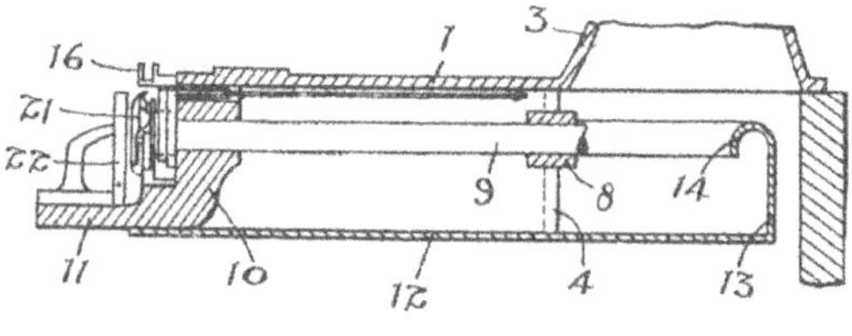

Fig.2.

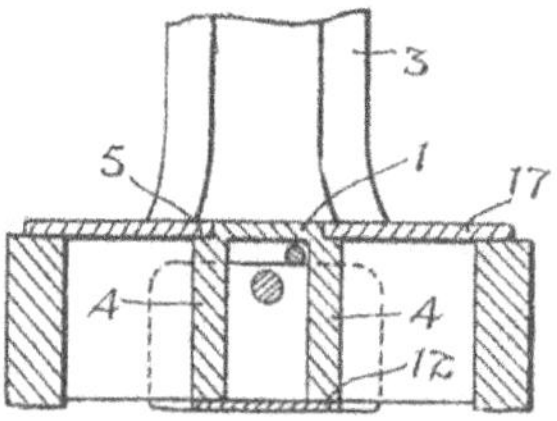

Fig.3.

Inventor.

Bertram Eaton

by H. J. S. Dennison atty

50

UNITED STATES PATENT OFFICE

BERTRAM EATON, OF TORONTO, ONTARIO, CANADA, ASSIGNOR TO ARTHUR LATCHAM, OF YORK, ONTARIO, CANADA, AND CLARK TAYLOR PURVIS, OF TORONTO, ONTARIO, CANADA

SEWING MACHINE

Application filed June 7, 1928. Serial No. 283,484.

The principal objects of this invention are, to provide a general utility form of machine which may be used for sewing flat or tubular articles and which may be very quickly changed to suit either purpose.

The principal feature of the invention consists in the novel construction of the bed frame and bed plate, whereby the major portion of the bed plate may be removed presenting an arm containing the bobbin and feed mechanism over which the tubular goods may be inserted.

In the drawings, Figure 1 is a perspective view of the improved machine showing a portion of the bed plate removed, disclosing the arm structure for cylindrical sewing.

Figure 2 is a longitudinal mid-sectional view through the arm structure.

Figure 3 is a cross sectional view taken on the line 3—3 of Figure 1.

In the ordinary types of sewing machines the bed plate is flat allowing only the sewing of flat goods thereon and where the cylindrical or tubular goods are to be machine sewn, special machines are provided wherein the operating mechanism is contained in an arm open at the end to allow the goods to be inserted thereover.

It is very desirable that a sewing machine be produced which will enable the ordinary seamstress to sew tubular goods and this invention has been produced to effect that result.

The bed plate 1 of the machine is of substantial T shape, the back portion 2 of which supports the standard 3 carrying the needle operating mechanism. The forwardly extending portion is preferably centrally arranged and extending downwardly therefrom are the parallel side walls 4. These side walls are formed with a longitudinal ledge 5 level with the under side of the back portion 2.

The back portion 2 is adapted to rest upon a suitable frame 6 and vertical webs 7 extend laterally from the walls 4 beneath the portion 2. Between these lateral webs and arranged centrally between the side walls 4 is a journal bearing 8 supporting one end of the main shaft 9 and the forward end of the shaft 9 is supported in a downwardly extending lug

structure 10 which is provided with a forwardly extending foot 11.

A sheet metal bottom plate 12 is secured to the bottom edges of the side walls 4 and extends underneath the standard 3 having at the rear portion beneath said standard an upward flange 13 provided with an inturned edge 14.

This structure completes the bobbin arm upon the top of which is secured the throat plate 15 through which the feed dog 16 extends.

This structure is complete for the purpose of receiving and operating upon tubular forms of goods but when flat goods are to be sewn it is desirable to have a flat bed plate.

A plate 17 is formed with a longitudinal slot extending inwardly from one end and the said plate rests upon the ledges 5 fitting snugly to the central portion of the bed plate 1 and having the ends abutting the forward edges of the back portion 2.

The plate 17 is preferably provided with lugs 18 adapted to extend under the portion 2 of the main bed plate to hold it firmly in place. The plate 17 extends forward of the throat plate and is provided with an opening 19 closed by a slide plate 20 of the usual form which enables the operator to reach in to manipulate the bobbin which is carried in the holder 21 on the main shaft 9.

The gate 22 is pivotally supported upon the foot 11 and is held in a vertical position against the holder 21 to hold the bobbin in place.

When the plate 17 is in position, a broad flat surface is provided to support the goods being operated upon but when it is desired to sew a tubular member the plate 17 is merely lifted upwardly from the supporting frame 6 and drawn forwardly, thus leaving a projecting arm in the center of the recess of the frame.

A machine as thus described is extremely simple in its construction and may be handled without difficulty by the ordinary user.

What I claim as my invention is:—

1. A sewing machine comprising a frame support having a rectangular opening in the top, a bed frame formed with lateral flanges

Hohmann & Osann

A better design for converting to a free arm came in 1939 from Hohmann & Osann, a sewing machine research organization in New York City. The partners in the organization were inventors Richard K. Hohmann and Frederick Osann.

What is so strange about this is that R.K. Hohmann was the designer of the Sewhandy sewing machine that the SINGER Featherweight replaced. And Frederick Osann was the owner of the Frederick Osann Company that produced the Sewhandy machines in the early 1930's. But that is another story... For more information about that sewing machine, see my book *"before the Featherweight - SEWHANDY"*

The partners filed two patent applications on December 26, 1939 related to this design. One on "Sewing Machine Drive Means" and one on "Convertible Flat-Bed Cylinder And Sewing Machine." The two became Patents 2,247,381 and 2,247,383 on July 1, 1941, and were assigned to the Sears Roebuck Corporation.

For those of you familiar with the Sewhandy sewing machine, you will recognize it in their drawings. They used it to show their ideas even though SINGER (manufacturing the Sewhandy since 1934) ended its production in 1938.

Their designs are on the following pages. A copy of the full patent is in the appendix

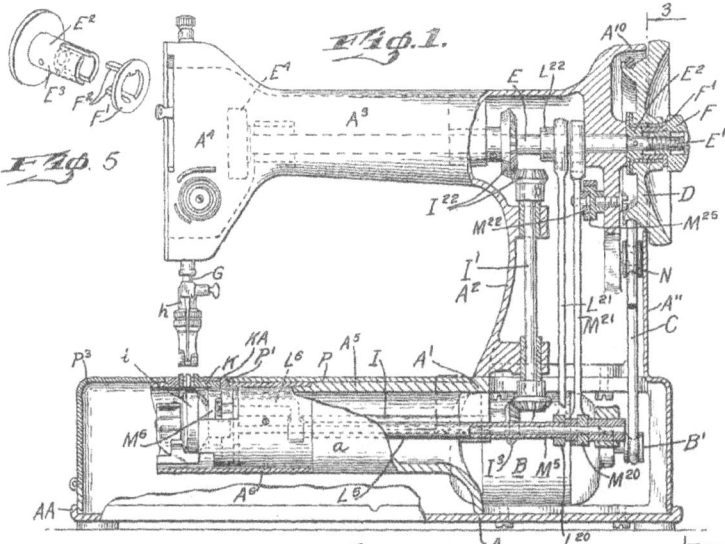

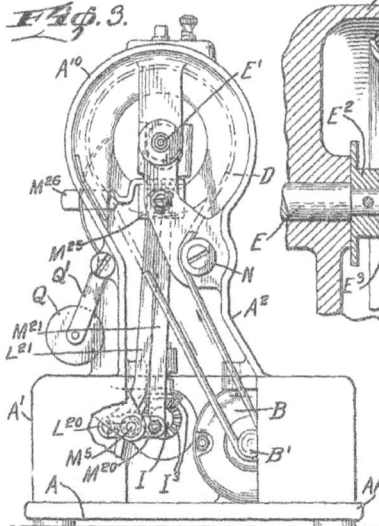

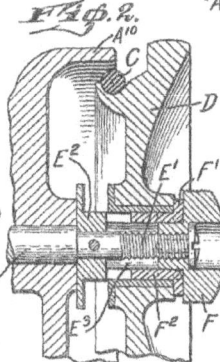

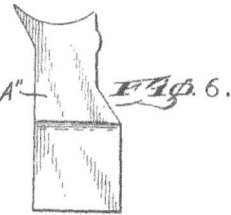

Inventors

Richard K. Hohmann
Frederick Osann

John E. Hubbell
Attorney

53

UNITED STATES PATENT OFFICE

2,247,381

SEWING MACHINE DRIVE MEANS

Richard K. Hohmann, Jamaica, and Frederick Osann, White Plains, N. Y., assignors to Sears, Roebuck and Co., Chicago, Ill., a corporation of New York

Original application December 29, 1939, Serial No. 311,486. Divided and this application August 3, 1940, Serial No. 351,013

4 Claims. (Cl. 112—220)

In our prior application, Serial No. 311,486, filed December 29, 1939, of which this application is a division, we have disclosed a simple and effective sewing machine devised by us especially for interchangeable use as a darning machine and for ordinary sewing operations.

That machine is readily convertible from one to the other of two conditions, in one of which it is adapted for plain sewing and includes a flat work bed, which may be generally similar in form and disposition to the conventional work bed of a plain sewing machine, and in the other of which it is adapted for darning and is adapted to support stockings, or other work to be darned, on a cylinder arm generally like, though preferably somewhat smaller in cross section than, the work supporting cylinder arms of ordinary darning machines. In its preferred form, the machine is adapted, however, for either plain sewing or darning operations, on flat bed and cylinder arm supported work.

The general object of the invention claimed herein is to provide an improved pulley and belt drive connection between a driving pulley mounted on the needle bar shaft and a driving electric motor located in the base of the sewing machine, and including novel provisions by which the portion of the belt above the base of the machine is normally enclosed within the standard and adjacent arm portion of the machine, but may be made readily accessible for belt removal and replacement operations.

The various features of novelty which characterize our novel work feed mechanism are pointed out with particularity in the claims annexed to and forming a part of this specification. For a better understanding of the invention, however, its advantages and specific objects attained with its use, reference should be had to the accompanying drawing and descriptive matter in which we have illustrated and described a preferred form of embodiment of the present invention.

Of the drawing:

Fig. 1 is an elevation, partly in section, of a sewing machine constituting a preferred embodiment of the present invention;

Fig. 2 is an enlarged reproduction of a portion of Fig. 1, showing parts in different relative positions;

Fig. 3 is a section on the line 3—3 of Fig. 1 with parts broken away and removed;

Fig. 4 is a perspective view showing parts of the cylinder arm and flat work bed of Fig. 1 in section;

Fig. 5 is a perspective view illustrating details of the main pulley mounting;

Fig. 6 is a small scale elevation of a removable cover plate at the right hand end of the machine as shown in Fig. 1.

The housing structure, or framework of the sewing machine illustrated in the drawing, comprises a rectangular supporting bottom plate A, and a sewing machine framework proper which is screw connected to the bottom plate and includes a rectangular base or bed portion A', a standard A², and a horizontal cylinder arm comprising a portion A⁵ and A⁶. The portion A⁵ is an integral tubular extension of the base portion A' and A⁶ is a tubular part detachably secured to the front end of the part A⁵ and forming an extension of the latter.

The machine comprises a driving motor B, mounted in the base portion A' and having a pulley B' on its shaft which is operatively connected by a belt C to a driving pulley D mounted on the adjacent end of the needle bar shaft E, which may be journalled in the arm A³ in any usual or suitable manner. In the preferred construction shown, the rear end E' of the needle bar shaft E is threaded, and supports a nut member F, which may be rotated about the shaft end E' to thereby clamp the hub portion of the pulley D between the head of the nut member F and the radially extending flange of a part E² carried by and secured to the shaft E and comprising a tubular hub portion E³ forming an elongated bearing for the pulley D. When the nut F is backed off, as shown in Fig. 2, the pulley E may be displaced axially of the shaft E, from its normal position, to thereby move the inner, belt groove portion of the pulley out of its normal position within the arm A³ so as to permit the belt C to be removed from and replaced on said pulley.

As shown, a washer member F' is interposed between the nut F and the hub of the pulley D, said washer member having integral arm extensions F² received in longitudinal slots formed for the purpose in the tubular portion E³ of the part E². The member F with its extensions F' and the part E² with the slots in its tubular portion E³, collectively form a split or extensible bearing for the pulley D, which provides a satisfactory support for the latter when in, and when displaced from, the position in which it is normally clamped by the nut F.

At its head end, the machine comprises means including a crank disc E⁴, carried by the shaft for actuating a needle bar G, mounted in the head

Fig.1.

Fig.3.

Fig.5.

Fig.6.

Fig.4.

Fig.2.

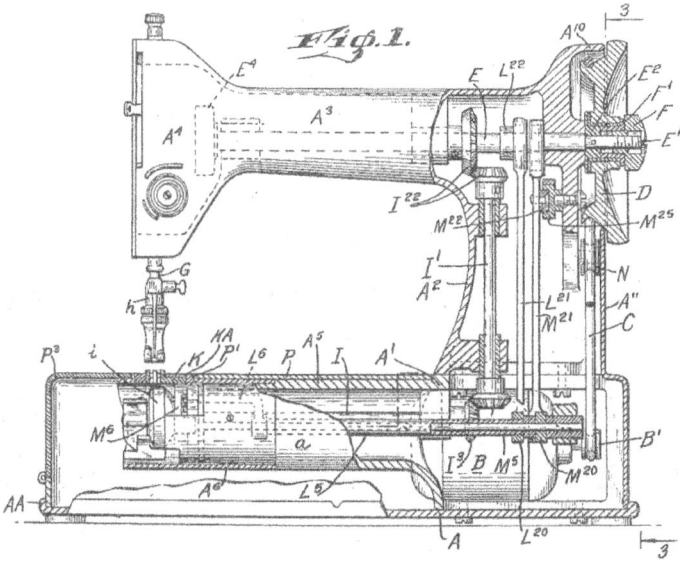

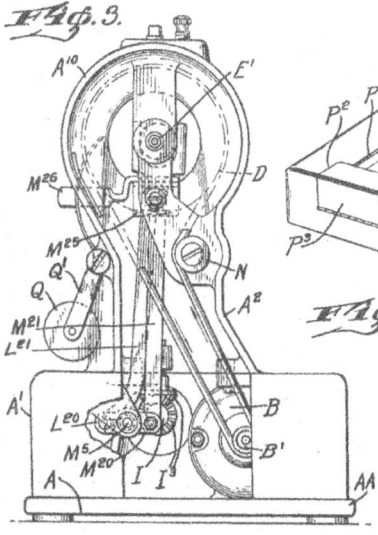

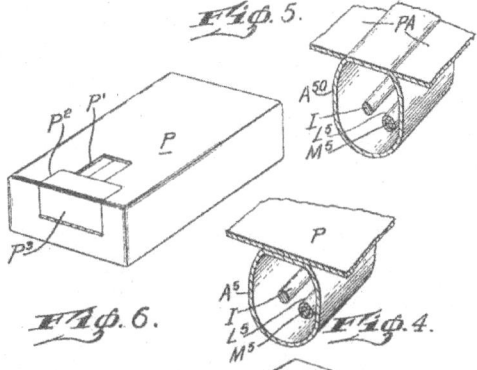

Richard K. Hohmann
Frederick Grann
John E. Hubbell Attorney

UNITED STATES PATENT OFFICE

2,247,383

CONVERTIBLE FLAT-BED CYLINDER ARM SEWING MACHINE

Richard K. Rohmann, Jamaica, and Frederick Osann, White Plains, N. Y., assignors to Sears, Roebuck and Co., Chicago, Ill., a corporation of New York

Original application December 29, 1939, Serial No. 311,486. Divided and this application August 3, 1940, Serial No. 351,014

3 Claims. (Cl. 112—260)

Our prior application Serial No. 311,486, of which this application is a division, discloses a simple and effective sewing machine devised by us for interchangeable use as a darning machine and for ordinary sewing operations.

That machine is readily convertible from one to the other of two conditions, in one of which it is adapted for plain sewing and includes a flat work bed, which may be generally similar in form and disposition to the conventional work bed of a plain sewing machine, and in the other of which it is adapted for darning and is adapted to support stockings or other work to be darned, on a cylinder arm generally like, though preferably somewhat smaller in cross section than, the work supporting cylinder arms of ordinary darning machines. In its preferred form, the machine is adapted, however, for either plain sewing or darning operations, on flat bed and cylinder arm supported work.

The general object of the present invention is to provide a sewing machine and a flat work bed part which can be readily put in place in or removed from the machine, of such character that with the work bed part in place, has the general form and work supporting characteristics of an ordinary flat bed portable sewing machine, and with said part removed, the cylinder arm of the machine is fully exposed, and accessible for the free and unobstructed movements of stockings and other tubular work pieces onto and off said arm.

The various features of novelty which characterize the present invention are pointed out with particularity in the claims annexed to and forming a part of this specification. For a better understanding of the invention, however, its advantages and specific objects attained with its use, reference should be had to the accompanying drawing and descriptive matter in which we have illustrated and described preferred forms of embodiment of the present invention.

Of the drawing:

Fig. 1 is an elevation, partly in section, of a sewing machine constituting a preferred embodiment of the present invention;

Fig. 2 is a perspective view of the removable flat work bed member shown in Fig. 5;

Fig. 3 is a section on the line 3—3 of Fig. 1 with parts broken away and removed;

Fig. 4 is a perspective view showing parts of the cylinder arm and flat work bed of Fig. 1 in section;

Fig. 5 is a view taken similarly to Fig. 4, illustrating the use of a flat work bed member of modified form; and

Fig. 6 is a perspective view of the removable flat bed part shown in Fig. 1.

The housing structure, or frame of the sewing machine illustrated in the drawing, comprises a rectangular supporting bottom plate A, and a sewing machine body frame member which is screw connected to the bottom plate and includes a rectangular base or bed portion A', a standard A², and a horizontal cylinder arm comprising portions A⁵ and A⁶. The portion A⁵ is an integral tubular extension of the base portion A', and A⁶ is a tubular part detachably secured to the front end of the part A⁵ and forming an extension of the latter.

The machine comprises a driving motor B, mounted in the base portion A' and having a pulley B' on its shaft which is operatively connected by a belt C to a driving pulley D mounted on the adjacent end of the needle bar shaft E, which may be journalled in the arm A³ in any usual or suitable manner. In the preferred construction shown, the rear end E' of the needle bar shaft E is threaded, and supports a nut member F, which may be rotated about the shaft end E' to thereby clamp the hub portion of the pulley D between the head of the nut member F and the radially extending flange of a part E² carried by and secured to the shaft E and comprising a tubular hub portion forming an elongated bearing for the pulley D. When the nut F is backed off, the pulley E may be displaced axially of the shaft E, from its normal position, to thereby move the inner belt groove portion of the pulley out of its normal position within the arm A³, so as to permit the belt C to be removed from and replaced on said pulley. As shown, a washer member F', specially shaped and disposed as described in said prior application, is interposed between the nut F and the hub of the pulley D.

At its head end, the machine comprises means including a crank disc E⁴ carried by the shaft E for actuating a needle bar G, mounted in the head A⁴ in any usual or suitable manner for vertical reciprocatory movement.

At its head end, the machine is also provided with a presser bar h, and in our said prior application we disclose and claim novel actuating means for lifting said presser bar during each upstroke of the needle bar G, when the machine is in condition for darning use, but said actuating means need not be illustrated or described herein. Our sewing machine also includes ten-

The Production Design

In 1944, a SINGER Engineer at the Bridgeport, Connecticut factory came up with an improvement to previous convertible designs. The engineer was a recent 39-year-old Russian emigrant named Sydney Zonis.

He filed a patent application for a "Convertible Flat-Bed And Cylinder-Arm Sewing Machine" on December 16, 1944. Zonis lists in his application that his design is partly based on the work of Hohmann and Osann in US Patent 2,247,383 (page 48).

The new design was issued as Patent 2,424,872 on July 29, 1947. Note that this application shows the first illustration of the actual design of the SINGER Model 222. Zonis assigned all rights to this patent to The SINGER Manufacturing Company, Elizabeth, N.J.

The first SINGER Model 222 sewing machines did not come out for sale to the public until mid 1951 (first ad that I have found for the Model 222 is June 1951). If that date is correct, that means that SINGER had this design for almost four years before getting it to the public. I was not able to discover why it took so long.

The Zonis convertible bed design is on the following pages. A copy of the full patent application is in the appendix at the end of this book.

CONVERTIBLE FLAT-BED AND CYLINDER-ARM SEWING MACHINE

Filed Dec. 16, 1944　　　　4 Sheets—Sheet 1

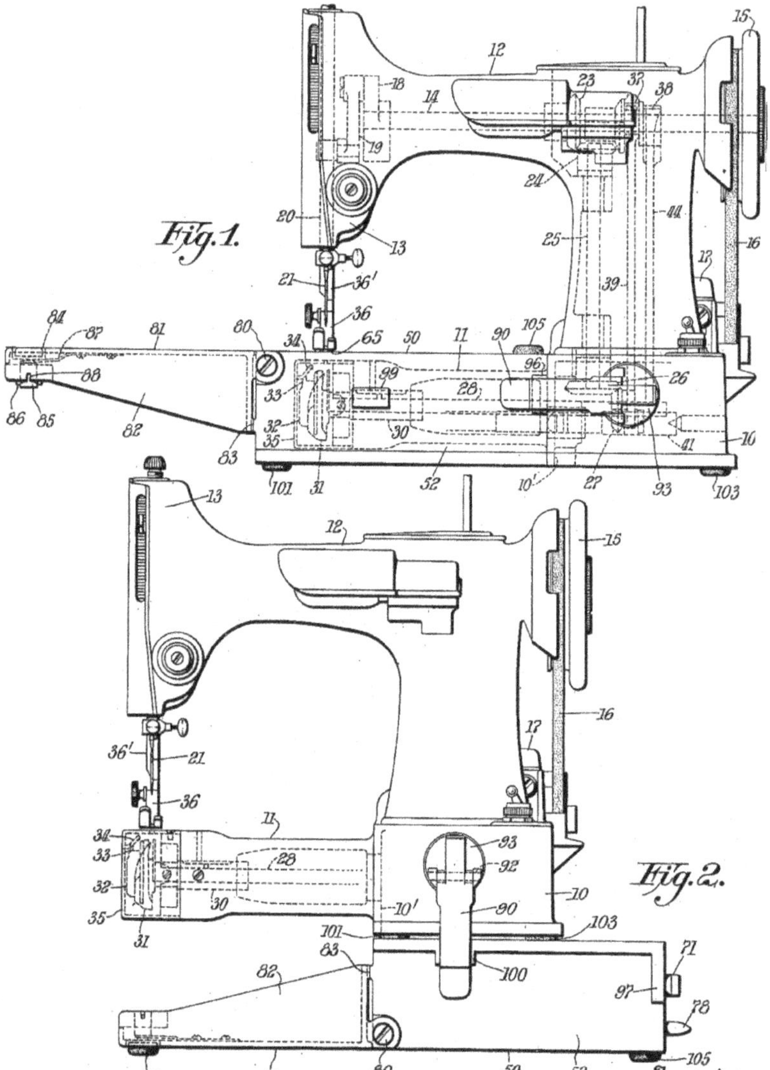

Fig.1.

Fig.2.

58

July 29, 1947.

S. ZONIS

2,424,872

CONVERTIBLE FLAT-BED AND CYLINDER-ARM SEWING MACHINE

Filed Dec. 16, 1944

4 Sheets—Sheet 2

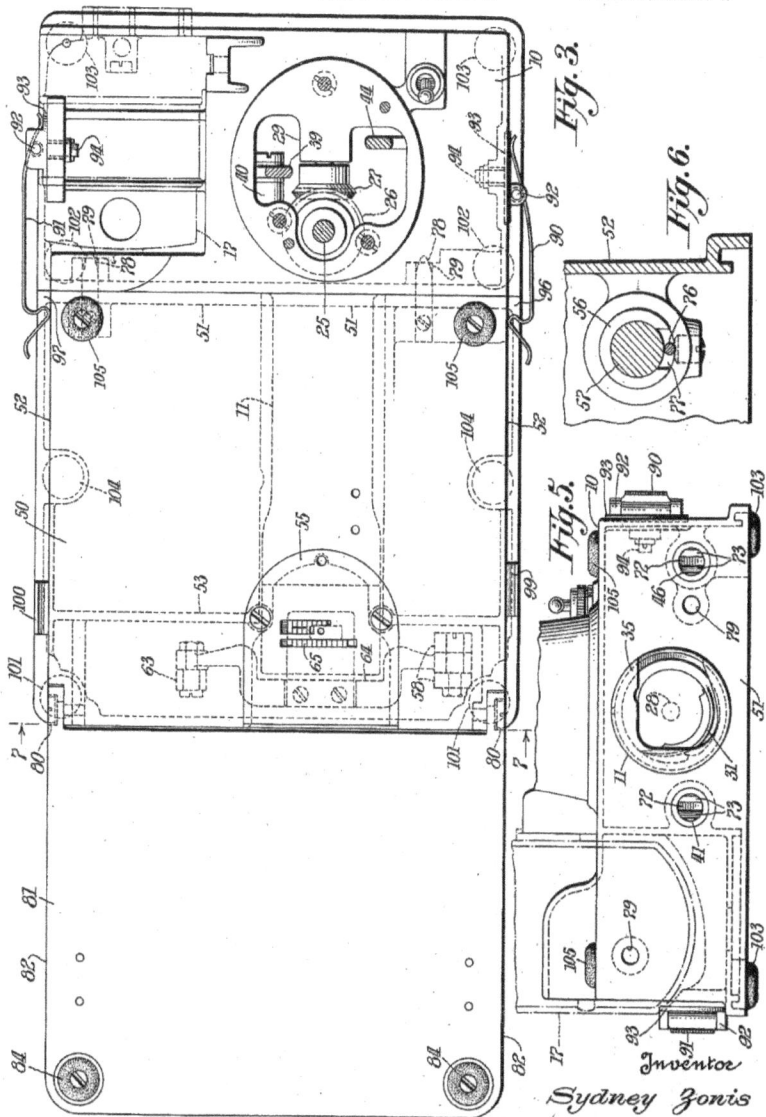

Fig. 3.

Fig. 6.

Fig. 5.

Witness:
Godfrey Pecina

Inventor
Sydney Zonis

By
William P. Stewart
Attorney

59

Fig. 8.

Fig. 4.

Fig. 7.

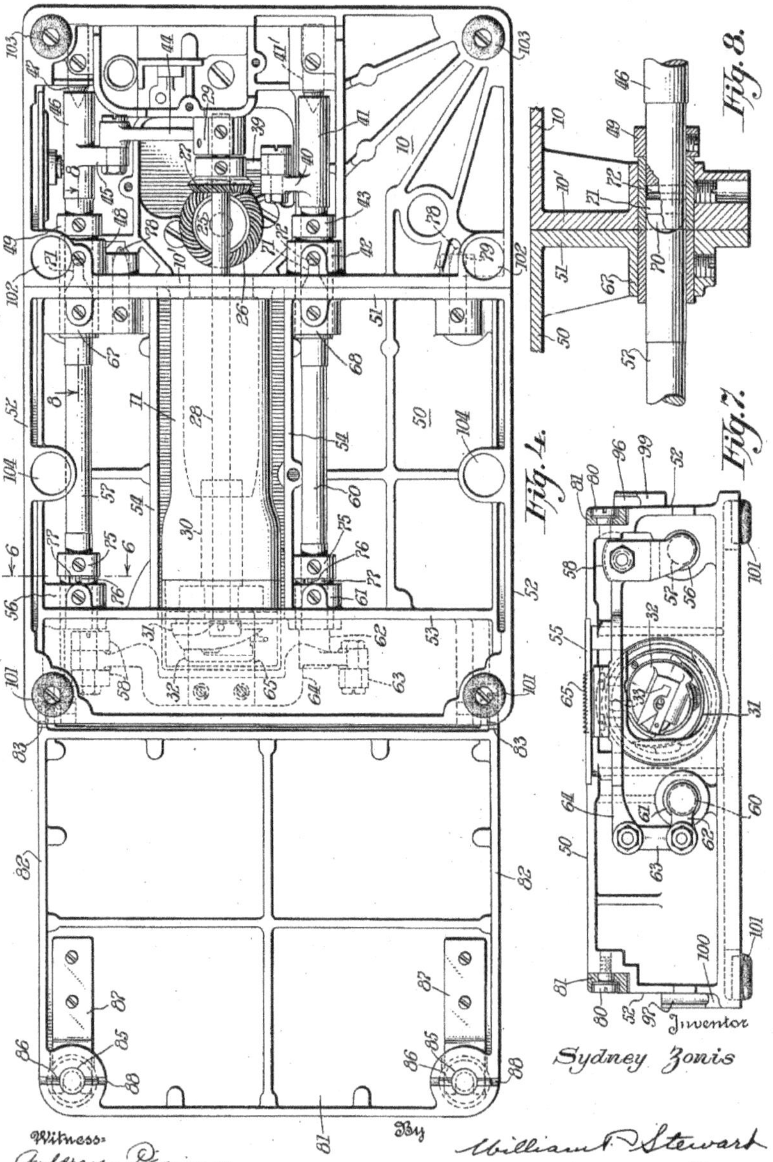

Inventor

Sydney Zonis

Witness

Godfrey Pecina

By

William F. Stewart

Attorney

60

CONVERTIBLE FLAT-BED AND CYLINDER-ARM SEWING MACHINE

Filed Dec. 16, 1944　　　　4 Sheets—Sheet 4

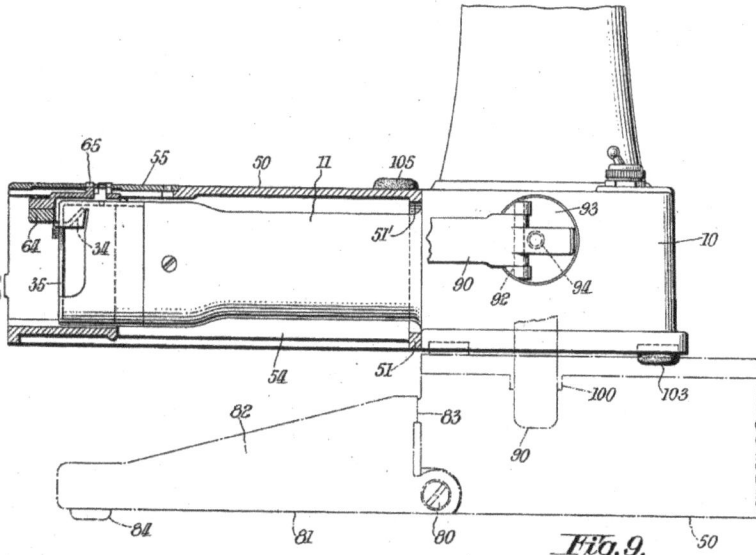

Fig. 9.

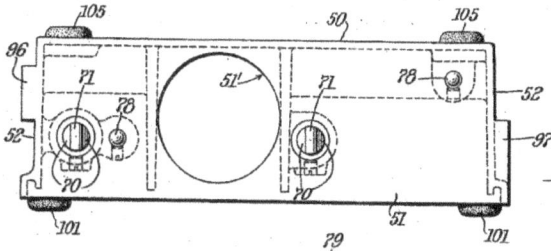

Fig. 10.

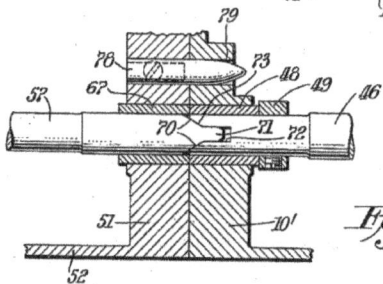

Fig. 11.

Inventor

Sydney Zonis

Witness:
Godfrey Pecina

By　William P. Stewart

Attorney

61

UNITED STATES PATENT OFFICE

2,424,872

CONVERTIBLE FLAT-BED AND CYLINDER-ARM SEWING MACHINE

Sydney Zonis, Bridgeport, Conn., assignor to The Singer Manufacturing Company, Elizabeth, N. J., a corporation of New Jersey

Application December 16, 1944, Serial No. 568,405

21 Claims. (Cl. 112—260)

1

This invention relates to sewing machines and more particularly to a sewing machine which may be readily changed from a flat-bed machine, used for general sewing purposes, to a cylinder-arm or bed machine.

A primary object of this invention is to provide a sewing machine which is quickly and easily convertible for use either as a flat-bed type sewing machine having work-feeding mechanism of the drop-feed type or as a cylinder work-arm type sewing machine in which the minimum size of the free end portion of the work-arm is limited solely by loop-taker mechanism which is complemental to the sewing machine needle in the formation of stitches.

This invention has also for its object to provide a sewing machine having a detachable flat work-supporting bed underlying the bracket-arm, which bed carries the work-advancing mechanism of the machine and, when removed, exposes a cylindrically shaped arm which carries the loop-taker and its actuating shaft.

Another object of this invention is to provide a sewing machine with a work-support and a feeding mechanism including a feed-dog operating through said work-support, in which sewing machine the work-support and the feeding mechanism in the stitch-forming region are together removable as a unit from the machine.

Another object of the invention is to provide a detachable flat work-supporting bed which may be removed from the machine to expose a cylinder arm, and the detached flat work-supporting bed used as a support for the machine for the purpose of providing substantial clearance beneath the cylinder arm.

Another object of this invention is to provide improved latching means for holding the detachable portion of the flat bed in position when it is used as a work-support and to hold the machine on the detachable flat bed when it is used as a support for the stitch-forming mechanism.

Another object of this invention is to provide the removable portion of the bed with end walls in which are journaled the feed-rock-shafts and to provide a feed-dog offset laterally from the feed-bar so as to overhang the end of the cylinder arm.

With the above and other objects in view, as will hereinafter appear, the invention comprises the devices, combinations and arrangements of parts hereinafter set forth and illustrated in the accompanying drawings of a preferred embodiment of the invention, from which the several features of the invention and the advantages

2

attained thereby will be readily understood by those skilled in the art.

The several features of the present invention will be clearly understood from the following description and accompanying drawings in which:

Fig. 1 is a front elevation of my improved combinational sewing machine showing the flat work-supporting bed in operative position, and the machine ready for use as a flat-bed machine.

Fig. 2 is a front elevation of my improved machine showing the flat bed removed for the purpose of converting the machine into a cylinder bed darning machine and the removable bed used as a support for the machine.

Fig. 3 is a top plan view of the machine shown in Fig. 1 with the bracket-arm removed.

Fig. 4 is a bottom plan view of the machine shown in Fig. 1.

Fig. 5 is a left end elevation of the cylindrical work-arm and base of the machine shown in Fig. 2.

Fig. 6 is a detailed sectional view taken along the line 6—6 of Fig. 4.

Fig. 7 is a view taken along the line 7—7 of Fig. 3.

Fig. 8 is a sectional view taken along the line 8—8 of Fig. 4.

Fig. 9 is a side elevation of the cylindrical arm with a central section through the flat bed and feed-dog, showing the position of the feed-dog and its relation to the cylindrical arm and the flat bed.

Fig. 10 is a right end elevation of the removable flat bed and Fig. 11 is an enlarged detail view showing the detachable connection between the rock-shaft in the bed and the actuating rock-shaft in the base.

In the embodiment of the invention selected for illustration, my improved convertible flat-bed and cylinder-arm machine comprises a base 10 having downturned side and end walls forming a rectangularly shaped enclosure. The bed 10 carries a laterally extending tubular-shaped work-supporting arm 11 and a bracket-arm 12 terminating in a hollow head 13.

Journaled in suitable bearings in the bracket-arm 12 is a shaft 14 having a balance-wheel 15 secured to one of its ends. The balance-wheel 15 is operatively connected by a belt 16 to an electric motor 17 carried by the base 10. A crank 18 is secured to the other end of the shaft 14 and is connected by a link 19 to a needle-bar 20 journaled in the hollow head 13 and carrying an eye-pointed needle 21. The above described mechanism is old and well known and reference

Appendix

Appendix

Model 221/222 Patents

1. Maud Pratt US Patent #1,394,396

2. Daniel Chason US Patent #1,820,119

3. HJ Goosman US Patent #2,031,562

4. HJ Goosman US Des. #91,816

5. HJ Goosman US Patent #2,063,841

6. HJ Goosman US Patent #2,007,894

7. Denis S. Craddock GB Patent #435,578

8. James Heggie GB Patent #545,156

9. James Heggie US Patent #2,325,510

10. GA Fleckenstein US Patent #2,276,246

11. Marsac-Graesser US Patent #2,282,071

12. Daniel Chason US Patent #2,341,975

Model 222 Patents

13. Bertram Eaton US Patent #1,778,107

14. Hohmann-Osann US Patent #2,247,381

15. Hohmann-Osann US Patent #2,247,383

16. Sydney Zonis US Patent #2,424,872

1,394,936

Patented Oct. 25, 1921

Fig. 1

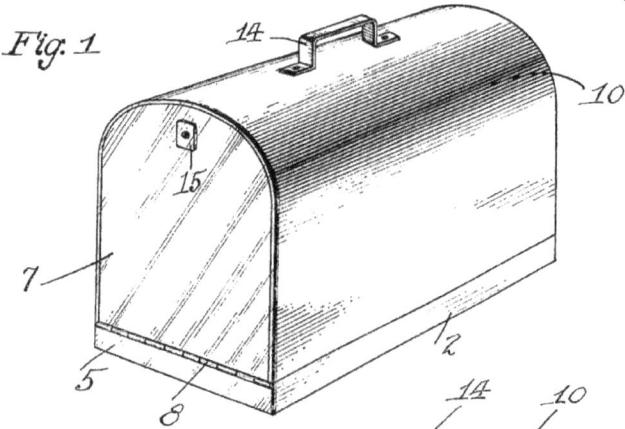

Fig. 2

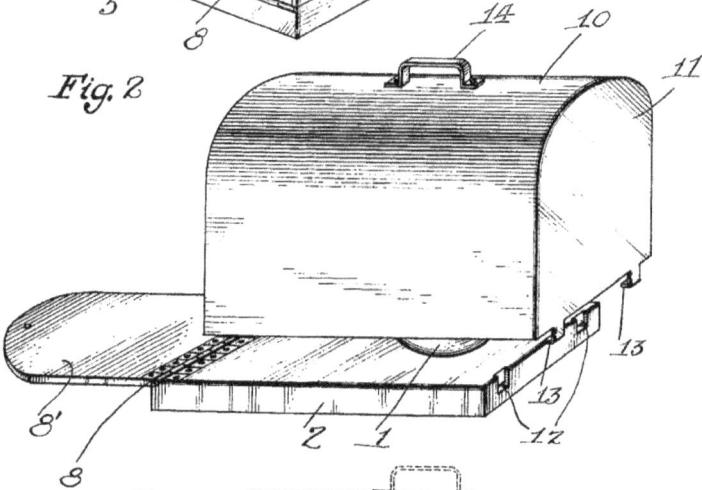

Fig. 3

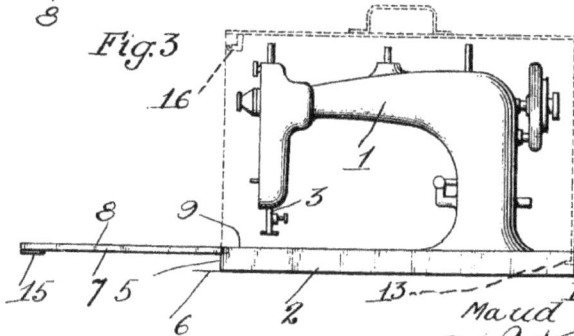

Inventor
Maud Pratt
By Arthur W. Nelson
Atty.

66

UNITED STATES PATENT OFFICE.

MAUD PRATT, OF CHICAGO, ILLINOIS.

HAND PORTABLE SEWING-MACHINE.

1,394,936.　　　　Specification of Letters Patent.　　Patented Oct. 25, 1921.

Application filed December 17, 1920.　Serial No. 431,354.

To all whom it may concern:

Be it known that I, MAUD PRATT, a citizen of the United States, and a resident of Chicago, county of Cook, and State of Illinois, have invented certain new and useful Improvements in Hand Portable Sewing-Machines, of which the following is a specification.

My invention relates generally to improvements in a type of sewing machine which is adapted to be carried by the hand from place to place, and which is usually operated by means of an electric motor. Such a machine as heretofore constructed embodies the elements of lightness, compactness and ready portability but has been open to some objections with respect to its use during the sewing operation.

The general object of my invention is to improve the hand portable type of sewing machine so as to make it generally more efficient, and in particular to provide means whereby the goods to be operated upon or sewed shall be held and supported in a position to secure the best results.

It is a further object of my invention to provide means whereby the above result can be attained without increasing the weight or appreciably affecting the cost and without affecting the durability or rigidity of the device.

My invention consists generally in the form, arrangement, construction and coöperation of the parts whereby the above named objects, together with others that will appear hereinafter are attainable; and my invention will be more readily understood by reference to the accompanying drawings which illustrate what I consider, at the present time, to be the preferred embodiment thereof.

In said drawings:

Figure 1 is a perspective view of a hand portable sewing machine embodying my invention, the parts being positioned as in carrying the machine.

Fig. 2 is a perspective illustrative view illustrating a step in the course of preparing the hand portable sewing machine for use; and

Fig. 3 is a side elevation of the machine ready for use.

As here shown, 1, represents what is usually termed the head of the sewing machine and which is mounted or supported upon a base 2. The base 2, as here shown, is of rectangular form and houses certain of the operating parts of the sewing machine (not shown). The size of the base 2 is usually no larger than is necessary properly to support the head 1 and the mechanism within the base 2. 3 represents the presser foot of the machine and is in the plane in which the needle of the sewing machine (not shown) operates and in which the sewing is done. The sewing, therefore, is performed relatively close to the end 5 of the sewing machine base. The base 2 in use is ordinarily placed upon a surface 6 which is representative of a table or some other suitable support.

In using machines of the hand portable type the goods being sewed, in many of the machines heretofore devised, drags over the end of the base corresponding to the end 5 of my base and interferes with the sewing operation. This is particularly objectionable when sewing relatively heavy cloth. Some attempt has been made to obviate this difficulty such for example as by the expedient shown in the Patent to Riddell No. 1344718 of June 29, 1920, but this involves certain objections, such as separate parts which are likely to become misplaced and also involves elements of added cost, weight and multiplicity of parts which are somewhat objectionable.

In my construction I provide a combined cover end and drop shelf or support 7 which is hingedly secured, as indicated at 8, to the end of the base 2 of the machine. The upper surface 8' of the combined cover end and support is in the same plane as the upper surface 9 of the base, and therefore, forms an unbroken continuation thereof when the member 7 is in the horizontal position shown in Figs. 2 and 3. This forms an ideal support for goods being sewed and makes practicable the use of the portable machine even upon a table or other support which is no larger than the base 2 of the sewing machine. It also assists very greatly in the successful use of the machine even when placed upon a relatively large table, as in either event it removes all tendency of the cloth or other goods to drag upon the needle and thus interfere with the free and proper functioning of the stitching mechanism. This also forms a support for the arm when threading the needle.

Being a hand portable machine it is essential that the weight of the device as a whole be kept down to the lowest possible minimum. This means that the parts must be made of as thin material as is possible without sacrificing features of strength and durability. The head of the machine, and the mechanism mounted in the base 2, is necessarily of considerable weight as a large part thereof is composed of castings and other metal parts. In order to preserve the mechanism against liability of injury and also to keep it clean a cover of some kind must be provided. Such covers, as heretofore constructed, have been provided with a handle and with means for securing same to the base of the machine so that the device, as a whole, may be carried about by the hand.

I likewise provide means to this end, and, as here shown, such means takes the form of a substantially U-shaped cover portion 10, which is open at one end, and which is closed at the other end by the portion 11 which is a rigid or integral part of the portion 10. That is to say the portions 10 and 11 are so firmly secured together as in effect to be integral in form. This enables great rigidity even in material of little weight. As here shown, the base is provided with recesses 12 for the reception of the tongue portions 13 of the cover. Thus to place the cover upon the base the handle 14 is grasped and the portion to which it is attached is moved longitudinally of the base so that the tongues 13 enter the said recesses 12 as is well shown by means of dotted lines in Fig. 3. To close the other end of the cover, so as to form a complete closure, the member 7 is swung upwardly to the position shown in Fig. 1 in which position it is locked to the other parts of the machine cover by means of the latch 15 which co-acts with the latch member 16 (shown by means of dotted lines in Fig. 3). This locking construction may vary in detail and is essentially only mechanism which will rigidly fix the member 7 to the remainder of the cover portion. When the device is in the form shown in Fig. 1 it appears much as an ordinary hand portable machine of the type heretofore employed; has all the strength and rigidity thereof; may therefore be carried about without danger of the parts shaking about and becoming loose; is no greater in weight than other similarly sized hand portable machines; and can be quickly and easily made ready for the more efficient use already described. To prepare for use it is but necessary to unlatch the combined cover end and support 7, swing the same to the horizontal position shown in Figs. 2 and 3, and then bodily withdraw the remainder of the cover formed by the portions 10 and 11.

The many advantageous characteristics of my hand portable sewing machine construction will be apparent to those skilled in this art without further comment.

I claim:—

1. The herein described improvements in hand portable sewing machines, embodying therein, a base having a sewing machine head thereon, a two-part cover for said head and connected parts, one part being a combined drop leaf and cover end and being hinged to the base, being swingable to a horizontal position to lie flush with said base and form a continuation of the top surface of the base, and being swingable to a vertical position to co-act with and form an end closure for the other cover part, said other cover part having means for detachably connecting it to the base.

2. The herein described improvements in hand portable sewing machines, embodying therein, a base having a sewing machine head thereon, a two-part cover for said head and connected parts, one part being a combined drop leaf and cover end and being hinged to the base, being swingable to a horizontal position to lie flush with said base and form a continuation of the top surface of the base, and being swingable to a vertical position, to co-act with and form an end closure for the other cover part, said other cover part having means for detachably connecting it to the base, and means for securing the cover parts together when said hinged part is in a vertical position.

3. The herein described improvements in hand portable sewing machines, embodying therein, a base having a sewing machine head thereon, a two-part cover for said head and connected parts, one part being a combined drop leaf and cover end and being hinged to one end of the base, being swingable to a horizontal position to lie flush with said base and form a continuation of the top surface of the base, and being swingable to a vertical position to co-act with and form an end closure for the other cover part, said other cover part having means for detachably connecting it to the base.

4. The herein described improvements in hand portable sewing machine, embodying therein, a base having a sewing machine head thereon, a two-part cover for said head and connected parts, one part being a combined drop leaf and cover end and being hinged to one end of the base, being swingable to a horizontal position to lie flush with said base and form a continuation of the top surface of the base, being swingable to a vertical position to coact with and form an end closure for the other cover part, said other cover part having means for detachably connecting it to the base, and means for securing the cover parts together when said hinged part is in a vertical position.

5. In the herein described improvements

in hand portable sewing machines embodying therein a base having a sewing machine
head thereon, a two part cover for said head
and connecting parts, one part being a combined drop leaf and cover end being hinged
to the base and being swingable to a horizontal position to form an extension of the
base and being swingable to a vertical position to coact and form an end closure wall
for the other cover part, and means for detachably connecting said other cover part
to the base and detachable coupling means
between said other cover part and the drop
leaf.

6. The herein described improvements in
hand portable sewing machines, embodying
therein, a base having a sewing machine
head thereon, means for covering said head
and connected parts, said means comprising a cover portion substantially U-shaped
in cross section, means for detachably securing same to said base, and a combined
cover end and drop leaf, means for securing
the combined cover end and drop leaf to the
end of the base to enable swinging movement to a horizontal position flush with the
base, thereby forming a continuation of the
upper surface of the base, and to a vertical
position to form an end closure for said substantially U-shaped cover portion.

7. The herein described improvements in
hand portable sewing machines, embodying
therein, a base having a sewing machine
head thereon, means for covering said head
and connected parts, said means comprising
a cover portion substantially U-shaped in
cross section, means for detachably securing
same to said base, a combined cover end and
drop leaf, means for securing the combined
cover end and drop leaf to the end of the
base to enable swinging movement to a horizontal position flush with the base, thereby
forming a continuation of the upper surface
of the base, and to a vertical position to
form an end closure for said substantially
U-shaped cover portion, and a lock for securing the cover parts together.

8. The herein described improvements in
portable sewing machines comprising a base
having a sewing machine head thereon, a
cover for said head, said cover having an
end wall removed, means for detachably connecting the cover to the base, a drop leaf
member hingedly connected to the base and
adapted to form an extension thereof when
disposed in horizontal position, said drop
leaf being swingable to a vertical position to
form an end closure wall for the cover and
means for connecting the drop leaf member
to the cover when said drop leaf member is
in vertical position.

In testimony whereof, I have hereunto set
my hand this 14th day of December, A. D.
1920.

MAUD PRATT.

GRADUATED TENSION REGULATOR FOR SEWING MACHINES

Filed May 9, 1930

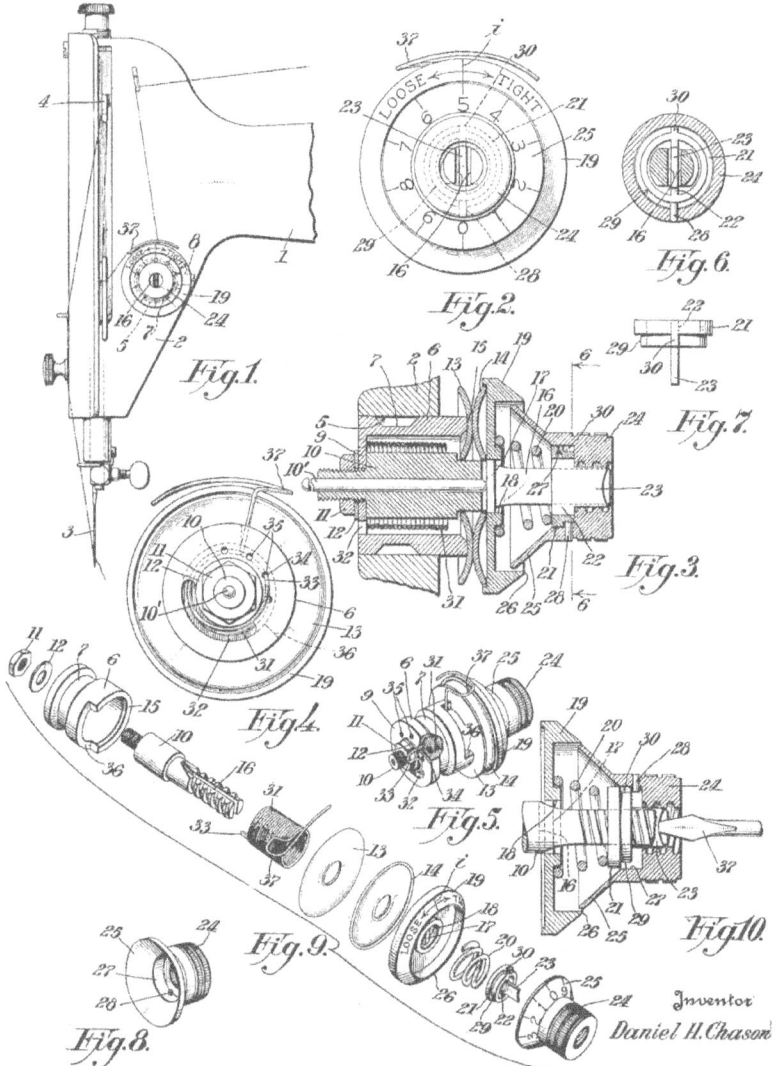

Fig.1.

Fig.2.

Fig.6.

Fig.7.

Fig.3.

Fig.4.

Fig.5.

Fig.9.

Fig.8.

Fig.10.

Inventor
Daniel H. Chason

Witness:
Godfrey Secing

By Henry J. Miller

Attorney

70

UNITED STATES PATENT OFFICE

DANIEL H. CHASON, OF ELIZABETH, NEW JERSEY, ASSIGNOR TO THE SINGER MANU-
FACTURING COMPANY, OF ELIZABETH, NEW JERSEY, A CORPORATION OF NEW
JERSEY

GRADUATED TENSION REGULATOR FOR SEWING MACHINES

Application filed May 9, 1930. Serial No. 450,952.

This invention relates to sewing machines and has for an object to provide an improved device for tensioning the sewing thread or threads of such machines.

With the above and other objects in view, as will hereinafter appear, the invention consists in the devices, combinations and arrangements of parts hereinafter set forth and illustrated in the accompanying drawings of a preferred embodiment of the invention, from which the several features of the invention and the advantages attained thereby will be readily understood by those skilled in the art.

In the accompanying drawings Fig. 1 is a side elevation of a portion of a sewing machine bracket-arm fitted with a tension device embodying the invention. Fig. 2 is a front elevation of the tension device. Fig. 3 is a longitudinal vertical section through the tension device. Fig. 4 is a rear elevation and Fig. 5 a perspective view of the tension device. Fig. 6 is a section on the line 6—6, Fig. 3. Fig. 7 is a top plan view of the slidably mounted dial stop member. Fig. 8 is a rearward perspective view of the dial member. Fig. 9 is a disassembled perspective view of the device, and Fig. 10 is a view similar to Fig. 3 but showing how the dial may be removed for disassembly of the device.

1 represents the bracket-arm of a sewing machine terminating in the head 2 for the usual reciprocating needle 3 and take-up 4. The head 2 is formed with an aperture 5 which receives the hollow cylindrical shank 6 of the tension device, which shank is formed with a circumferential groove 7 entered by the set-screw 8 in the head 2 to fix the tension device in working position on the sewing machine.

The shank 6 is of hollow cylindrical form and has an inner end-wall 9 formed with a central aperture through which passes the reduced and threaded inner end of the hollow stem 10 which is tightly fixed to the shank 6 by the nut 11 and washer 12. Surrounding the stem 10 are the opposed tension disks 13, 14, of which the disk 13 rests against the rim 15 of the hollow shank-member 6. The outer end-portion of the stem 10 is

formed with a longitudinal diametrical slot 16 through which passes the diameter-bar 17 crossing the central stem-embracing aperture 18 in the shallow base-cup 19 which is pressed against the tension disk 14 by the bee-hive spring 20.

The spring 20 is engaged at its outer end by the ring-shaped member, preferably in the form of a washer 21, formed with a diameter-bar 22 having a forwardly extending stem-portion 23 disposed in the slot 16 in the stem 10. The washer 21 is engaged or backed by a dial-nut 24 having an outwardly flaring conical skirt 25, the rim of which is slightly smaller than and is received within the rim 26 of the base-cup 19. The skirt 25 is preferably formed integral with and non-adjustable relative to the screw-threaded head of the nut 24. It overhangs and encloses the major portion of the bee-hive spring 20. The nut 24 is preferably screw-threaded onto the split stem 10 and has an inner cylindrically recessed portion 27 which receives the washer 21 and into which cylindrically recessed portion projects the stop-pin 28 fixed in the nut 24. The stop-pin 28 normally works in a clearance groove 29 in the washer 21, and this clearance groove is interrupted at one point in its circumference by the stop-wall 30 which limits the turning movement of the nut 24 to one rotation during which the spring 20 is stressed from minimum to maximum requirements; the strength and stiffness of the spring 20 and the pitch of the screw-threads on the stem 10 for the nut 24 being proportioned to attain this result. The washer 21 thus constitutes a stop between the nut 24 and spring 20, which stop is engaged by the stop 28 on the nut 24.

There is disposed within the hollow stem 10 the usual presser-controlled tension-release pin 10' which engages the diameter-bar 17 of the base-cup 19 and relieves the tension-disks of the pressure of the spring 20 when the usual presser-foot (not shown) is lifted.

Surrounding the stem 10 within the shank 6 is the check-spring 31 one end of which extends through the arcuate slot 32 in the end wall 9 of the shank member 6 and is formed with a loop 33 and inturned end 34 which projects into one of the several apertures 35 in the end wall 9 and is thus anchored to the shank 6 and stem 10. The other end of the check-spring 31 extends outwardly through the slot 36 in the rim of the shank 6 and is formed with the usual thread-engaging loop 37.

The tension on the check-spring may be readily adjusted by removing the entire tension device from the aperture 5 in the head 2 and by inserting the end 34 of the check-spring in another of the anchor-holes 35. The loop 33 affords a convenient means for retraction and reinsertion of the end 34 from and in the anchor-holes 35. It is also useful in assembling the device as it permits the end 34 to be readily extracted from the arcuate slot 32 preparatory to being inserted in one of the apertures 35.

The base-cup 19 is preferably provided with an index mark i and the skirt 25 of the nut 24 is graduated so that, when the user has the tension correctly adjusted for a certain grade of work, the figure on the dial may be noted and the desired tension immediately restored whenever required.

The device may be taken apart by first turning the dial-nut 24 to the left or unscrewing it as far as it will go and by then depressing the washer 21 with the aid of a screw-driver blade 37, as shown in Fig. 10, to carry the stop-shoulder 30 inwardly out of range of the stop-pin 28, whereupon the dial-nut 24 may be entirely unscrewed and removed from the stem 16. The other parts may then be readily slipped off.

The stop-pin 28 is fixed in or made integral with the nut 24 and there are no small stop-screws which are likely to work loose or be lost.

Having thus set forth the nature of the invention, what I claim herein is:—

1. In a sewing machine tension-device, the combination with the thread-engaging means, a stem, and a tension-spring, of a screw-threaded tension-regulating nut on said stem, a washer interposed between said nut and spring, said washer being keyed to said stem to slide lengthwise of the latter without rotation, and coacting stop-elements on said washer and nut to limit the movement of the latter to one rotation.

2. In a sewing machine tension-device, the combination with the thread-engaging means, a stem, and a tension-spring, of a tension-regulating dial rotatably mounted on said stem, and a ring-shaped member interposed between said dial and one end of said tension-spring, said ring-shaped member being keyed to said stem to slide lengthwise of the latter without rotation.

3. In a sewing machine tension-device, the combination with the thread-engaging means, a longitudinally slotted stem, and a tension-spring, of a screw-threaded tension-

regulating nut on said stem, a stop interposed between said nut and spring, said stop having a portion disposed in the slot in said stem, and a coacting stop on said nut to limit the movement of the latter to one rotation.

4. In a sewing machine tension-device, the combination with the thread-engaging means, a diametrically slotted stem, and a tension-spring, of a screw-threaded tension-regulating nut on said stem, a washer interposed between said nut and spring, said washer having a diameter-bar disposed in the slot in said stem, and coacting stop-elements on said washer and nut to limit the movement of the latter to one rotation, said stop-elements being permanently fixed on their respective carriers.

5. In a sewing machine tension-device, the combination with the thread-engaging means, a diametrically slotted stem, and a tension-spring, of a screw-threaded tension-regulating nut on said stem, a washer having a diameter-bar disposed in the slot in said stem, said diameter-bar having a forwardly extending stem-portion, and coacting stop-elements on said washer and nut to limit the movement of the latter to one complete rotation.

6. In a sewing machine tension-device, the combination with the thread-engaging means, a stem, and a tension-spring, of a two-part casing for said spring, one of said parts being a shallow base-cup, and the other a dial-nut screw-threaded onto said stem and having an outwardly flaring conical skirt the rim of which overhangs said spring and is slightly smaller than and is received within the rim of said cup.

7. In a sewing machine tension-device, the combination with the thread-engaging means, a stem, and a tension-spring, of a two-part casing for said spring, one of said parts being a shallow base-cup and the other a dial-nut screw-threaded onto said stem and having an outwardly flaring conical skirt the rim of which is slightly smaller than and is received within the rim of said cup, a washer interposed between said dial-nut and the outer end of said spring, said washer and said base-cup being keyed against rotation relative to said stem, and coacting stop-elements on said washer and dial-nut.

8. In a sewing machine tension-device, the combination with the thread-engaging means, a stem, a tension-spring and a tension-regulating nut, of a hollow cylindrical shank having an end-wall on which said stem is mounted, said end-wall having in it a check-spring clearance slot and a series of anchor holes, and a check-spring surrounding said stem within said hollow shank and having one of its ends extending through said clearance slot and anchored in one of said anchor holes.

9. In a sewing machine tension-device,

the combination with the thread-engaging means, a stem, a tension-spring and a tension-regulating nut, of a hollow cylindrical shank having an end-wall on which said stem is mounted, said end-wall having in it a check-spring clearance slot and a series of anchor holes, and a check-spring surrounding said stem within said hollow shank and having one of its ends extending through said clearance slot and formed with a rearwardly extending loop terminating in a forwardly extending end anchored in one of said anchor holes.

In testimony whereof, I have signed my name to this specification.

    DANIEL H. CHASON.

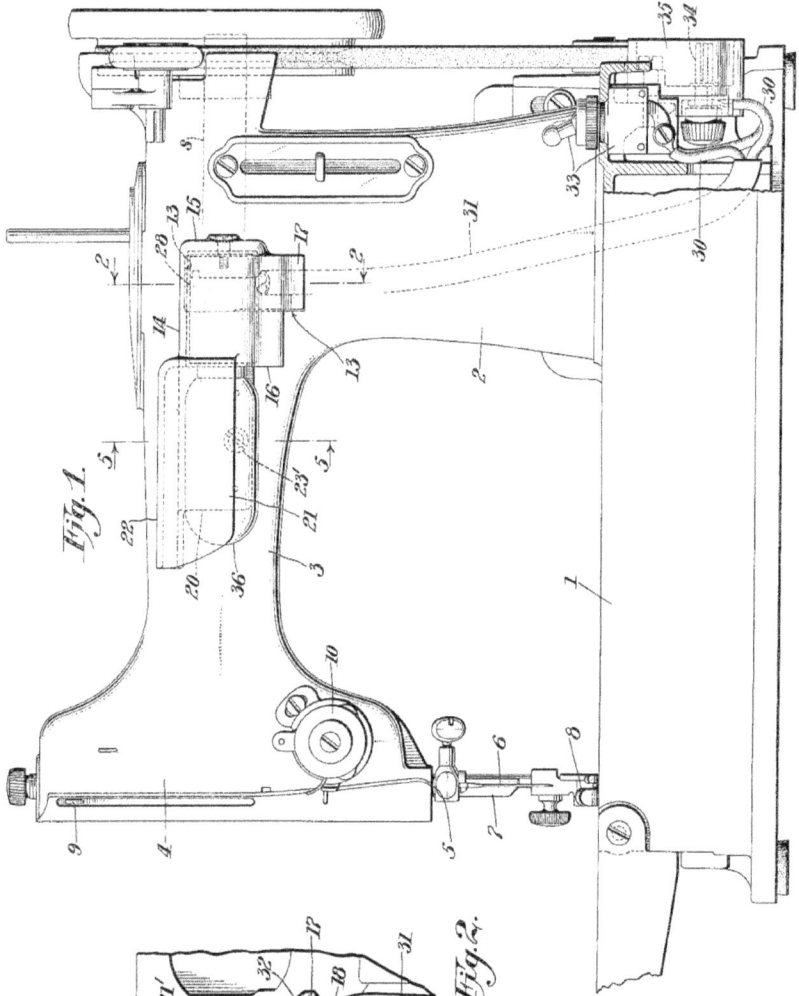

Fig. 1.

Fig. 2.

Inventor

Herbert J. Goosman

Witness:

By   *Harry J. Miller*

Attorney

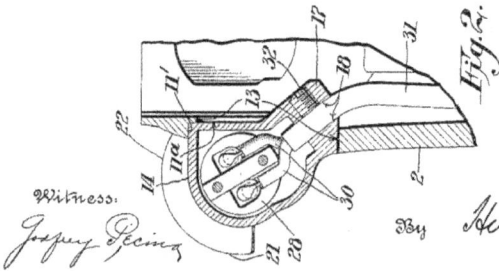

74

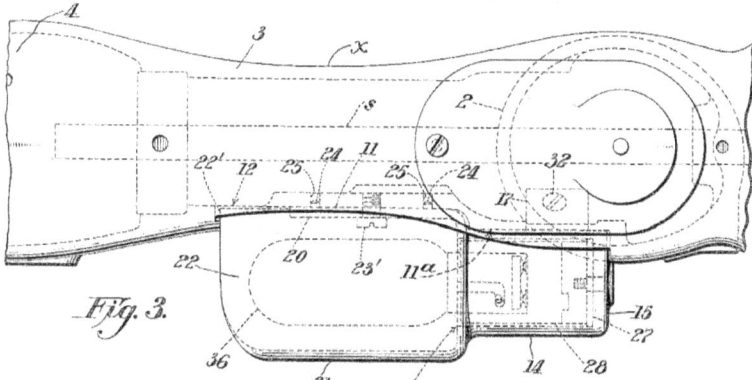

Fig. 3.

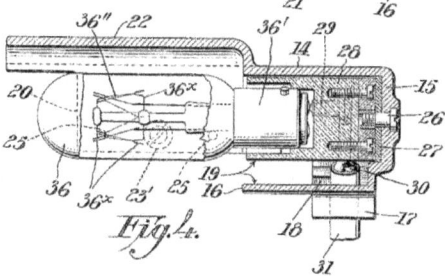

Fig. 4.

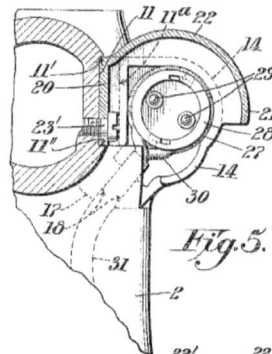

Fig. 5.

Fig. 4.ª

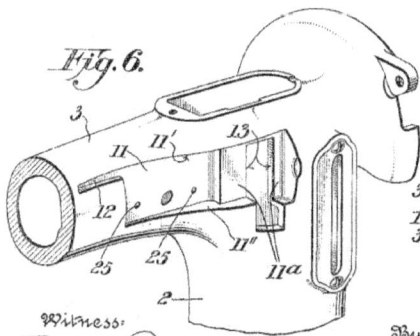

Fig. 6.

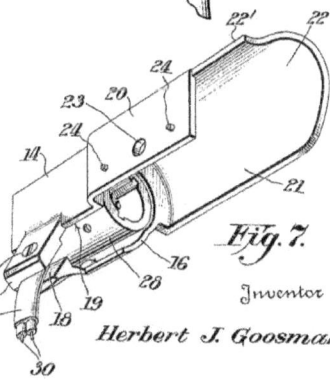

Fig. 7.

Inventor

Herbert J. Goosman

By Henry J. Miller

Attorney

Witness:

Joseph Steiner

75

UNITED STATES PATENT OFFICE

2,031,562

ELECTRICALLY LIGHTED SEWING MACHINE

Herbert J. Goosman, Elizabeth, N. J., assignor to The Singer Manufacturing Company, Elizabeth, N. J., a corporation of New Jersey

Application July 13, 1933, Serial No. 680,219

10 Claims. (Cl. 240—2.14)

Electric sewing machine lighting devices as heretofore constructed and applied to the sewing machine, when of ample illuminating capacity, have been objected to in some cases because of their inordinate size relative to the sewing machine frame and in general because of the high temperature to which the lamp-shade is raised by the heat from the lamp; such high temperature making the lamp-shade a radiator of a discomforting amount of heat into the operator's face and further making it necessary for the operator to use great care not to touch the hot lamp-shade.

It has heretofore been proposed to overcome the objection of discomforting heat radiation by placing the lighting device horizontally directly in rear of the overhanging member of the sewing machine gooseneck, which member functioned as a barrier to radiant heat between the lighting device and the operator's face. In cases where, for any reason, it is desired to position the lighting device in front of the gooseneck, the desirable heat-barrier function of the gooseneck is lost.

It has also been proposed to prevent overheating of the lamp-shade by interposing between it and the lamp-bulb a thin sheet-metal liner separated from the shade by an air-gap through which cooling currents of air may freely flow by convection.

The present invention has for an object to provide simple, sturdy, inexpensive, unobtrusive, easily constructed, and readily assembled means for the electric illumination of a sewing machine, which will adequately illuminate the work being stitched without danger or discomfort to the operator, and which does not depend upon an additional liner or upon the heat barrier function of the sewing machine gooseneck to shield the operator from discomforting heat radiation from the lighting device.

Another object of the invention is to provide an electrically lighted sewing machine, the lighting device of which, while of relatively small physical size and relatively high wattage, is so contrived and combined with the sewing machine as to afford generous illumination of the work without discomforting radiation of heat.

A further object of the invention is to provide a sewing machine with a built-in lighting device which is simple in construction, inexpensive to manufacture, easy to assemble and apply to the sewing machine, and which does not interfere in any manner with the normal operation and use of the sewing machine or with the assembling or disassembling of the parts of the machine.

With the above and other objects in view, as will hereinafter appear, the invention comprises the devices, combinations, and arrangements of parts hereinafter set forth and illustrated in the accompanying drawings of a preferred embodiment of the invention, from which the several features of the invention and the advantages attained thereby will be readily understood by those skilled in the art.

In the accompanying drawings Fig. 1 is a front side elevation of a sewing machine embodying the invention. Fig. 2 is a section on the line 2—2, Fig. 1. Fig. 3 is a fragmentary top plan view of the machine. Fig. 4 is a vertical longitudinal section through the electric lighting device of the machine. Fig. 4a is a detail view of a portion of the lamp filament used in this device. Fig. 5 is a section on the line 5—5, Fig. 1. Fig. 6 is a fragmentary perspective view of the sewing machine gooseneck from which the lighting device has been removed and Fig. 7 is a perspective view of the lighting device removed from the machine.

For the purposes of the present disclosure the invention is described as embodied in a preferred form in a sewing machine having a hollow bed 1 from which rises the standard 2 of the hollow inverted L-shaped gooseneck 3 terminating in the head 4 carrying the usual needle-bar 5, needle 6, presser-bar 7, presser-foot 8, take-up 9 and tension device 10. Disposed within and lengthwise of the overhanging member 3 of the gooseneck is the sewing machine main shaft s which is connected in the usual manner to drive the needle-bar 5, take-up 9 and the usual loop-taking and feeding devices (not shown) customarily located below or within the bed 1. The overhanging member 3 of the gooseneck is preferably of curved contour and is tapered inwardly, Fig. 3, from the standard 2, or gradually reduced in section, to a point x intermediate the standard 2 and head 4, from which intermediate point x the gooseneck is tapered outwardly or enlarged in section toward the head 4. The gooseneck is preferably formed in its curved and tapered front side wall, Fig. 6, with a flat vertical seat 11 which may be sunk somewhat below the normal curved and tapering surface of the gooseneck and made parallel to the main shaft s. The gooseneck 3 may be formed in its side wall at one end of the seat 11 with a slot 12 and is preferably formed adjacent the other end of the seat 11 with a step or auxiliary seat 11a in which there is an aperture 13 opening into the hollow interior of the gooseneck 3.

The electric lighting device preferably comprises an electric lamp-socket shell 14 of hollow tubular form closed at one end 15 and open at its other end 16. Projecting rearwardly from the socket-shell 14 is a lug 17 formed with a lateral slot 18. The socket-shell 14 has a slot 19 in its lower wall opening into the lateral slot 18 in the lug 17.

Preferably, cast integral with the lamp-socket

shell 14 is the inverted trough-shaped lamp-shade having preferably a flat vertical rear wall 20, a front wall 21 and an arched top connecting wall wall 22. The rear wall 20 of the shade preferably extends below the lever of the free edge of the front wall 21 and is preferably provided with an aperture 23 for the fastening screw 23' and with a pair of dowel pins 24 which enter the dowel pin apertures 25 in the seat 11 when the lighting device is applied to its seat in the gooseneck.

Preferably yieldingly mounted within the shell 14 by means of the screw 26 and intervening felt washer 27 is the lamp-socket 28 having the usual spring-pin lamp-base-engaging contacts 29 to which are connected the conductor wires 30 of the lead-sheathed conductor cable 31 passing downwardly through the slotted conductor lead-in lug 17 and through the aperture 13 into the hollow gooseneck.

By virtue of the provision of the slots 18 and 19 in the socket-shell 14 and conductor lead-in lug 17, the lamp-socket 28 may first be wired and assembled with the cable 31 and the wired socket assembly slid into the socket-shell 14; the cable 31 passing along the slot 19 and into the slot 18 in which it is secured by the clamp-screw 32. One conductor of the cable 31 may be connected at its lower end through a conventional toggle-switch 33 to a contact element 34 of the usual terminal block 35. The other conductor 30 may be connected directly to another contact element (not shown) of the block 35.

In accordance with the principles of the present invention it is important that the lamp-shade be made to function as an extremely good or rapid conductor of heat and, to this end, the shell 14 and walls 20, 21, 22 of the lamp-shade are preferably die cast in metal of high heat-conductivity, such as one of the well known aluminum alloys of high aluminum content. Such an alloy may contain, say, from 6 to 8 percent of copper and from 2 to 3 percent of silicon with the balance of commercially pure aluminum. The walls of the cast aluminum shade are relatively thick, as compared with rolled sheet metal such as is customarily used for making lampshades, and insure mechanical strength as well as large heat-conductive capacity and a rapid heat flow into the gooseneck from the shade 21, 22, 20 and shell 14, the preferably offset flat rear walls of which shade and shell are in intimate thermal contact over a relatively large vertical surface area with the stepped seats 11, 11ᵃ. The corner 22' of the shade is preferably received in the slot 12 in the gooseneck and is protected by the gooseneck. The socket-shell 14 and shade wall 20 are also preferably in juxtaposition with the top and bottom ledges 11' and 11'' of the stepped seats 11, 11ᵃ. It will be observed, particularly in Figs. 1 and 4, that the area of thermal contact between the sewing machine arm 3 and the lamp-shade and socket-shell unit detachably seated thereon, is approximately equal to the axial sectional area of the lamp-bulb 36. This extensive area of thermal contact permits of a very rapid flow of heat from the lamp-shade into the sewing machine arm in accordance with the principle of the invention.

According to the present invention, the gooseneck of the machine is made to function as a primary reservoir and radiator of heat from the lighting device and, to this end, should have a large surface area relative to the surface area of the lamp-shade and socket-shell elements. It should also be so constructed that it will function to rapidly conduct the heat stream away from its area of contact with lamp-shade and socket-shell elements and spread the heat well over its relatively large surface, from which the heat is readily dissipated to the surrounding air without an objectionable rise in temperature in any of the parts of the lamp-shade, lamp-socket shell or gooseneck. While it is preferred to cast the gooseneck also of aluminum alloy, it may be made of cast-iron or other metal of lower heat-conductivity than aluminum, provided its metallic cross-sectional area is sufficient to insure large heat-conductive capacity and a sufficiently rapid spread of heat to and over a relatively large proportion of its surface to prevent an excessive or objectionable localized temperature rise in the lamp-shade or adjacent the position of attachment of the lamp-shade and socket-shell casting. Because of the high degree of accuracy with which aluminum die-castings can be made, the gooseneck 3 and shell and shade castings may, when cast in aluminum, be secured together in intimate thermal contact over a relatively large contact area as compared with the total area of the lamp-shade, without subsequent machining operations, to insure a very free and rapid flow of heat from the lamp-shade and socket-shell into the relatively large gooseneck 3.

In the preferred embodiment of the invention illustrated the vertical height of the stepped seats 11, 11ᵃ is at least equal to the diameter of the lamp-bulb 36. Excellent heat-conductive contact with low impedance to the heat stream is thus afforded between the lamp-shade and the supporting gooseneck to insure against objectionable overheating of the lamp-shade. The lamp-bulb 36 is preferably of the conventional, horizontally disposed, commercial, sewing machine lighting type, of tubular form, approximately ⅞ inch in diameter and 2 inches long, exclusive of its base 36', and has the usual concentrated filament 36'' which is in the form of a fine helix, as shown in Fig. 4ᵃ and is draped back and forth as usual upon the hangers 36ˣ within a cylindrical space 7⁄16 inch in diameter by 7⁄16 inch long. Such a lamp may be connected directly to a commercial 120 volt lighting circuit and is rated at 15 watts.

I believe that I am the first to provide a sewing machine with a shaded electric lighting device having an illuminating capacity which is adequate for practical use, without objectionable operative or accompanying heat characteristics, and I accomplish this new result by utilizing the gooseneck of a sewing machine as the primary radiator or dissipator of heat from the shade of the lighting device and by providing for a rapid conduction of heat through the lamp-shade and from the lamp-shade into the gooseneck.

I am aware that it has been proposed to mount an electric lighting device including a lamp and reflector either partially or wholly within a recess in the under side of the overhanging gooseneck of a sewing machine, but in such outfits the lamp-bulb and reflector either encroach objectionably upon the space under the gooseneck or must be made small enough to avoid interference with the working parts of the machine within the gooseneck and, when so made, either do not give sufficient illumination to be of practical use or have objectionable heating characteristics.

The invention is not to be understood as limited to the specific embodiment thereof shown and described, as it is obviously susceptible of embodiment in various specifically different forms within the spirit and scope of the invention.

Having thus set forth the nature of the invention, what I claim herein is:—

1. The combination with a sewing machine formed with a frame including a bed and a hollow gooseneck of good heat conductivity and relatively large surface area, with stitch-forming mechanism incorporated in said frame, of a lighting device including an electric lamp-bulb of relatively high wattage and small physical size together with a lamp-socket and a correspondingly small one-piece highly heat-conductive inverted trough-shaped lamp-shade and tubular lamp-socket shell carrying said lamp and lamp-socket and detachably mounted on the front side of said gooseneck with a large portion of the surface of the lamp-shade and lamp socket shell in direct heat-conductive contact with said gooseneck, whereby a rapid flow of heat is had through and from the shade and shell elements into the gooseneck which functions as a primary heat radiator from the extensive surface area of which the heat is dissipated with only a moderate rise in temperature.

2. An electrically lighted sewing machine having a frame comprising a bed and overhanging hollow gooseneck, said gooseneck being formed at one side thereof with a seat and with an aperture adjacent to said seat, a one-piece metallic electric lamp-socket shell and lamp-shade member having a portion mating with and secured to said seat and a portion received in said aperture, an electric lamp-socket mounted in said shell, and an electric conductor cable housed within said hollow gooseneck and passing outwardly through said aperture to said lamp-socket.

3. An electrically lighted sewing machine having a frame comprising a bed and gooseneck, said gooseneck having a vertical standard and a horizontal arm overhanging said bed, said arm being formed at one side thereof with a flat vertical seat, an electric lamp-socket shell and lamp-shade member, said member having a hollow tubular socket-shell portion closed at one end and open at its other end, said member further having an inverted trough-shaped lamp-shade portion cast in one piece with and projecting beyond the open end of said shell-portion, said lamp-shade portion having a vertical inner wall extending downwardly below the level of its outer free edge and screwed to said seat, and an electric lamp-socket mounted in said socket-shell portion.

4. An electrically lighted sewing machine having a frame including a bed and an overhanging hollow gooseneck formed with an aperture in a side wall thereof, a one-piece hollow tubular socket-shell closed at one end and open at its other end and having a laterally slotted lug projecting rearwardly therefrom and entering the aperture in said gooseneck, said socket-shell having a slot in its lower wall extending from the open end thereof to and opening into the lateral slot in said lug, an electric lamp-socket mounted in said shell, an electric conductor cable extending from said lamp-socket through said lug and downwardly within said hollow gooseneck, and

means for securing said socket-shell to said gooseneck.

5. The combination with a hollow tubular sewing machine gooseneck of inverted L-shape with a seat at one side thereof and with an aperture adjacent to said seat, of a one-piece electric lamp-socket shell and lamp-shade member die-cast in aluminum, the lamp-socket shell portion of said member being formed with a conductor lead-in lug received in said aperture and the lamp-shade portion of said member being formed with a side wall portion secured flatwise to said seat, an electric lamp-socket mounted in said shell portion, and an electric conductor cable leading upwardly within said hollow gooseneck and through said lug to said lamp-socket.

6. The combination with a hollow sewing machine gooseneck of die-cast aluminum, said gooseneck being of inverted L-shape the overhanging horizontal portion of which is formed at one side thereof with a seat, of an electric lamp-shade of inverted trough shape die-cast of aluminum with front and back side walls and a connecting top wall, means for securing one of the side walls of said shade flatwise against said seat, an electric lamp-socket shell cast integrally with said shade, and an electric lamp-socket mounted in said shell.

7. The combination with a sewing machine having a frame including a bed and a gooseneck formed with a hollow standard rising from said bed and with an overhanging hollow arm terminating at its free end in a head, said arm being of curved contour and tapered inwardly and reduced in cross-section between said standard and head and formed at one side thereof with a stepped seat, of an electric lighting device including a lamp-socket shell and lamp-shade member cast in one piece in aluminum with a stepped rear wall secured to said seat, and an electric lamp-socket and lamp mounted in said socket-shell and shade member.

8. An electrically lighted sewing machine having a frame including a bed and an overhanging tapered gooseneck formed with stepped seats, and an electric lighting device having metallic lamp-socket-shell and lamp-shade elements in engagement, respectively, with said seats.

9. An electrically lighted sewing machine having a frame including a bed and an overhanging tapered gooseneck formed at one side with stepped parallel seats, a one-piece detachable electric lamp-socket-shell and lamp-shade member having offset parallel walls in engagement, respectively, with said seats, an electric lamp-socket mounted in the socket-shell portion of said member, and an electric lamp-bulb carried by said lamp-socket.

10. The combination with a sewing machine having a bed and a gooseneck with a relatively large heat-radiating surface, of an electric lighting device including a tubular electric lamp of at least 15 watts power consumption disposed entirely at one side of the central vertical plane of the gooseneck and having a one-piece inverted trough-shaped metallic lamp-shade and tubular lamp-socket shell of relatively high heat conductivity detachably seated in thermal contact with said gooseneck over a surface area approximately equal to the axial sectional area of said lamp-bulb.

HERBERT J. GOOSMAN.

Fig.1.

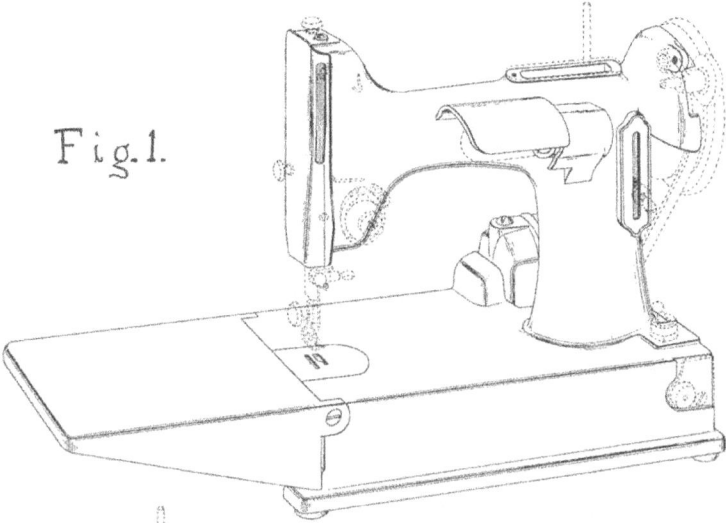

Fig. 2.

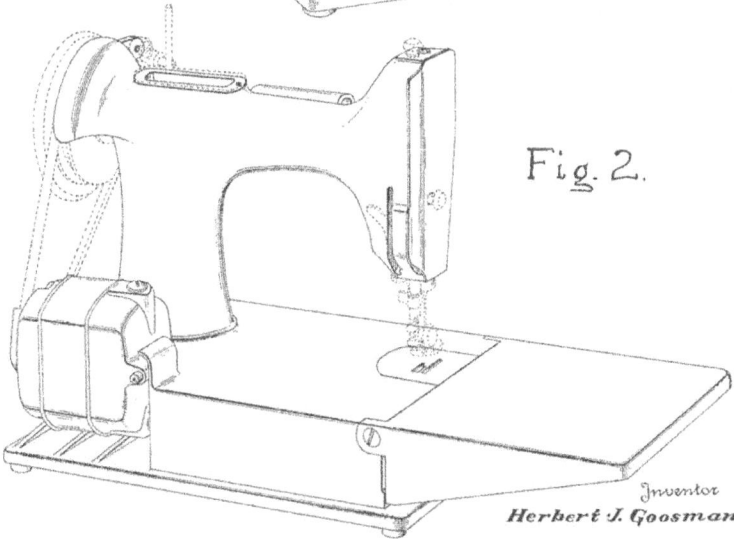

Inventor

Herbert J. Goosman

Witness:

John H. Cave

By Henry J. Miller

Attorney

79

Des. 91,816

UNITED STATES PATENT OFFICE

91,816

DESIGN FOR AN ELECTRIC SEWING
MACHINE

Herbert J. Goosman, Elizabeth, N. J., assignor to
The Singer Manufacturing Company, Elizabeth, N. J., a corporation of New Jersey

Application January 25, 1934, Serial No. 50,502

Term of patent 14 years

To all whom it may concern:

Be it known that I, HERBERT J. GOOSMAN, a citizen of the United States, residing at Elizabeth, in the county of Union and State of New Jersey, have invented a new, original, and ornamental Design for an Electric Sewing Machine, of which the following is a specification, reference being had to the accompanying drawing, forming a part thereof.

Figures 1 and 2 are perspective views of an electric sewing machine showing my new design; the parts shown in dotted lines being conventional.

I claim:

The ornamental design for an electric sewing machine, as shown and described.

In testimony whereof I have signed my name to this specification.

HERBERT J. GOOSMAN

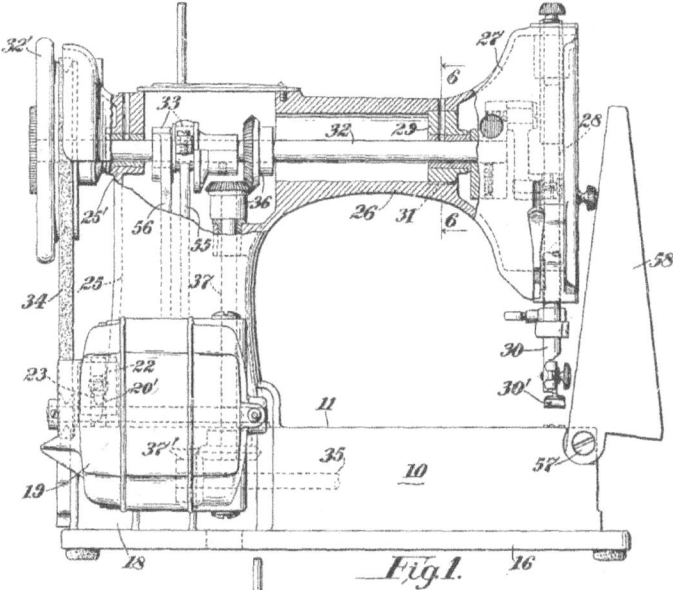

Fig.1.

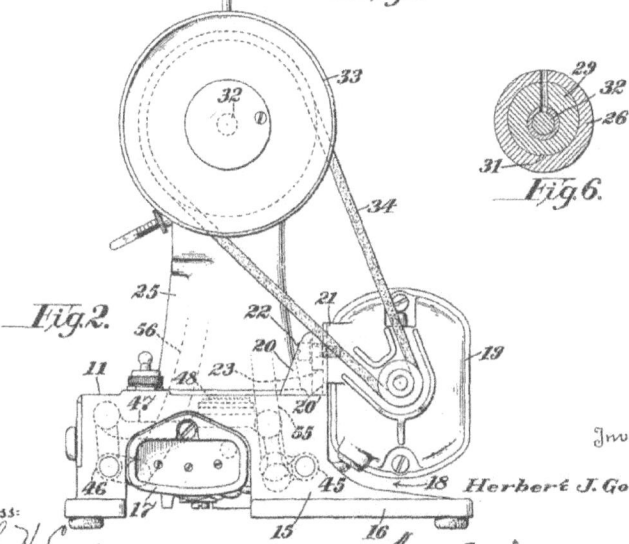

Fig.2.   Fig.6.

Inventor

Herbert J. Goosman

Witness:

John N. Cave

By Amy J. Miller

Attorney

Dec. 8, 1936.
H. J. GOOSMAN
2,063,841

SEWING MACHINE FRAME

Filed April 11, 1934
3 Sheets—Sheet 2

Fig.3.

Fig.4.

Fig.5.

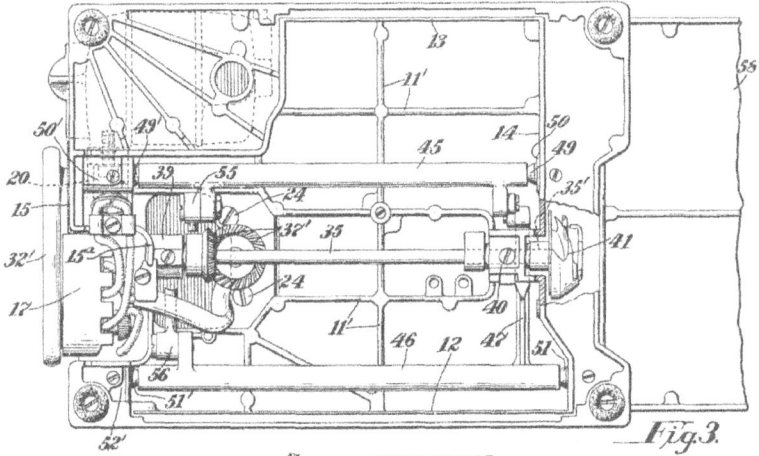

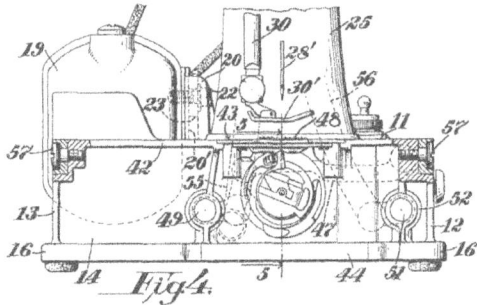

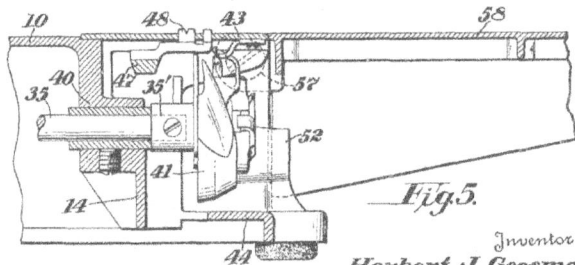

Inventor
Herbert J. Goosman

Witness:
John H. Cave

By Henry J. Miller

Attorney

82

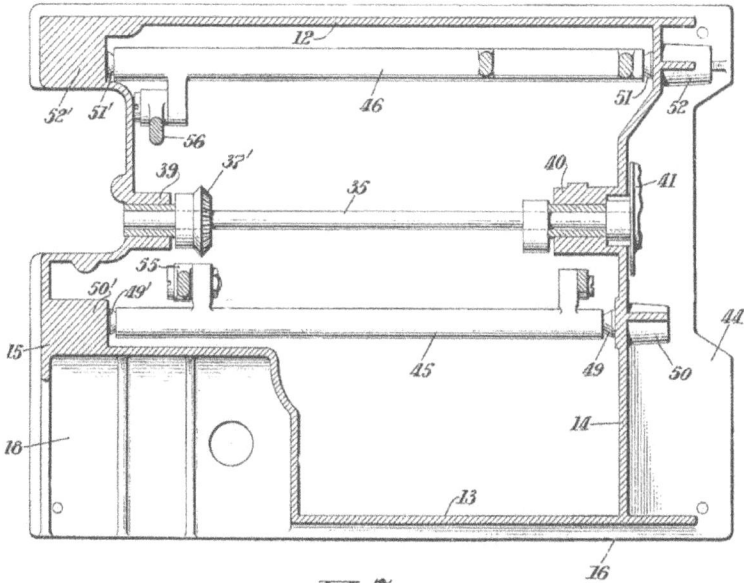

Fig.7.

Inventor

Herbert J. Goosman

Witness:
Godfrey Pecing

By Henry J Miller
                                                   Attorney

83

UNITED STATES PATENT OFFICE

2,063,841

SEWING MACHINE FRAME

Herbert J. Goosman, Elizabeth, N. J., assignor to
The Singer Manufacturing Company, Elizabeth, N. J., a corporation of New Jersey

Application April 11, 1934, Serial No. 719,996

8 Claims. (Cl. 112—258)

This invention relates to sewing machines and more particularly to sewing machines of the domestic portable type and has for its object to produce a sewing machine which is compact and exceedingly light in weight.

Another object of the present invention is to provide a frame for such machine having the bearing supports for the operating parts die-cast with the frame and to provide a die-cast frame which requires a minimum of machining.

Another object of the invention is to provide a sewing machine bed having an enclosure in which the loop-taker and feed-actuating mechanism are housed and the loop-taker disposed outside of the housing in a position where the bobbin may be removed and the loop-taker inspected, cleaned and repaired.

With the above and other objects in view, as will hereinafter appear, the invention comprises the devices, combinations, and arrangements of parts hereinafter set forth and illustrated in the accompanying drawings of a preferred embodiment of the invention, from which the several features of the invention and the advantages attained thereby will be readily understood by those skilled in the art.

The several features of the present invention will be clearly understood from the following description and accompanying drawings:—

Figure 1 is a rear elevation of my improved sewing machine, a portion of the bracket-arm being broken away to show the operating parts and their supports.

Figure 2 is an end elevation looking from the left of Figure 1.

Figure 3 is a bottom plan view.

Figure 4 is an end elevation of the bed and upper and lower stitch-forming mechanisms.

Figure 5 is a sectional view taken substantially along the line 5—5 of Figure 4, the loop-taker and its actuating shaft being shown in elevation.

Figure 6 is a section taken along the line 6—6 of Figure 1.

Figure 7 is a horizontal sectional view of the bed taken in a plane passing substantially through the shaft 35.

The frame of the machine is die-cast in metal of aluminum alloy of high aluminum content. Such an alloy may contain, for instance, from 6 to 8 percent of copper and from 2 to 3 percent of silicon with the balance of commercially pure aluminum. Due to the precision with which a frame may be die-cast only a minimum amount of machining, reaming and drilling are necessary.

As illustrated in the drawings the frame of the machine comprises a substantially rectangular shaped bed or base, indicated generally as 10, having a work-supporting plate 11 provided on its under face with transversely arranged strengthening ribs 11', downwardly extending side-walls 12 and 13 and end-walls 14 and 15 forming an enclosure. The side-walls terminate in a flange portion 16. The end-wall 15 is recessed to receive an electrical terminal 17 and the side-wall 13 and end-wall 15 are inwardly offset to form a recess 18 for the reception of an electric motor 19. Fixed to the work-supporting plate 11 is a motor-supporting bracket 20 formed with a channel 20' which slidably receives the rectangular shaped lug 21 carried by the frame of the motor 19. The lug 21 is adjustably fixed to the bracket 20 by means of a screw 22 which extends through a slot 23 in the bracket 20 and is threaded into the lug 21. From the above it will be obvious that the motor 19 may be raised or lowered on its support.

Fixed to the hollow bed 10 by the screws 24 is the standard 25 which carries the overhanging bracket-arm 26 terminating in a hollow head 27 carrying the usual reciprocatory needle-bar 28, needle 28', presser-bar 30 and presser-foot 30'. Disposed within and lengthwise of the overhanging bracket-arm 26 is the sewing machine main shaft 32 having a balance-wheel 32' fixed thereto and driven from the motor 19 by the belt 34. The shaft 32 is connected in the usual manner to drive the needle-bar 28 and the loop-taker actuating shaft 35 is driven through the gears 36, vertical shaft 37 and gears 37'.

The main shaft 32 adjacent the balance-wheel 32' is carried by the bearing support 25' die-cast with the standard 25. The standard 25, bracket-arm 26 and head 27 are die-cast in a single piece and the interior diameter of the bracket-arm 26 is made greater at the end of the arm adjacent the head 27 to facilitate the removal of the core after the casting operation. To support the shaft 32 in the bracket-arm there is provided a bearing support 29 which is fixed in the interior of the arm by a driving fit or by spinning a portion of the metal in the bracket-arm over the bearing support 29 to securely hold it against endwise displacement. As shown in Figures 1 and 6, the aperture in the support 29 through which the shaft 32 extends is off center, the purpose being to align this aperture with the aperture in the bearing support **25′**. The arm **26** is cast with a feather **31** which extends into a keyway in the support **29** to prevent the support from turning in the arm.

The loop-taker actuating shaft **35** has one of its ends journaled in a bearing lug **39** die-cast to the offset portion **15a** of the end-wall **15** and the other end of the shaft **35** extends through the bearing-lug **40** die-cast to and forming part of the end-wall **14**. To the end **35′** of the shaft **35** there is secured a loop-taker **41** preferably of the lock-stitch type. As shown in Figures 3, 4, and 5, to protect the loop-taker the cloth-plate **11** is formed with an overhanging portion **42** which carries a throat-plate **43** and the bed **10** is provided with a lower extension **44**. The loop-taker **41** is disposed in the space between the throat-plate **43** and the extension **44**.

Also disposed within the hollow bed **10** are rock-shafts **45** and **46** which impart to the feed-bar **47** carrying a feed-dog **48** the usual feed-lift and feed-advance and return movements. The rock-shaft **45** is supported on the pivot-lugs **49** and **49′** carried by the bearing supports **50** and **50′** die-cast with the walls **14** and **15** of the bed **10** and the rock-shaft **46** is supported on the pivot-lugs **51** and **51′** carried by the bearing supports **52** and **52′** which are also die-cast with the walls **14** and **15** of the bed. The rock-shafts **45** and **46** are actuated by the pitmen **55** and **56**, respectively, the pitmen receiving their motion from the usual feed-actuating eccentrics **33** carried by the main-shaft **32**.

The overhanging portion **42** of the cloth-plate terminates a little to the left of the stitch-forming and feeding mechanism and to support the work at the left of the stitch-forming mechanism, I have pivotally secured to the corners of the bed **10** by the screws **57** an extension-plate **58**. As shown in Figure 5, the extension-plate **58** abuts the overhanging edge of the throat-plate **43** and the overhang of the cloth-plate **42**. By terminating the bed and work-support slightly to the left of the stitch-forming and feeding mechanism and pivoting an extension-plate to the bed so that it may be tilted to the position shown in Figure 1, the length of the bed of the machine is reduced which is highly desirable in the portable type machine.

Having thus set forth the nature of the invention, what I claim herein is:—

1. A sewing machine having, in combination a bed having depending side-walls and end-walls forming an enclosure, a loop-taker actuating shaft journaled in said bed and having one of its ends extending through one of the end-walls, a loop-taker fixed to the end of the shaft extending beyond said wall in an exposed position outside of the enclosure defined by said side-walls and end-walls, and an extension-plate pivotally secured to said bed, said extension plate being swingable upwardly to provide access to said loop-taker.

2. A sewing machine having in combination, a die-cast aluminum bed having depending side-walls and end-walls forming an enclosure, a standard rising from said bed, an overhanging bracket-arm terminating in a hollow head and carried by said standard, a loop-taker actuating shaft located within the enclosure formed by the side-walls and end-walls of said bed and one of its ends journaled in a bearing carried by one of the end-walls and its other end extending through a bearing carried by the other of the end-walls to a position beneath the hollow head, a loop-taker fixed to the extending end of said

actuating shaft in an exposed position outside of the enclosure defined by said side-walls and end-walls, and mechanism for imparting movement to said shaft.

3. A sewing machine having, in combination, an overhanging bracket-arm terminating in a hollow-head, a standard carrying said bracket-arm and head, a bed supporting said standard and having depending side-walls and end-walls defining a substantially rectangular shaped enclosure, one of said end-walls being disposed in a vertical plane passing through said hollow head, loop-taker and feed-dog actuating mechanism disposed entirely at one side of said end-wall and within the enclosure and a loop-taker and feed-dog disposed on the other side of said wall in an exposed position beneath the hollow head.

4. A sewing machine having, in combination, a standard carrying an overhanging bracket-arm terminating in a hollow-head, a base to which said standard is fixed, said base being substantially rectangular in shape and having depending side-walls and end-walls forming an enclosure, one of said side-walls and one of said end-walls being inwardly offset to provide a recess adjacent the standard, a bracket carried by said base, and an electric motor partially received within the recess and adjustably secured to said bracket.

5. A sewing machine having, in combination, a standard carrying an overhanging bracket-arm terminating in a hollow head, a base to which said standard is fixed, said base being substantially rectangular in shape and having depending side-walls and end-walls forming an enclosure, one of said side-walls and one of said end-walls being offset inwardly to provide a recess adjacent the standard for the reception of an electric motor, a loop-taker actuating shaft journaled in said base and having one of its ends extending through one of the end-walls, and a loop-taker secured to the end of the shaft extending beyond said wall and in an exposed position beneath the hollow head.

6. A sewing machine having, in combination, a standard carrying an overhanging bracket-arm terminating in a hollow head, a base to which said standard is fixed, said base being substantially rectangular in shape and having depending side-walls and end-walls forming an enclosure, one of said side-walls and one of said end-walls being offset inwardly to provide a recess adjacent the standard for the reception of an electric motor, a loop-taker actuating shaft journaled in said base and having one of its ends extending through one of the end-walls, a loop-taker secured to the end of the shaft extending beyond said wall in an exposed position beneath the hollow head, and an extension-plate forming a continuation of the bed and pivotally secured to the depending side-walls of the bed whereby it may be swung upwardly about its pivotal connection to a substantially vertical position adjacent said hollow head to provide access to said loop-taker.

7. A sewing machine having, in combination, an overhanging bracket-arm terminating in a hollow head, a standard carrying said bracket-arm and head, a base supporting said standard and having depending side-walls and end-walls defining a substantially rectangular shaped enclosure, one of said end-walls being disposed in a vertical plane passing through said hollow head, loop-taker and feed-dog actuating mechanism disposed entirely at one side of said end-wall and within the enclosure, a loop-taker and feed-dog disposed on the other side of said wall in an ex-

posed position beneath the hollow head, and an extension plate pivotally secured to said bed, said extension plate being swingable upwardly to a substantially vertical position to provide access to said loop-taker.

8. A sewing machine having in combination, a frame comprising a standard carrying a bracket-arm terminating in a hollow head, a work-supporting plate to which said standard is fixed, said work-supporting plate having depending side-walls and end-walls made integral therewith and forming an enclosure for the feed and loop-taker

actuating mechanism, sewing instrumentalities including a reciprocatory needle located above said work-supporting plate, a throat-plate fixed to said work-support, and an extension plate forming a continuation of said work-supporting plate and pivotally secured to said side-walls at points located in a vertical plane passing through said throat-plate, said extension plate abutting the edge of said throat-plate and being shiftable about its pivot points to a substantially vertical position adjacent said hollow head.

HERBERT J. GOOSMAN.

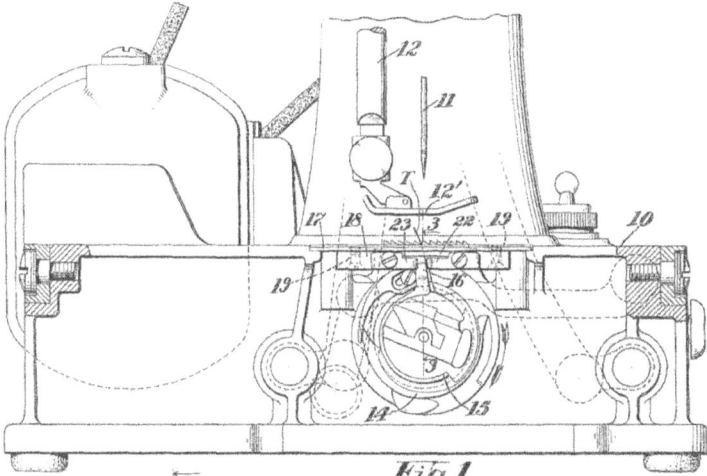

Fig.1.

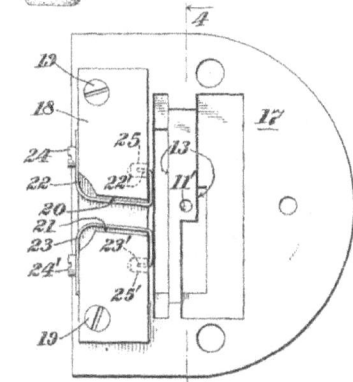

Fig.2.

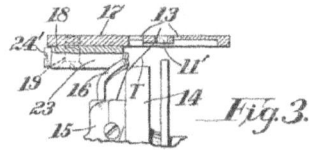

Fig.3.

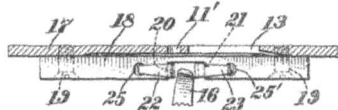

Fig.4.

Inventor

Herbert J. Goosman

Witness:

John N. Cave

By Henry J. Miller, Attorney

87

Patented July 9, 1935

2,007,894

UNITED STATES PATENT OFFICE

2,007,894

THREAD-CASE ROTATION-RESTRAINING
MEANS

Herbert J. Goosman, Elizabeth, N. J., assignor to
The Singer Manufacturing Company, Elizabeth, N. J., a corporation of New Jersey

Application May 12, 1934, Serial No. 725,291

5 Claims.   (Cl. 112—181)

This invention relates to sewing machines and more particularly to sewing machines of the lock-stitch type and has for its objective the provision of sound and vibration absorbing elements which will absorb the impact of the thread-case rotation restraining finger during the operation of the stitch-forming mechanism.

With the above and other objects in view, as will hereinafter appear, the invention comprises the devices, combinations, and arrangements of parts hereinafter set forth and illustrated in the accompanying drawing of a preferred embodiment of the invention, from which the several features of the invention and the advantages attained thereby will be readily understood by those skilled in the art.

The several features of the present invention will be clearly understood from the following description and accompanying drawing in which—

Figure 1 is an end elevation representing the stitch-forming mechanism of a sewing machine with my improved thread-case rotation-restraining elements embodied therein.

Figure 2 is a bottom plan view of the throat-plate.

Figure 3 is a fragmentary sectional view taken substantially along the line 3—3 of Figure 1, the loop-taker and thread-case being shown in elevation.

Figure 4 is a section of the throat-plate taken along the line 4—4 of Figure 2.

The present invention is shown embodied in a sewing machine such as that disclosed in my co-pending application, Serial No. 719,996, filed April 11, 1934. This machine comprises the usual bed 10, reciprocatory needle 11, presser-bar 12 and presser-foot 12'. Mounted for rotary movement on the bed 10 is a loop-taker 14 having a journaled therein a thread-case 15 formed with a rotation-restraining finger 16. The loop-taker and thread-case are shown and described in detail in my copending application, Serial No. 692,934, filed October 10, 1933.

Fixed to and carried by the bed of the machine is a throat-plate 17 formed with the usual needle-aperture 11' and feed-dog slots 13 and having a rotation-restraining bar 18 fixed by the screws 19 to the lower face thereof. The throat-plate and rotation-restraining bar, for the purpose of this improvement, are parts of the sewing machine bed. The bar 18 is provided with a groove defined by the walls 20 and 21 and fixed to the bar are two U-shaped cushioning flat-springs 22 and 23. The springs 22 and 23 each have one of their limbs fixed to one edge of the bar 18 by the screws 24

and 24' and the bends are spaced from and substantially parallel to the walls 20 and 21. The other limbs, which are free, extend along the other edge of the bar and terminate in portions 22' and 23', respectively, which extend into apertures 25 and 25' of larger diameter than the width of the springs 22 and 23.

The cushion springs 22 and 23 are spaced from each other to provide an opening for the finger 16 on the thread-case, the space between the springs being slightly greater than the width of the finger 16. As is well known in sewing machines of this type, the loop of needle-thread is seized by the loop-taker beak, which moves in the direction of the arrow in Figure 1, and casts it around the thread-case 15 and, as the needle-thread loop is drawn up by the take-up, the thread must pass between the spring 22 and finger 16. It will be understood that the friction between the thread-case and loop-taker causes the finger 16 to press against the spring 22, and when the machine is operated the passage of the thread between the spring and finger occurs very quickly and with a snap-like action with the result that the finger 16, in some instances, is thrown against the bend of the spring 22 which absorbs the impact and reduces the noise. The friction between the thread-case and loop-taker then causes the thread-case to move in the direction of movement of the thread-case as indicated by the arrow in Figure 1 and this movement of the thread-case throws the finger 16 against the bend of the spring 22 which deadens this blow. Also, due to the fact that the lead of the lower thread T is at one side of a vertical plane passing through the center of the thread-case when the stitch is set, the lower thread T, which is under tension at this time, moves the thread-case in a counter-clockwise direction, as viewed in Figure 1, thereby causing the finger 16 to strike the spring 23 which absorbs the blow.

It will be obvious from the above description that the springs 22 and 23 will absorb the blow of the thread-case rotation-restraining finger as it vibrates back and forth in the space between the springs thereby reducing noise and vibration.

Having thus set forth the nature of the invention, what I claim herein is:—

1. A sewing machine having in combination, stitch-forming mechanism including a reciprocatory needle, a circularly moving loop-taker cooperating with said needle, a thread-case carried by said loop-taker and having a rotation-restraining finger, a throat-plate, a bar located beneath said throat-plate, said bar having a groove which re-

ceives the finger on said thread-case, and means carried by said bar and disposed on opposite sides of said finger for cushioning the latter.

2. A sewing machine having in combination, stitch-forming mechanism including a reciprocatory needle, a circularly moving loop-taker cooperating with said needle, a thread-case carried by said loop-taker and having a rotation-restraining finger, a throat-plate, a bar fixed to the under side of said throat-plate and a flat spring fixed to said bar and spaced from one of the walls of said groove for absorbing the impact of said finger.

3. A sewing machine having in combination, stitch-forming mechanism including a reciprocatory needle, a circularly moving loop-taker cooperating with said needle, a thread-case carried by said loop-taker and having a rotation-restraining finger, a throat-plate, and cushion springs secured to said throat-plate and provided with finger-engaging portions spaced apart to form a resilient pocket for said rotation-restraining finger.

4. A sewing machine having in combination, stitch-forming mechanism including a reciprocatory needle, a circularly moving loop-taker cooperating with said needle, a thread-case journaled in said loop-taker and having a rotation-restraining finger, a throat-plate, a bar carried by said throat-plate and formed with a groove, and cushion springs secured to said bar on opposite sides of said groove, said cushion springs being spaced apart to form a resilient pocket for the rotation-restraining finger on said thread-case.

5. A sewing machine having in combination, stitch-forming mechanism including a reciprocatory needle, a circularly moving loop-taker cooperating with said needle, a thread-case carried by said loop-taker and having a rotation-restraining finger, a throat-plate, and a pair of spring members carried on the lower face of said throat-plate, said springs being spaced from each other to provide a resilient pocket for the finger of said thread-case.

                                    HERBERT J. GOOSMAN.

PATENT SPECIFICATION

Application Date: May 18, 1934. No. 15012/34.

Complete Specification Left: May 20, 1935.

Complete Specification Accepted: Sept. 24, 1935.

435,578

PROVISIONAL SPECIFICATION

Improvements in Sewing Machines

We, THE SINGER MANUFACTURING COMPANY LIMITED, a British Company of Singer, Clydebank, Dumbartonshire, and DENIS SHAW CRADDOCK, of British Nationality, of 3, Gray Street, Glasgow, do hereby declare the nature of this invention to be as follows:—

This invention relates to improvements in sewing machines.

In a sewing machine constructed in accordance with the present invention the mechanism below the bed-plate is enclosed within a sheet metal box structure attached to the bed-plate and provided with a hinged bottom wall openable to afford access to the lower mechanism.

Hinged on a horizontal axis to the box structure at the forward end of the bed-plate is a sheet metal flap adapted, when the machine is in use, to form an extension of the bed-plate. In order to permit the machine to be accommodated within a travelling case of minimum capacity, the extension plate is foldable into a position above and perpendicular to the bed-plate adjacent to the head of the arm of the machine.

According to a preferred arrangement the bed-plate rests at each corner on a resilient pad supported by a strut member within and unitary with the box structure and extending the full depth of said box structure so that its lower end engages the bottom wall of the box structure at a point in vertical register with a resilient supporting foot on the exterior of said bottom wall for engagement with a table or other machine-supporting surface. As will be understood, the construction is such that the weight of the machine is transmitted through the strut members to the resilient feet.

The box structure is conveniently pivotally attached to the bed-plate on an axis transverse to and located about midway of the length of the bed-plate, by means of two short pivot-forming bolts each of which penetrates an aperture in one longitudinal wall of the box structure and a registering aperture in a longitudinal rib depending from the adjacent edge of the bed-plate. It will thus be seen that, by virtue of its pivotal connection with the box structure, the machine is permitted readily to accommodate itself to its resilient supports.

The bottom wall of the box structure is hinged along its rear longitudinal edge to the rear wall of said structure so that, to gain access to the mechanism below the bed-plate, it is necessary only to tip the machine backwardly on to its side, whereupon the bottom wall may be opened forwardly and downwardly.

Dated this 17th day of May, 1934.
CRUIKSHANK & FAIRWEATHER,
86, St. Vincent Street, Glasgow, and
65/66, Chancery Lane, London, W.C.2,
Agents for the Applicants.

COMPLETE SPECIFICATION

Improvements in Sewing Machines

We, THE SINGER MANUFACTURING COMPANY LIMITED, a British Company of Singer, Clydebank, Dumbartonshire, and DENIS SHAW CRADDOCK, of British Nationality, of 3, Gray Street, Glasgow, do hereby declare the nature of this invention and in what manner the same is to be performed, to be particularly described and ascertained in and by the following statement:—

This invention relates to improvements in sewing machines.

[*Price 1/-*]

In a sewing machine constructed in accordance with the present invention the mechanism below the bed-plate is enclosed within a box structure attached to the bed-plate and provided with a hinged bottom wall openable to afford access to the lower mechanism.

A sewing machine constructed in accordance with the present invention is illustrated in the accompanying drawings in which Fig. 1 is a front elevation, Fig. 2 an inverted plan view, the bottom wall of the box structure being omitted, and Fig. 3 an end elevation showing the machine tipped backwardly on its side and the bottom wall of the box structure in partially opened position.

As shown, 1 denotes the bed-plate, and 2 the bracket-arm terminating in the head 3 of the sewing machine.

The mechanism below the bed-plate 1 is enclosed within a sheet metal box structure 4 attached to the bed-plate 1 and provided with a hinged bottom wall 5 openable to afford access to the lower mechanism.

Hinged at 6 on a horizontal axis to the box structure 4 at the forward end of the bed-plate 1 is a sheet metal flap 7 adapted, when the machine is in use, to form an extension of the bed-plate 1. In order to permit the machine to be accommodated within a travelling case of minimum capacity, the extension flap 7 is foldable into a position above and perpendicular to the bed-plate 1 adjacent to the head 3 of the bracket-arm 2, as shown in dotted lines in Fig. 1.

In the construction shown, the bed-plate 1 rests at each corner on a resilient pad 8 supported by a strut member 9 within and unitary with the box structure 4 and extending the full depth of the box structure 4 so that its lower end normally engages the bottom wall 5 at a point in vertical register with a resilient supporting foot 10 on the exterior of the bottom wall 5 for engagement with a table or other machine-supporting surface. As will be understood, the construction is such that the weight of the machine is transmitted through the strut members 9 to the resilient feet 10.

The box structure 4 is conveniently pivotally attached to the bed-plate 1 on an axis transverse to and located about midway of the length of the bed-plate 1, by means of two short-pivot-forming bolts 11 each of which penetrates an aperture in one longitudinal wall of the box structure 4 and a registering aperture in a longitudinal rib 12 depending from the adjacent edge of the bed-plate 1. A tubular distance piece 13 is fitted on each of the bolts 11 between the rib 12 and the adjacent longitudinal wall of the box structure 4. It will thus be seen that, by virtue of its pivotal connection with the box structure 4, the machine is permitted to accommodate itself to its resilient sup-

port pads 8.

The bottom wall 5 is hinged at 14 at its rear longitudinal edge to the rear wall of the box structure 4 so that, to gain access to the mechanism below the bed-plate 1, it is only necessary to tip the machine backwardly on to its side, whereupon the bottom wall 5 may be opened forwardly and downwardly, as shown in Fig. 3.

A spring detent 15 provided on the front longitudinal wall of the box structure 4 is engageable with the front edge of the bottom wall 5 so as normally to hold the bottom wall 5 in shut position.

Having now particularly described and ascertained the nature of our said invention and in what manner the same is to be performed, we declare that what we claim is:—

1. A sewing machine attached to the bed-plate of which is a box structure enclosing the mechanism below the bed-plate and provided with a hinged bottom wall openable to afford access to the lower mechanism.

2. A sewing machine as claimed in claim 1, in which there is hinged to the box structure at the forward end of the bed-plate a flap adapted to form an extension of the bed-plate and foldable into a position perpendicular to the bed-plate.

3. A sewing machine as claimed in claim 1, in which the bed-plate rests at the corners on resilient pads supported by strut members located within the box structure and normally engaging the bottom wall of the box structure at points in vertical register with resilient supporting feet fitted to said bottom wall.

4. A sewing machine as claimed in claim 1, in which the box structure is pivotally attached to the bed-plate on an axis disposed transverse to and about midway of the length of the bed-plate.

5. A sewing machine as claimed in claim 1, in which the bottom wall of the box structure is hinged along its rear longitudinal edge to the rear wall of said structure.

6. A sewing machine constructed and arranged as hereindescribed with reference to the accompanying drawings.

Dated this 18th day of May, 1935.
CRUIKSHANK & FAIRWEATHER,
86, St. Vincent Street, Glasgow, and
65/66, Chancery Lane, London, W.C.2,
Agents for the Applicants.

Leamington Spa: Printed for His Majesty's Stationery Office, by the Courier Press.—1935.

435,578 COMPLETE SPECIFICATION

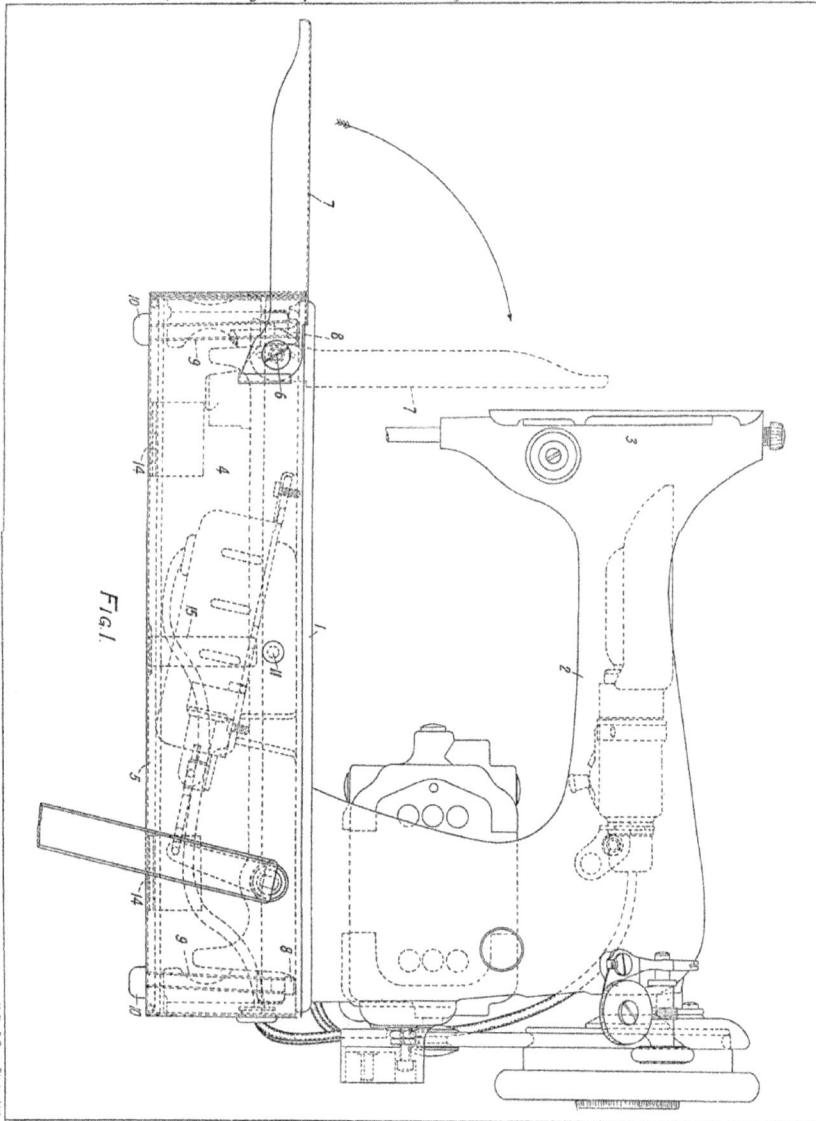

FIG.1.

Malby & Sons, Photo-Lith.

3 SHEETS
SHEET 1

92

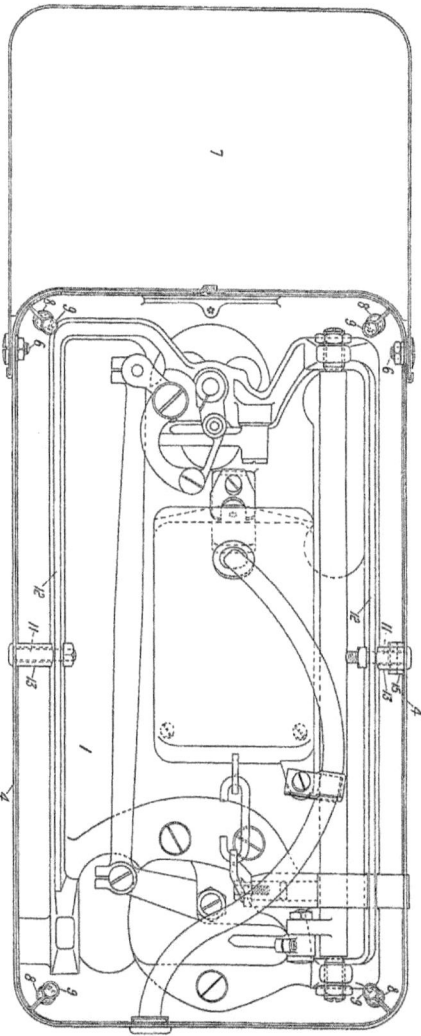

FIG. 2.

93

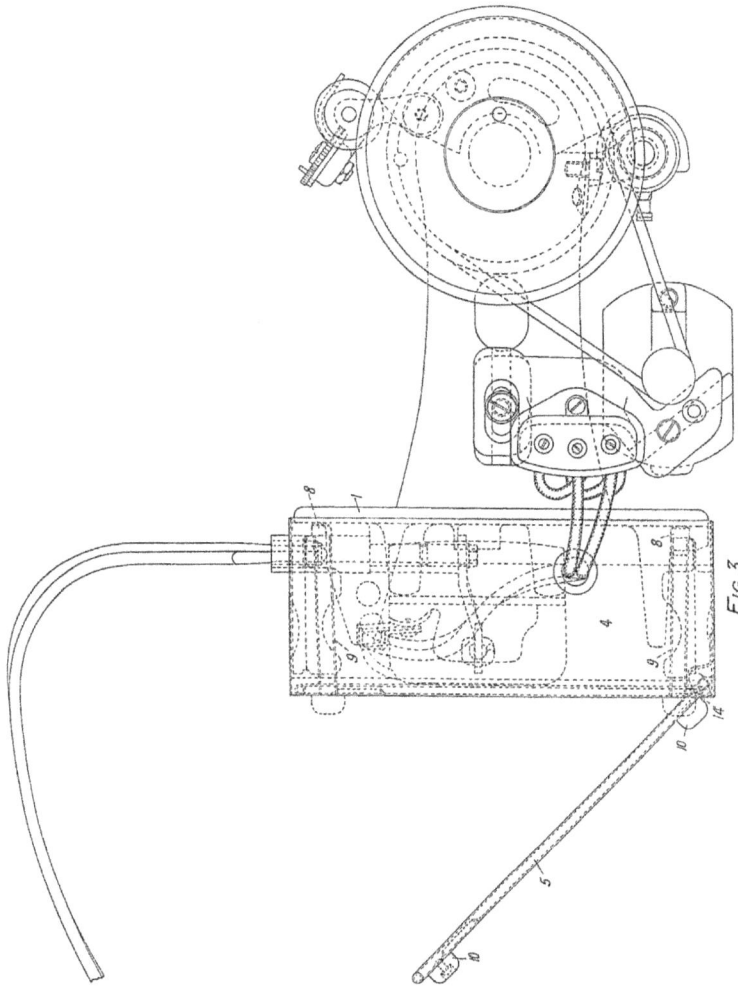

Malby & Sons, Photo-Lith.

FIG 3.

94

PATENT SPECIFICATION

Application Date: Nov. 11, 1940. No. 16326/40.

Complete Specification Left: Nov. 5, 1941.

Complete Specification Accepted: May 13, 1942.

545,156

PROVISIONAL SPECIFICATION

Feeding Mechanism for Sewing Machines

We, THE SINGER MANUFACTURING COMPANY LIMITED, a British Company, of Singer, Clydebank, Dumbartonshire, and JAMES HEGGIE, of British Nationality, of 7, Drumry Road, Clydebank, Dumbartonshire, do hereby declare the nature of this invention to be as follows:—

This invention relates to feeding mechanism for sewing machines, more particularly applicable to sewing machines of the type formed with a cylindrical work-arm as used, for example, in the stitching and trimming of footwear.

An object of the invention is to produce a construction in which the free end or head of the work-arm is rendered compact by reason that certain elements of the feeding mechanism, in lieu of being located in the work-arm head, are located within the contour of the arm but spaced from said head.

In a construction of cylinder arm machine according to the invention a bifurcated feed-dog-carrier mounted within the head of the work-arm in front of a rotary loop-taker derives its rising and falling movements from a feed-lift shaft journalled within the work-arm and actuated by pitman mechanism from the main shaft journalled in the usual overhanging bracket arm. The feed-lift-rock shaft carries, within the work-arm, a bracket in which is journalled a feed shaft carrying, at its forward end, the feed-dog-carrier. Mounted on the rear end of said feed-shaft within a laterally exposed part of the work-arm is a forked lever which straddles a sleeve journalled on a boss carried by a lever secured on one end of a short feed-rock-shaft journalled within the work-arm and operatively connected at its other end by means of pitman mechanism with the main shaft. The boss loosely surrounds a shaft which drives the lower stitch-forming mechanism and which is operatively connected at its rear end by gearing with the lower end of a vertical shaft of which the upper end is geared to the main-shaft.

Lateral cut-aways in the work-arm permit ready access to the feed actuating shafts.

Dated this 9th day of November, 1940.
CRUIKSHANK & FAIRWEATHER,
29, St. Vincent Place, Glasgow, C.1,
Agents for the Applicants.

COMPLETE SPECIFICATION

Feeding Mechanism for Sewing Machines

We, THE SINGER MANUFACTURING COMPANY LIMITED, a British Company, of Singer, Clydebank, Dumbartonshire, and JAMES HEGGIE, of British Nationality, of 7, Drumry Road, Clydebank, Dumbartonshire, do hereby declare the nature of this invention and in what manner the same is to be performed, to be particularly described and ascertained in and by the following statement:—

This invention relates to feeding mechanism for sewing machines, more particularly applicable to sewing machines of the type formed with a cylindrical work-arm as used, for example, in the stitching and trimming of footwear.

An object of the invention is to produce a construction in which the free end or head of the work-arm is rendered compact by reason that certain elements of the feeding mechanism, in lieu of being located in the head of the work-arm, are located within the contour of the arm but spaced from said head.

The invention consists of feeding mechanism for a sewing machine of the type equipped with a work-arm, including a feed-shaft located within the work-arm, a feed-dog-carrier secured on the forward end of said feed-shaft, a feed-lift-shaft journalled within the work-arm and carrying a bracket in which the feed-shaft is journalled eccentrically to said feed-lift-shaft, whereby the feed-shaft and the feed-dog-carrier derive rising and falling movements from oscillatory movements of the feed-lift-shaft, a feed-

[*Price* 1/-]

rock-shaft journalled within the work-arm, and coupling means connecting the feed-rock-shaft with the feed-shaft whereby oscillatory feeding movements are transmitted from the feed-rock-shaft to the rising and falling feed-shaft, said feed-lift-shaft and said feed-rock-shaft deriving oscillatory movements from the main shaft of the sewing machine.

A practical construction of feeding mechanism includes a bifurcated feed-dog-carrier mounted within the head of the work-arm in front of a rotary loop-taker or shuttle and deriving its rising and falling movements from a feed-lift-shaft journalled within the work-arm and actuated by crank and pitman mechanism from an eccentric on the main shaft journalled in the usual overhanging bracket arm. The feed-lift-shaft carries, within the work-arm, the bracket in which is journalled the feed-shaft, said feed-shaft carrying, at its forward end, the feed-dog-carrier. Mounted on the rear end of the feed-shaft within a laterally exposed body part of the work-arm is a forked lever which straddles a bush journalled on a boss carried by a lever secured on the forward end of a short feed-rock-shaft journalled within the work-arm and operatively connected at its other end by means of crank and pitman mechanism with an eccentric on the main shaft. The boss loosely surrounds a shaft which drives the lower stitch-forming element and which is operatively connected at its rear end by gearing with the lower end of a vertical shaft of which the upper end is geared to the main-shaft.

The invention is illustrated in the accompanying drawings in which Fig. 1 is a side elevation of a sewing machine incorporating the improved feeding mechanism. Fig. 2 is a fragmentary transverse vertical section mainly on the line A—A of Fig. 1. Fig. 3 is a vertical transverse section on the line B—B of Fig. 1. Fig. 4 is an end elevation looking on the front end of the work-arm. Figs. 3 and 4 are drawn to a larger scale than Figs. 1 and 2.

Referring to the drawings, the machine frame comprises a cylindrical work-arm 20, a standard 21 uprising from the rear end of the work-arm 20, and an overhanging bracket-arm 22 terminating in a head 23.

Journalled in the bracket-arm 22 is a main shaft 24 provided at its rear end with a driving pulley and balance wheel 25 and at its front end with a crank disc which drives, through the medium of a connecting rod, a reciprocatory needle-bar 28 which is journalled in the head 23

and which carries at its lower end a needle 29. 30 denotes a presser-bar also mounted in the head 23 and carrying at its lower end a bracket 31 to which is connected an arm 32 carrying a presser-wheel 33 which co-operates with a feed-dog 2 adapted to project upwardly through a throat-plate 3 attached to the head of the work-arm 20.

Mounted within the head of the work-arm 20, in front of a rotary loop-taker 4 which co-operates with the needle 29, is a bifurcated feed-dog-carrier 1 secured on the forward end of a feed-shaft 8. The feed-shaft 8 and therewith the feed-dog-carrier derive rising and falling movements from a feed-lift-shaft 5 journalled within the work-arm 20 and having fixed on its rear end a crank-arm 5^1 which is operatively connected to the lower end of a pitman 6 of which the upper end is formed as a strap 6^1 embracing an eccentric 34 secured on the main shaft 24. Fixed to the shaft 5, within the work-arm 20, is a bracket 7 in which is journalled, eccentrically of the shaft 5, the feed-shaft 8. Mounted on the rear end of the feed-shaft 8, within a laterally exposd body part of the work-arm 20, is a forked lever 9 which slidably straddles a bush 10 journalled on a boss 11 carried by a lever 12 secured on the forward end of a short feed-rock-shaft 13 journalled within the work-arm 20, the construction being such that the feed-shaft 8 rises and falls under the action of the shaft 5 and is also oscillated, i.e., performs feeding movements, about its own axis under the action of the feed-rock-shaft 13. Fixed on the rear end of the feed-rock-shaft 13 is a crank-arm 13^1 to which is operatively connected the lower end of a pitman 14 provided at its upper end with a strap 14^1 embracing an eccentric 35 secured on the main shaft 24.

The loop-taker 4 is secured on the forward end of a shaft 15 journalled within the work-arm 20 and loosely surrounded by the boss 11. At its rear end the shaft 15 is connected by bevel gear wheels 37, 38 with the lower end of an upright shaft 39 connected at its upper end by bevel gear wheels 40, 41 with the shaft 24.

Lateral cut-aways 20^1 in the work-arm 20 permit ready access to the feed-actuating mechanism.

Having now particularly described and ascertained the nature of our said invention and in what manner the same is to be performed, we declare that what we claim is:—

1. Feeding mechanism for a sewing machine of the type equipped with a work-arm, including a feed-shaft located within the work-arm, a feed-dog-carrier

;45,156 COMPLETE SPECIFICATION

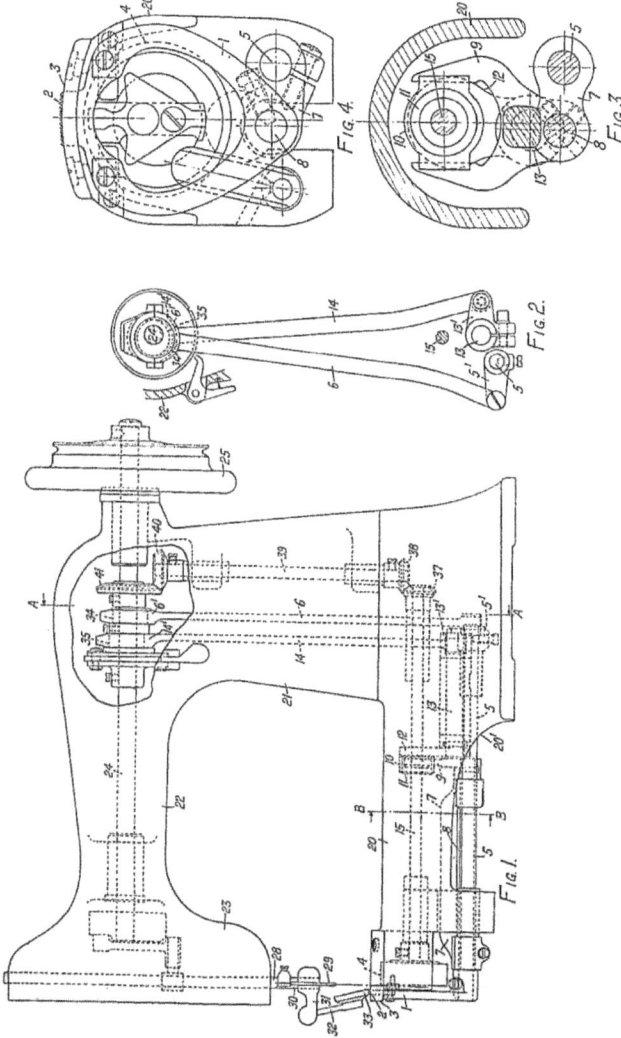

FIG. 1.

FIG. 2.

FIG. 3.

FIG. 4.

Malby & Sons, Photo-Lth

97

secured on the forward end of said feed-shaft, a feed-lift-shaft journalled within the work-arm and carrying a bracket in which the feed-shaft is journalled eccentrically to said feed-lift-shaft, whereby the feed-shaft and the feed-dog-carrier derive rising and falling movements from oscillatory movements of the feed-lift-shaft, a feed-rock-shaft journalled within the work-arm, and coupling means connecting the feed-rock-shaft with the feed-shaft whereby oscillatory feeding movements are transmitted from the feed-rock-shaft to the rising and falling feed-shaft, said feed-lift-shaft and said feed-rock-shaft deriving oscillatory movements from the main shaft of the sewing machine.

2. Feeding mechanism as claimed in claim 1 in which the coupling means comprises a pair of levers secured on the respective shafts, one of said levers being forked so as slidingly to straddle a member carried by the other lever.

3. Feeding mechanism as claimed in claim 2 in which the forked lever slidingly straddles a bush mounted on a boss carried by the other lever and loosely surrounding a shaft which drives the lower stitch-forming element of the machine.

4. Feeding mechanism as claimed in claim 1 in which the feed-lift-shaft and the feed-rock-shaft are provided with crank-arms which are operatively connected by pitmen with eccentrics on the main shaft.

5. Feeding mechanism for a sewing machine, constructed and arranged for operation substantially as hereindescribed with reference to the accompanying drawings.

Dated this 27th day of October, 1941.
CRUIKSHANK & FAIRWEATHER,
Chartered Patent Agents,
29, St. Vincent Place, Glasgow, C,1, and
29, Southampton Buildings,
London, W.C.2,
Agents for the Applicants.

Leamington Spa : Printed for His Majesty's Stationery Office, by the Courier Press.—1942.

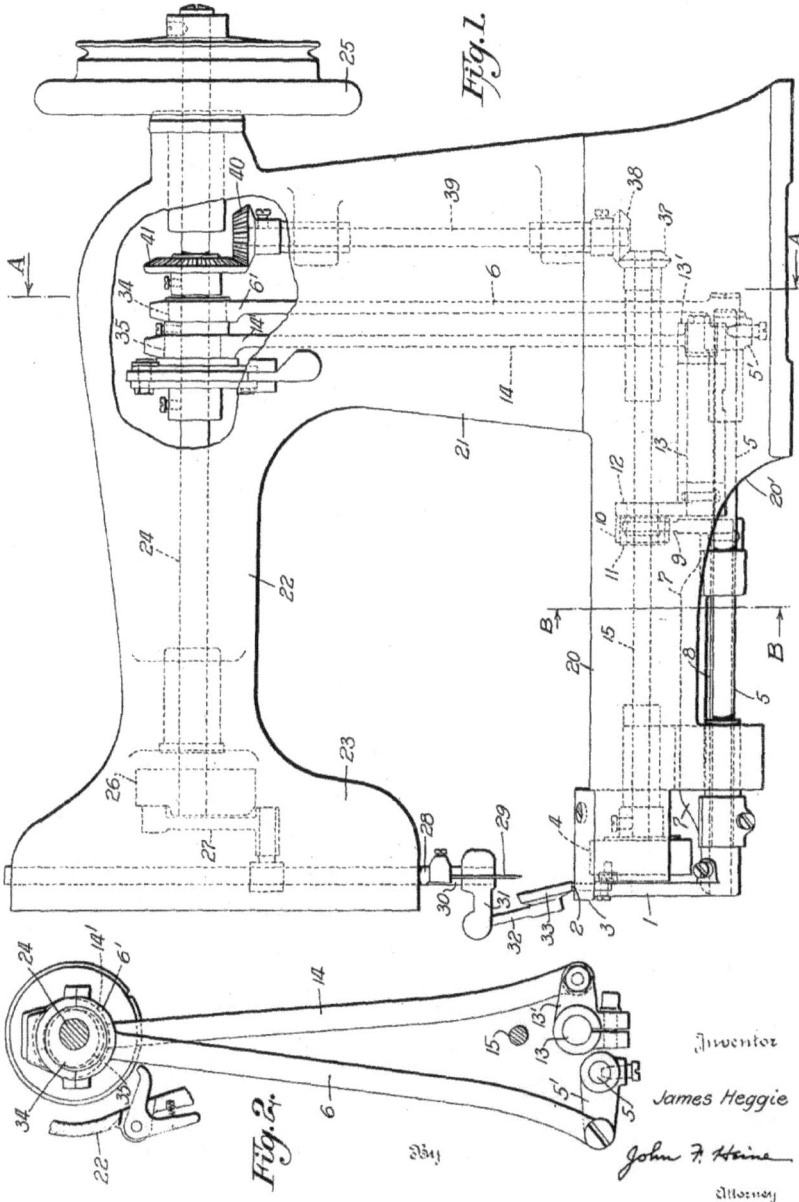

Fig. 1.

Fig. 2.

Inventor

James Heggie

John F. Heine

Attorney

99

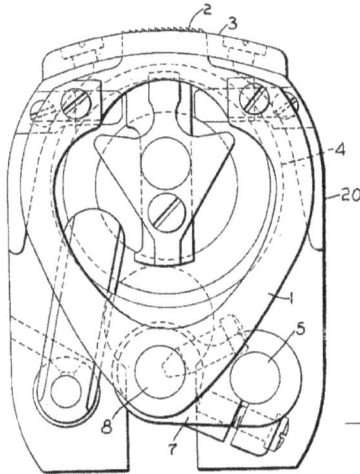

Fig. 4.

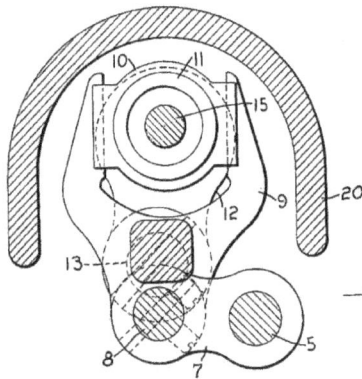

Fig. 3.

Inventor
James Heggie

Witness:
John H. Cave

By John F. Heine

Attorney

100

Patented July 27, 1943

2,325,510

UNITED STATES PATENT OFFICE

2,325,510

FEEDING MECHANISM FOR SEWING
MACHINES

James Heggie, Clydebank, Scotland, assignor to
The Singer Manufacturing Company, Elizabeth, N. J., a corporation of New Jersey

Application November 12, 1941, Serial No. 418,821
In Great Britain November 11, 1940

5 Claims. (Cl. 112—215)

(Granted under the provisions of sec. 14, act of
March 2, 1927; 357 O. G. 5)

This invention relates to feeding mechanism for sewing machines, more particularly applicable to sewing machines of the type formed with a cylindrical work-arm as used, for example, in the stitching and trimming of footwear.

An object of the invention is to produce a construction in which the free end or head of the work-arm is rendered compact by reason that certain elements of the feeding mechanism, in lieu of being located within the work-arm head, are located within the contour of the arm but spaced from, i. e., rearward of, said head.

Feeding mechanism according to the invention includes a feed-dog-carrier mounted within the work-arm head on the forward end of a feed-shaft which is operatively connected within the body of the work-arm to a feed-rock-shaft, and a feed-lift-shaft journalled within the work-arm and carrying a bracket fixed thereto in which said feed-shaft is journalled, said feed-rock-shaft and said feed-lift-shaft deriving actuation from the main or upper shaft of the sewing machine.

The invention is illustrated in the accompanying drawings in which Fig. 1 is a side elevation of a sewing machine incorporating the improved feeding mechanism. Fig. 2 is a fragmentary transverse vertical section mainly on the line A—A of Fig. 1. Fig. 3 is a vertical transverse section on the line B—B of Fig. 1. Fig. 4 is an end elevation looking on the front end of the work-arm. Figs. 3 and 4 are drawn to a larger scale than Figs. 1 and 2.

Referring to the drawings, 20 denotes a cylindrical work-arm, 21 a standard uprising from the rear end of the work-arm 20, and 22 an overhanging bracket-arm terminating in a head 23, constituting the frame of the sewing machine.

Journalled in the bracket-arm 22 is a main shaft 24 provided at its rear end with a driving pulley and flywheel 25 and at its front end with a crank disc 26 which drives the medium of a connecting rod 27, a reciprocatory needle-bar 28 which is journalled in the head 23 and is equipped at its lower end with a needle 29. 30 denotes a presser-bar also mounted in the head 23 and equipped at its lower end with a bracket 31 to which is connected an arm 32 carrying a presser-wheel 33 which co-operates with a feed-dog 2 projecting upwardly through a throat-plate 3 attached to the head of the work-arm 20.

Mounted within the head of the work-arm 20, in front of a rotary loop-taker 4 which co-operates with the needle 29, is a bifurcated feed-dog-carrier 1 secured on the forward end of a feed-shaft 8. The feed-shaft 8 and therewith the feed-dog-carrier derive rising and falling movements from a feed-lift-shaft 5 journalled within the work-arm 20 and having fixed on its rear end a crank-arm 5' which is operatively connected to the lower end of a pitman 6 of which the upper end is formed as a strap 6' embracing an eccentric 34 secured on the main shaft 24. Fixed on the shaft 5, within the work-arm 20, is a bracket 7 in which is journalled, eccentrically of the shaft 5, the feed-shaft 8. Mounted on the rear end of the feed-shaft 8, within a laterally exposed body part of the work-arm 20, is a forked lever 9 which slidably straddles a bush 10 journalled on a boss 11 carried by a lever 12 secured on the forward end of a short feed-rock-shaft 13 journalled within the work-arm 20, the construction being such that the feed-shaft 8 rises and falls under the action of the shaft 5 and is also oscillated, i. e., performs feeding movements, about its own axis under the action of the feed-rock-shaft 13. Fixed on the rear end of the feed-rock-shaft 13 is a crank-arm 13' to which is operatively connected the lower end of a pitman 14 provided at its upper end with a strap 14' embracing an eccentric 35 secured on the main shaft 24.

The loop-taker 4 is secured on the forward end of a shaft 15 journalled within the work-arm 20 and loosely surrounded by the boss 11. At its rear end the shaft 15 is connected by bevel gear wheels 37, 38 with the lower end of an upright shaft 39 connected at its upper end by bevel gear wheels 40, 41 with the shaft 24.

Lateral cut-aways 20' in the work-arm 20 permit ready access to the feed-actuating mechanism.

What is claimed is:

1. In a sewing machine having a frame including a bracket-arm and a work-arm formed with a head, in combination, a main shaft journalled in said bracket-arm, a feed-rock-shaft journalled within said work-arm, a feed-lift-shaft journalled within said work-arm, a bracket fixed to said feed-lift-shaft within said work-arm, a feed-shaft journalled in said bracket and eccentric to said feed-lift-shaft, operative connections within the body of said work-arm for communicating oscillatory movements to said feed-shaft from said feed-rock-shaft, a feed-dog carrier mounted within the head of said work-arm on the forward end of said feed-shaft, and operative connections between said feed-rock-shaft and feed-lift-shaft and said main shaft.

2. In a sewing machine having a frame including a bracket-arm and a work-arm formed with

a head, in combination, a main shaft journalled in said bracket-arm, a feed-rock-shaft journalled within said work-arm, a lever secured on the forward end of said feed-rock-shaft, a bush mounted on said lever, a feed-lift-shaft jour- [5] nalled within said work-arm, a bracket fixed to said feed-lift-shaft, a feed-shaft journalled in said bracket and eccentric to said feed-lift-shaft, a forked lever mounted on the rear end of said feed-shaft within the body of said work-arm and [10] slidably engaging said bush whereby oscillatory movements are imparted to said feed-shaft by said feed-rock-shaft, a feed-dog carrier mounted within the head of said work-arm on the forward end of said feed-shaft, and operative con- [15] nections between said feed-rock-shaft and feed-lift-shaft and said main shaft.

3. In a sewing machine having a frame including a bracket-arm and a work-arm formed with a head, in combination, a main shaft journalled [20] in said bracket-arm, a loop-taker shaft journalled within said work-arm, a feed-rock-shaft journalled within said work-arm, a lever secured on the forward end of said feed-rock-shaft, a boss carried by said lever and loosely surround- [25] ing said loop-taker-shaft, a bush journalled on said boss, a feed-lift-shaft journalled within said work-arm, a bracket fixed to said feed-lift-shaft within said work-arm, a feed-shaft journalled in said boss, a feed-lift-shaft journalled within said work-arm, a bracket fixed to said feed-lift-shaft within said work-arm, a feed-shaft journalled in said bracket and eccentric to said feed-lift-shaft whereby to rise and fall with rocking movements [30] of said feed-lift-shaft, a forked lever mounted on the rear end of said feed-shaft within the body of said work-arm and slidably engaging said bush, whereby oscillatory movements are im- [35] parted to said feed-shaft by said feed-rock-shaft, a feed-dog carrier mounted within the head of said work-arm on the forward end of said feed-shaft, and operative connections between said feed-rock-shaft and feed-lift-shaft and said main shaft.

4. In a sewing machine having a frame including a bracket-arm and a work-arm formed with a head, in combination, a main shaft journalled in said bracket-arm, a feed-lift-shaft journalled within said work-arm, a bracket fixed to said feed-lift-shaft within said work-arm, a feed-shaft journalled in said bracket, a pair of interconnected levers within the body of said work-arm carried, respectively, by said feed-shaft and said feed-rock-shaft, a feed-dog carrier mounted within the head of said work-arm on the forward end of said feed-shaft, and operative connections including cranks and pitmans between said feed-rock-shaft and feed-lift-shaft and said main shaft.

5. In a sewing machine having a frame including a bracket-arm and a work-arm formed with a head, in combination, a main shaft journalled within said work-arm, a feed-lift-shaft journalled within said work-arm, a bracket fixed to said feed-lift-shaft within said work-arm, a feed-shaft journalled in said bracket and eccentric to said feed-lift-shaft, connections within the body of said work-arm for communicating feeding movements from said feed-rock-shaft to said feed-shaft, a feed-dog carrier mounted within the head of said work-arm on the forward end of said feed-shaft, and operative connections between said feed-rock-shaft and feed-lift-shaft and said main shaft.

JAMES HEGGIE.

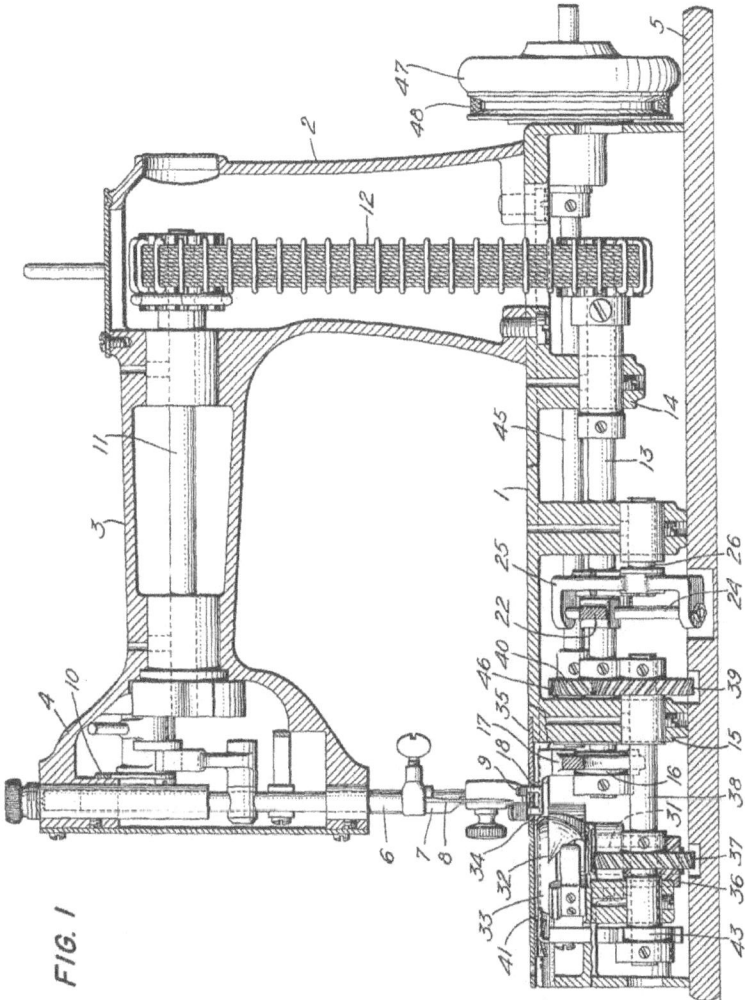

FIG. I

Inventor

GEORGE A. FLECKENSTEIN

By Henry J. Miller

Attorney

103

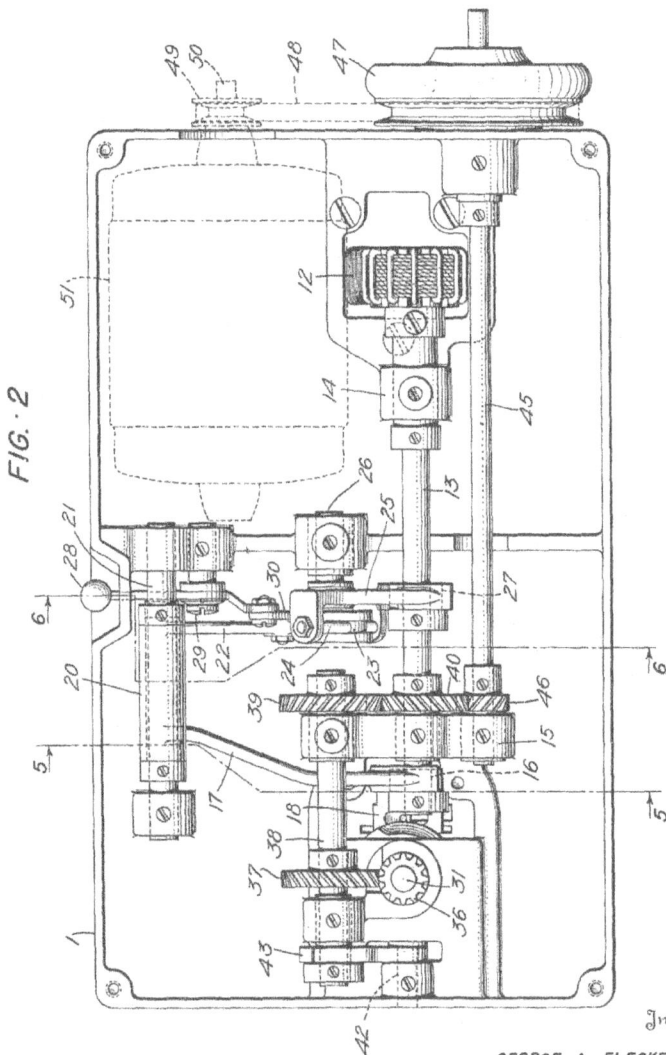

FIG. 2

Inventor

GEORGE A. FLECKENSTEIN

By Henry J Miller
Attorney

104

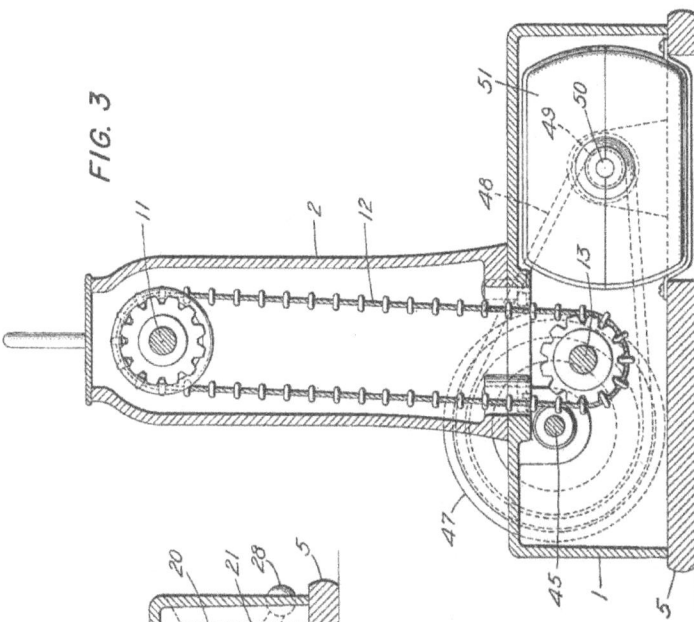

FIG. 3

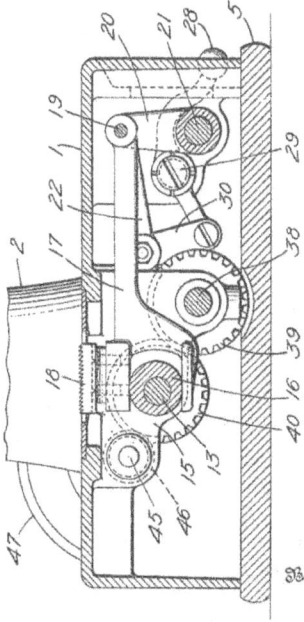

FIG. 5

Inventor

GEORGE A. FLECKENSTEIN

By Henry J Miller

Attorney

105

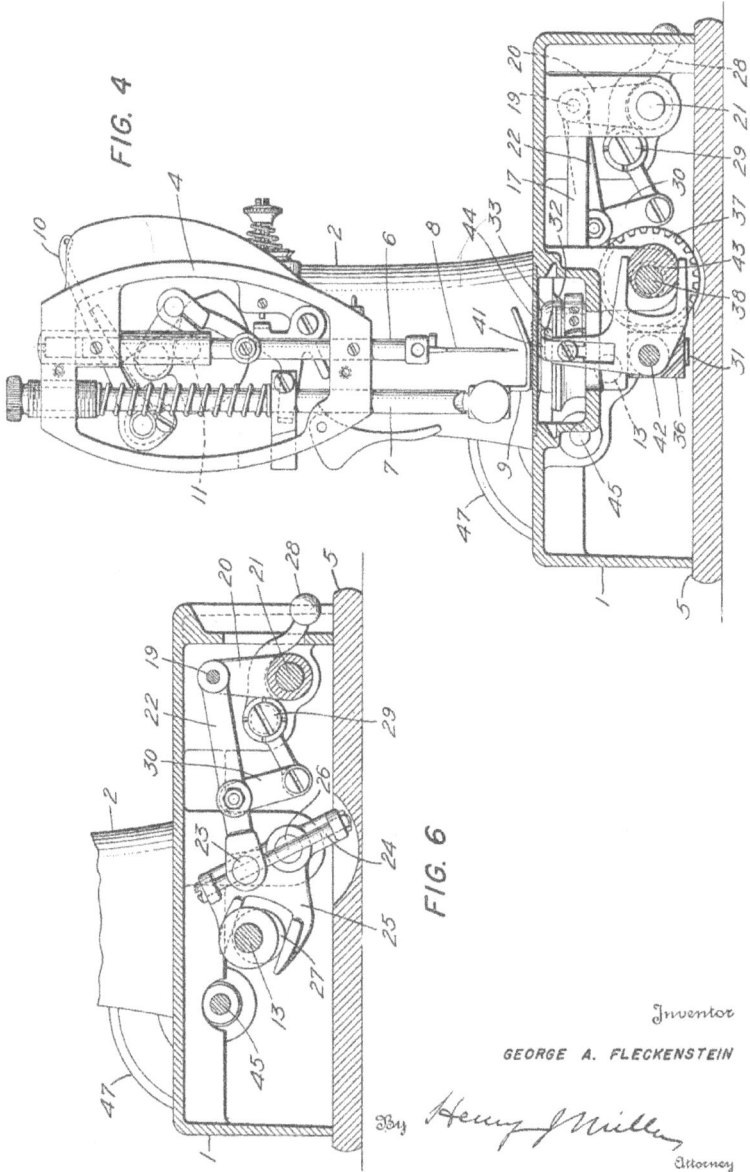

Inventor

GEORGE A. FLECKENSTEIN

By Henry J. Miller

Attorney

106

UNITED STATES PATENT OFFICE

2,276,246

SEWING MACHINE

George A. Fleckenstein, Stratford, Conn., assignor
to The Singer Manufacturing Company, Elizabeth, N. J., a corporation of New Jersey

Application October 24, 1939, Serial No. 300,903

8 Claims. (Cl. 112—220)

This invention relates to sewing machines more particularly of the small portable family type machines having a box bed and overhanging bracket-arm containing the stitch-forming and work-feeding mechanisms of the machine. The bed of the machine houses the work-feeding mechanism and vertical axis rotary loop-taker, which require to be driven at different speeds. The bed also houses the main-shaft of the machine and the electric motor for driving it by means of the usual belt and balance-wheel or belt-pulley, the latter being carried by an outboard projection of the main-shaft.

An object of the present invention is to provide a simplified arrangement of shafting and gearing for such a machine within the limited space available in the machine frame, using a small high speed motor with a small driving pulley belted to a balance-wheel on a main-shaft so located as to afford a belt drive of adequate length while keeping the rim of the balance-wheel above the base-plate of the machine upon which the bed is fastened.

With the above and other objects in view, as will hereinafter appear, the invention comprises the devices, combinations and arrangements of parts hereinafter set forth and illustrated in the accompanying drawings of a preferred embodiment of the invention, from which the several features of the invention and the advantages attained thereby will be readily understood by those skilled in the art.

Of the accompanying drawings, Fig. 1 is a longitudinal vertical section through a sewing machine embodying the invention. Fig. 2 is a bottom plan view of the machine with the bottom or base-plate removed from the machine bed. Fig. 3 is a transverse vertical section through the bed and bracket-arm standard. Fig. 4 is a transverse vertical section through the machine bed, showing the bracket-arm head and needle-mechanism therein in elevation. Fig. 5 is a transverse vertical section substantially on the line 5—5, Fig. 2, and Fig. 6 is a transverse vertical section substantially on the line 6—6, Fig. 2.

The machine is formed with a frame including the box bed 1 and overhanging bracket-arm with a vertical standard 2 and horizontal portion 3 terminating in the head 4. The open bottom of the bed 1 is closed by the bottom or base-plate 5.

The bracket-arm head 4 carries the usual reciprocatory needle-bar 6 and spring-pressed presser-bar 7 fitted, respectively, with the needle 8 and presser-foot 9. The head 4 also carries the needle-thread take-up lever 10. The needle-bar 6 and take-up lever 10 are actuated in the usual manner by the top rotary shaft 11 which is journaled in the horizontal member 3 of the bracket-arm and is connected at its rear end by the clip-belt 12 to the bottom free-ended rotary shaft 13 which is disposed directly below the bracket-arm and is journaled in bearing lugs 14, 15 between the ends of the shaft 13 in the bed 1.

Mounted on the free end of the bottom rotary shaft 13, remote from the clip-belt 12, is at least one of the feed-eccentrics, preferably the feed-lift eccentric 16, which is embraced by the feed-bar 17 carrying the feed-dog 18. The feed-bar 17 is fulcrumed at its rearward end upon the pin 19 carried by the feed-rocker 20 which is journaled on the pivot-shaft 21 fixed in lugs in the bed.

Connected to the pin 19, Fig. 6, is one end of the link 22 the opposite forked end of which pivotally carries a cross-pin 23 which is free to slide on the pin 24 carried by the rocking yoke 25 fulcrumed at 26 in the bed 1 and rocked by the feed-advance eccentric 27 on the bottom shaft 13. The stitch-length may be regulated, or even reversed, by shifting the link 22 to carry the cross-pin 23 toward or across a position of axial coincidence with the yoke-fulcrum 26. Such regulation may be effected by movement of the feed-regulator lever 28 which is frictionally fulcrumed at 29 in the bed 1 and connected by the link 30 to the link 22.

Complemental to the needle 8 in the formation of stitches is the loop-taker or rotary hook which is a cup-shaped body carried by the vertical hook-shaft 31 and formed with a loop-taking beak 32. Within the hook-cup is disposed the usual stationary bobbin-case 33 which carries the usual bobbin or under thread mass, not shown. This bobbin-case is restrained against rotation with the hook by means of the usual rotation-restraining tongue 34, Fig. 1, which freely enters a notch in the under side of the throat-plate 35.

The vertical hook-shaft 31 carries the spiral gear 36 which meshes with the spiral gear 37 on the countershaft 38 journaled parallel to and in front of the bottom rotary shaft 13. The countershaft 38 carries a gear 39 which meshes with a gear 40 of equal size on the bottom rotary shaft 13. The rotary hook preferably makes two revolutions to one revolution of the bottom shaft 13.

The machine is preferably provided with a bobbin-case opener or kicker 41, Fig. 4, which is pivoted at 42 in the bed 1 and actuated by the eccentric 43 on the countershaft 38. At the time when the needle-loop which has been cast about the bobbin-case 33 is being drawn up by the take-up 10 and is about to be drawn between the rotation-restraining tongue 34 and the engaged wall of the notch in the under side of the throat-plate, the kicker 41 engages the shoulder 44, Fig. 4, on the bobbin-case and turns the bobbin-case slightly or enough to open a gap or

2

2,276,246

passageway for the needle-loop adjacent the tongue 34.

Journaled high in the bed I, in rear of the bottom rotary shaft 13, is the main-shaft 45. The main-shaft carries a small pinion 46 which meshes with the larger gear 40 on the shaft 13. The main-shaft 45 also carries the balance-wheel and belt-pulley 47 which is connected by the belt 48 to the small pulley 49 on the shaft 50 of the small high-speed motor 51 disposed in the bed I, in front of the bottom rotary shaft 13. The balance-wheel 47, Fig. 1, due to the high position of the main-shaft, does not drag or encroach upon the base-plate 5, yet is of adequate size to effect a material speed reduction by the belt-connection 48. The speed-reducing gears 46, 40, effect a further speed reduction enabling the machine to be operated at a moderate speed from a small high-speed electric motor within the bed I.

By mounting the balance-wheel on a shaft which is geared down to the sewing machine mechanism, the weight of the balance-wheel may be reduced below the dictates of conventional practice, without loss of the necessary balancing effect required for slow operation of the machine, as in embroidering and darning operations. This is an important advantage in an electrically driven family type machine where the driving motor is permanently connected in driving relation with the machine and must be started and held at the desired running speeds by manual operation of the usual rheostatic controller furnished with such machines.

Having thus set forth the nature of the invention, what I claim herein is:

1. A sewing machine having a bed and overhanging bracket-arm, a bottom rotary shaft, feed-eccentrics thereon, a loop-taker driving countershaft parallel to and driven by said bottom rotary shaft, a loop-taker driven by said countershaft, a reciprocatory needle, a top rotary shaft for actuating said needle, a driving connection between said bottom and top rotary shafts, a main-shaft journaled in said bed, a balance-wheel carried thereby, and speed-reducing gearing connecting said main-shaft to drive said bottom rotary shaft.

2. A sewing machine having a bed and overhanging bracket-arm, a reciprocatory needle, a complemental loop-taker, a work-feeder, means interconnecting said needle, loop-taker and work-feeder to cause them to operate in timed relation to each other, a conventional small high-speed electric motor in said bed, a small driving belt pulley thereon, a balance-wheel shaft in said bed, a balance-wheel and belt-pulley thereon, a belt-connection between said pulleys, and speed-reduction gearing in said bed between said balance-wheel shaft and said means.

3. A sewing machine having a box-type bed and overhanging bracket-arm, a reciprocatory needle and top rotary needle-driving shaft carried by the bracket-arm, a lower rotary shaft connected to drive the top rotary shaft, a gear on said bottom rotary shaft, a vertical axis rotary hook complemental to said needle, a hook-driving countershaft parallel to said bottom rotary shaft and driven one-to-one by the gear on the latter, two-to-one gearing connecting said vertical axis rotary hook to said hook-driving countershaft, work-feeding mechanism including feed-eccen-

trics carried by said lower rotary shaft, a main-shaft journaled high in said bed, a balance-wheel on said shaft externally of said bed, and a pinion on said shaft meshing with said gear on said bottom rotary shaft.

4. The construction set forth in claim 3 with the hook-driving shaft set lower than and forwardly of the bottom rotary shaft which latter is set lower than and forwardly of the main-shaft.

5. A sewing machine having a box-bed, a hollow standard rising therefrom and an overhanging bracket-arm carried by said standard, top and bottom shafts journaled, respectively, in said bed and bracket-arm, a belt connection in said standard between said shafts, feed-eccentrics on said bottom shaft, feeding means actuated by said eccentrics, a reciprocatory needle actuated by said top shaft, a rotary hook-shaft journaled vertically in said bed beyond one end of said bottom shaft, a countershaft journaled in said bed forwardly of said vertical hook-shaft and bottom rotary shaft and geared to both of said last mentioned shafts, and a main-shaft journaled in said bed and geared to said bottom shaft.

6. A sewing machine having a box bed and overhanging bracket-arm, a bottom rotary shaft journaled in said bed directly below said bracket-arm, a reciprocatory needle carried by said bracket-arm, needle-driving mechanism actuated by said bottom rotary shaft and located within said bracket-arm, an electric motor disposed in said bed in front of said bottom rotary shaft, a main shaft journaled in said bed in rear of said bottom rotary shaft, a balance-wheel carried thereby, a speed-reducing belt-connection between said motor and main-shaft externally of said bed, a reduction gear connection between said main shaft and said bottom rotary shaft within said bed, work-feeding mechanism in said bed including feed eccentrics on said bottom rotary shaft, and a loop-taker complemental to said needle located in said bed and actuated by said bottom rotary shaft.

7. A sewing machine having a bed and overhanging bracket-arm, a free-ended lower rotary shaft journaled in said bed, feed-eccentrics carried by said lower rotary shaft at least one of which eccentrics is at one free end of said shaft, work-feeding mechanism actuated by said eccentrics, a reciprocatory needle carried by said bracket-arm, means at the other free end of said lower rotary shaft connected to drive said needle, a loop-taker in said bed complemental to said needle in the formation of stitches, a countershaft parallel to and driven by said lower rotary shaft for actuating said loop-taker, and a main-shaft in said bed and connections for driving said lower rotary shaft therefrom.

8. A sewing machine having interconnected stitch-forming and work-feeding mechanisms and including a machine shaft for driving said mechanisms, a balance-wheel shaft, speed-reducing means permanently connecting said balance-wheel shaft and said machine shaft, whereby said balance-wheel shaft is caused to run faster than said machine shaft, a balance-wheel on said balance-wheel shaft, and an electric motor permanently connected at all times to drive said balance-wheel shaft at a speed less than the motor speed.

GEORGE A. FLECKENSTEIN.

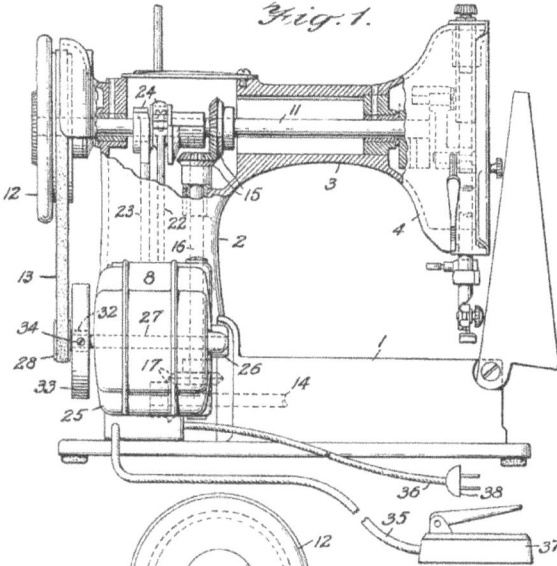

Fig. 1.

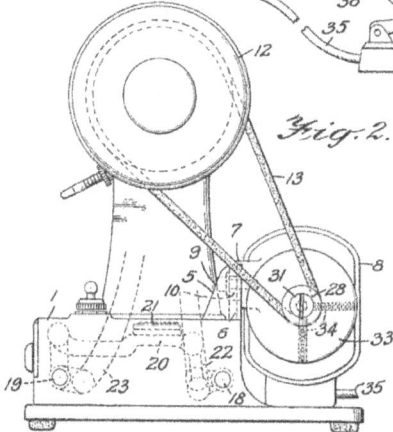

Fig. 2.

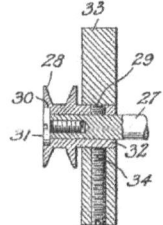

Fig. 4.

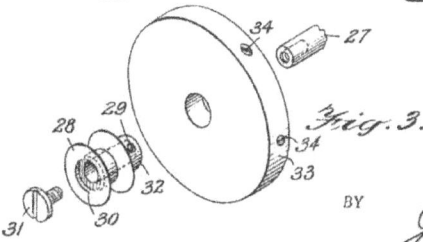

Fig. 3.

BY

INVENTORS
LEONARD C. MARSAC
DAVID A. GRAESSER

John F. Heine

ATTORNEY

UNITED STATES PATENT OFFICE

2,282,071

SEWING MACHINE DRIVE

Leonard C. Marsac, Cranford, and David A. Graesser, Elizabeth, N. J., assignors to The Singer Manufacturing Company, Elizabeth, N. J., a corporation of New Jersey

Application February 19, 1941, Serial No. 379,588

2 Claims. (Cl. 112—220)

This invention relates to motor-driven sewing machines, and more particularly to variable speed sewing machines which are driven by small individual motors permanently connected in driving relation therewith. These driving motors are usually of the high-speed series wound type and their speed is controlled by a manually actuated rheostat connected in series therewith.

This type of sewing machine is most commonly used in the home where a light compact sewing outfit having a moderate operating speed is required. Such a high-speed motor is therefore usually provided with a small driving pulley which is at all times operatively connected, by means of a belt, to a larger driven pulley mounted on the sewing machine. Thus a proper speed reduction is effected between the motor and the sewing machine.

Unfortunately this type of machine has had the undesirable characteristic of running unevenly in the low-speed range. This characteristic is highly objectionable as it is within the low-speed range that this type machine is often used in order to perform such work as embroidering, darning and hemstitching. This type of work is best accomplished with a sewing machine producing about fifty to seventy-five stitches per minute as compared to a regular sewing speed of about twelve hundred stitches per minute.

Some prior motor-driven sewing machines have been proposed, with little or no success, to overcome the above noted objectionable characteristic by the use of a heavier balance-wheel on the main shaft, or by the use of gears in lieu of the driving belt, or by generally strengthening the machine itself. Such expedients make for a heavy, slow running and costly machine.

It is therefore, an object of the present invention to provide an inexpensive, practical and light-weight family sewing machine including a motor-drive that will deliver a steady flow of power to the machine at all speeds and, particularly, in the low speed range used, for example, in embroidering and darning operations.

It is known that a machine of the above described type will operate smoothly at low speeds if a balance-wheel of relatively heavy weight is applied to the sewing machine main-shaft. However, such a machine is found to be sluggish in operation and too great a starting load is thereby applied to the small driving motor. The present applicants have drastically reduced the weight of the main shaft balance-wheel and have mounted a relatively small, light-weight balance-wheel upon the motor shaft. The weight of the motor

balance-wheel is much less than the weight which was removed from the above mentioned machine balance-wheel.

The applicants have found that by providing a small balance-wheel on the motor-shaft and by reducing the weight of the main-shaft balance-wheel, a steady flow of power will be available at all speeds, thus permitting a fine speed control at all times and particularly while in the low-speed range. In addition, it has been found that by removing weight from the main-shaft balance-wheel, slippage between the motor-driving pulley and the sewing machine driving belt is reduced to a marked extent. In the present machine the weight of the combined main shaft balance-wheel and driven pulley is reduced to a minimum by constructing the same of cast aluminum, light gauge sheet-metal or some similar material. This unit in the present machine now functions primarily, not as a balance-wheel, but as a hand-wheel, it being understood that hand-wheels on family sewing machines are required by their operators so that the machine may be turned over by hand, as in raising the needle for removal of work.

To more concretely illustrate the results of the present invention, the following figures are cited. It must be understood however that the invention is not limited in any manner by these figures and that they merely illustrate one specific form in which the invention may be applied.

The sewing machine herein illustrated is a Singer No. 221 class machine of the light-weight portable type weighing about eleven pounds and utilizing, prior to the application of the present invention, a main-shaft balance- and pulley-wheel weighing one pound and a half. Upon the application of the present invention, this old balance- and pulley-wheel was replaced by a combined hand-wheel and belt-pulley weighing ten ounces, and a seven ounce fly-wheel was mounted upon the motor-shaft. Thus it was found that not only were the slow-speed running qualities of the machine improved but an overall weight saving of seven ounces was made, such a saving representing four percent of the total weight of the prior machine.

The invention both in structure and in operation, as well as additional objects thereof, will be best understood from the following description taken in conjunction with the accompanying drawing in which:

Fig. 1 is a rear elevation of the improved sewing machine, a portion of the bracket-arm being broken away to show the operating elements thereof.

Fig. 2 is an end elevation looking from the left of Fig. 1.

Fig. 3 is a disassembled perspective view of a portion of the driving means.

Fig. 4 is a vertical section view of the assembled unit shown in Fig. 3.

Referring more specifically to the drawing, the invention is disclosed in connection with a sewing machine comprising a frame including a hollow base 1 carrying a standard 2 from which extends an overhanging bracket-arm 3 terminating in the hollow-head 4.

Fixed to the base 1 is a motor-supporting bracket 5 formed with a channel 6 which slidably receives the rectangular shaped boss 7 carried by the frame of the driving motor 8. The boss 7 is adjustably fixed to the bracket 5 by means of a bolt 9 which extends through a slot 10 in the bracket 5 and is threaded into the boss 7. Thus from the above it will be understood that the motor 8 may be raised or lowered on its support.

Journaled lengthwise within the overhanging bracket-arm 3 is the sewing machine rotary main-shaft 11 which actuates the usual needle-bar mechanism located within the hollow head 4. Mounted upon the outboard end of the main-shaft 11 is an extremely light-weight combined hand- and pulley-wheel 12 which is driven from the motor 8 by means of the V-belt 13. The shaft 11 is connected in the usual manner to drive the needle-bar mechanism and the loop-taker actuating shaft 14 is driven through the gears 15, vertical shaft 16 and gears 17.

The loop-taker actuating shaft 14 is disposed within the hollow base 1, as are the rock-shafts 18 and 19 which impart to the feed-bar 20, carrying a feed-dog 21, the usual feed-lift and feed-advance and return movements. The rock-shafts 18 and 19 are actuated by the pitmans 22 and 23, respectively, the pitmans receiving their motion from the usual feed-actuating eccentrics 24 carried by the main-shaft 11.

The motor 8 is provided with end-caps 25 and 26 and journaled within said motor is the usual motor-shaft 27 which is disposed in substantially parallel relation with said main-shaft 11. Upon the outboard end of the motor-shaft 27, which projects through end-cap 25, is mounted a driving pulley 28 secured thereto by means of set-screws 29. The outer end of the driving pulley 28 is provided with a countersunk hole 30 which receives the screw 31. As best shown in Figs. 3 and 4, the end of the motor-shaft 27 is tapped to receive the pulley-screw 31, thus securing the pulley 28 upon the shaft 27. A hub 32 is provided on the pulley 28 upon which is mounted a fly-wheel 33 secured thereto by means of set-screws 34.

The driving pulley 28 is operatively connected with the hand and driven pulley 12 by means of the above noted V-belt 13. The diameters of the driving pulley 28 and the driven pulley 12 are of such proportion that they effect a reduction in speed of about three or four to one.

In order to effectively control the speed of the motor 8 a foot-controlled rheostat 37 is connected in series therewith by means of an electrical conductor 35. A lead-in electrical conductor 36, connected with the motor, 8, is adapted to be connected to a suitable source of electrical energy as by means of a connector-plug 38.

Thus from the above description it may be understood that the sewing machine main-shaft 11 is actuated by the motor-shaft 27 through the speed-reducing unit comprising the driving pulley 28, the V-belt 13 and the driven pulley 12.

Having thus set forth the nature of the invention, what we claim herein is:

1. A motor driving attachment for sewing machines having a frame, a rotary shaft journaled within said frame, and a driven pulley and hand-wheel mounted upon said rotary shaft, comprising, an electric motor having end-caps and a motor-shaft, said motor-shaft extending through one of said end-caps, a driving pulley having an elongated hub mounted upon the outboard end of said motor-shaft, said driving pulley adapted to be operatively connected to said driven pulley by means of a belt, and a balance-wheel having at least one set-screw, said balance-wheel being secured upon said elongated hub.

2. In a sewing machine having a frame including a bed and a gooseneck, a rotary shaft journaled within said frame, a driven pulley and hand-wheel mounted upon said rotary shaft, an electric motor mounted upon said frame and having end-caps and a motor-shaft, said motor shaft extending through one of said end caps, a driving pulley mounted upon the outboard end of said motor-shaft, and a belt connecting said driving and driven pulleys; the improvement which consists in the provision of an elongated hub-portion integral with said driving pulley, and a balance-wheel having at least one set-screw, said balance-wheel being secured upon said elongated hub between said driving pulley and said end-cap by means of said set-screw.

LEONARD C. MARSAC.
DAVID A. GRAESSER.

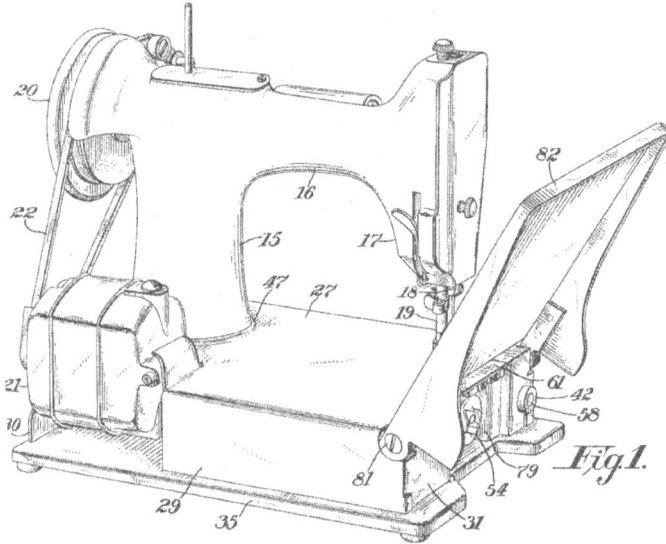

Fig.1.

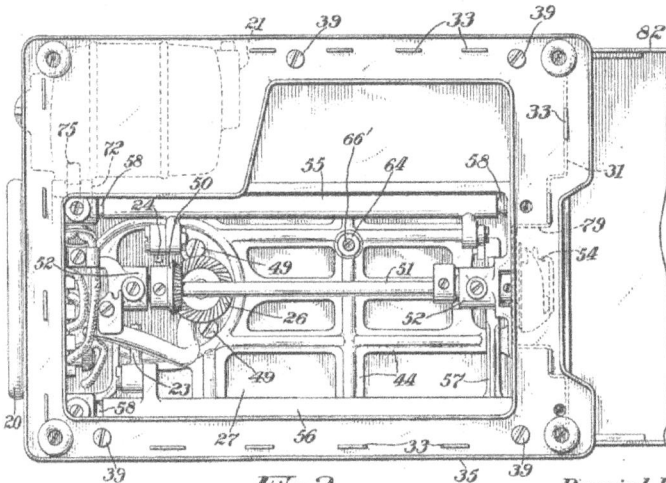

Fig.2.

Inventor

Daniel H. Chason

Witness:

John H. Cave

By William T. Stewart

Attorney

Feb. 15, 1944. D. H. CHASON 2,341,975

SEWING MACHINE BED

Filed June 8, 1942 3 Sheets-Sheet 2

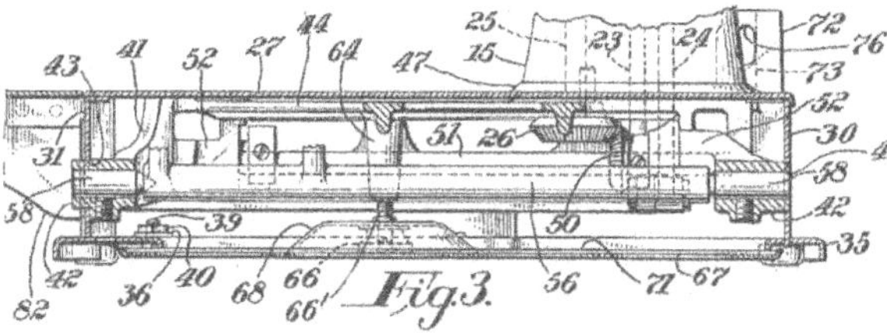

Fig.3.

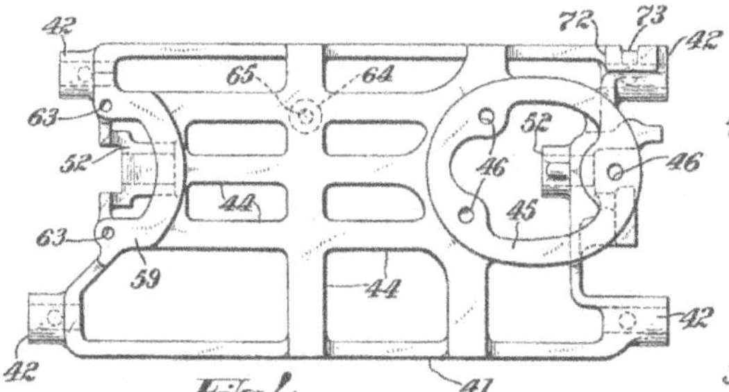

Fig.4.

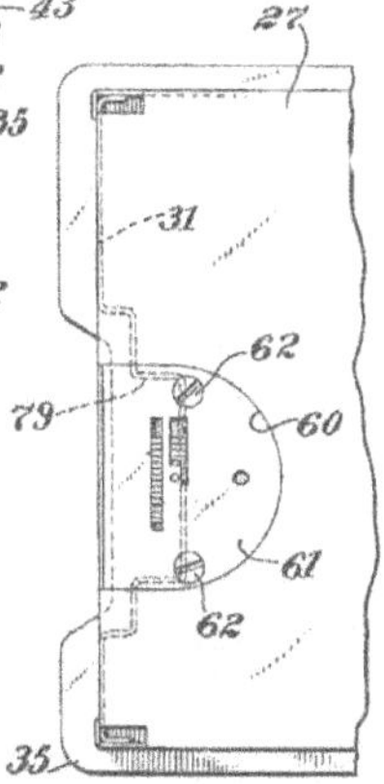

Fig.8.

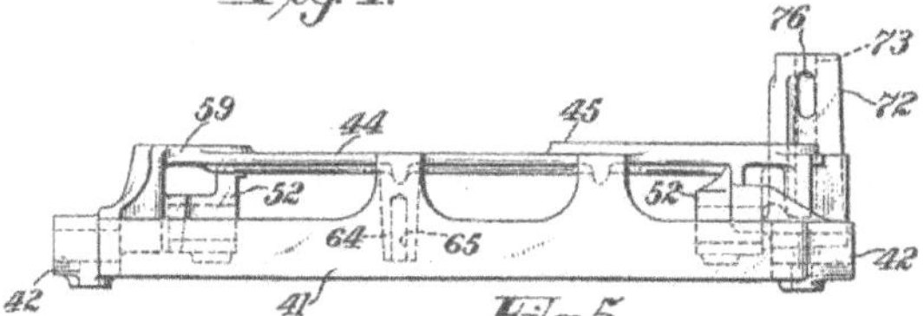

Fig.5.

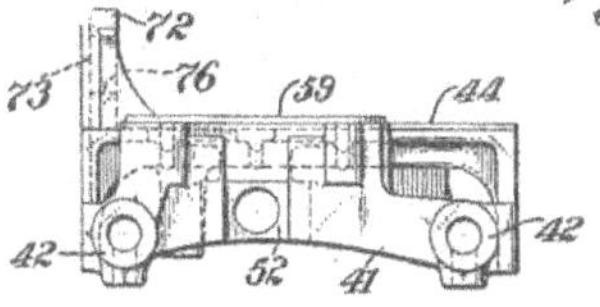

Fig.6.

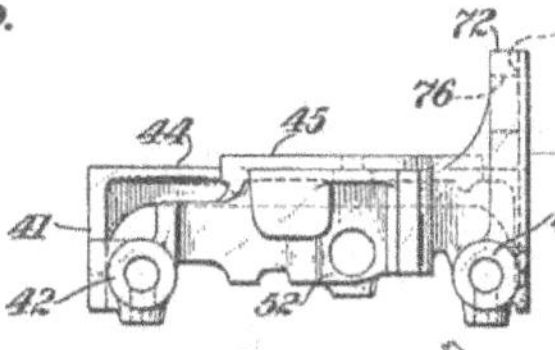

Fig.7.

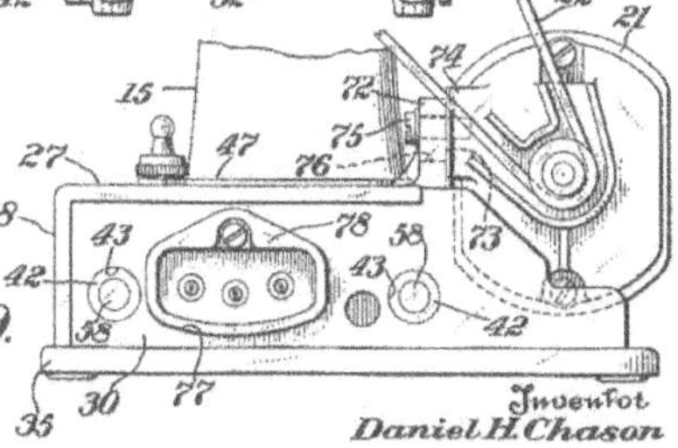

Fig.9.

Witness:

John H. Cave

Inventor
Daniel H. Chason

By William P. Stewart
Attorney

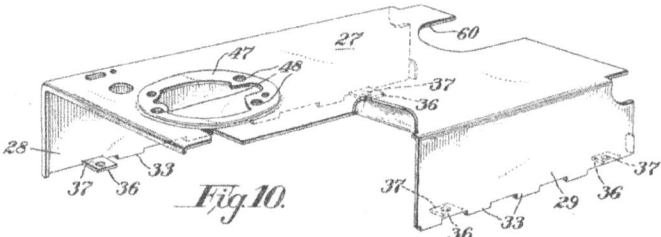

Fig 10.

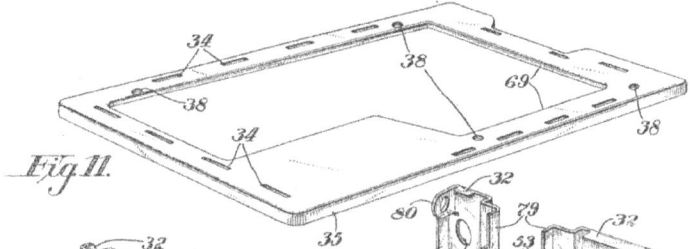

Fig 11.

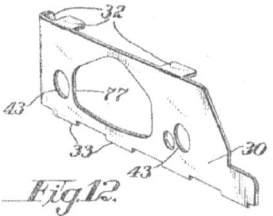

Fig 12.

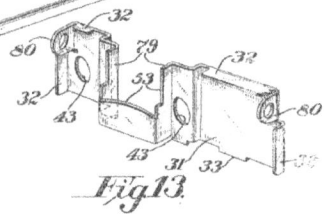

Fig 13.

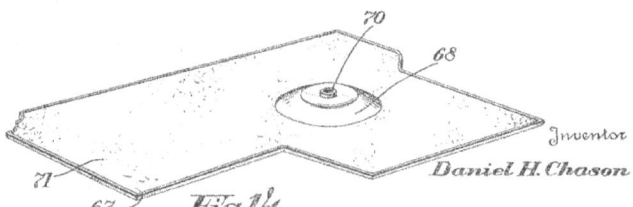

Fig 14.

Inventor
Daniel H. Chason

Witness:
John H. Cave

By
William P. Stewart
Attorney

114

UNITED STATES PATENT OFFICE

2,341,975

SEWING MACHINE BED

Daniel H. Chason, Elizabeth, N. J., assignor to
The Singer Manufacturing Company, Elizabeth, N. J., a corporation of New Jersey

Application June 8, 1942, Serial No. 446,179

8 Claims. (Cl. 112—258)

This invention relates to sewing machines and more particularly to sewing machines of the portable type and has for its primary object to produce a sewing machine which is light in weight.

Another object of the present invention is to provide such a machine with a bed which will be not only light in weight but exceedingly rigid and inexpensive to manufacture.

A further object of the invention is to provide a sewing machine bed having a receptacle portion which may be constructed of sheet-metal, plastic or equivalent light weight materials.

With the above and other objects in view, as will hereinafter appear, the invention comprises the devices, combinations and arrangements of parts hereinafter set forth and illustrated in the accompanying drawings of a preferred embodiment of the invention, from which the several features of the invention and the advantages attained thereby will be readily understood by those skilled in the art.

The invention, both in structure and in operation, as well as additional objects thereof, will be best understood from the following description taken in conjunction with the accompanying drawings, in which:

Fig. 1 is a perspective view from the back side of a sewing machine incorporating the present invention.

Fig. 2 is a bottom plan view of the machine with the bottom closure-plate removed.

Fig. 3 is a vertical section taken longitudinally through the bed portion of the machine.

Fig. 4 is a top plan view of the bed-frame.

Fig. 5 is a side elevation of the bed-frame shown in Fig. 4.

Fig. 6 is a left-hand end elevation of the bed-frame shown in Fig. 5.

Fig. 7 is a right-hand end elevation of the bed-frame shown in Fig. 5.

Fig. 8 is a top plan view of a portion of the machine cloth-plate at the work-feeding end thereof.

Fig. 9 is a right-hand end elevation of the machine shown in Fig. 3.

Fig. 10 is a perspective view of the cloth-plate of the machine.

Fig. 11 is a perspective view of the platform member of the machine.

Fig. 12 is a perspective view of the right-hand end-wall shown in Fig. 3.

Fig. 13 is a perspective view of the left-hand end-wall shown in Fig. 3.

Fig. 14 is a perspective view of the bottom closure-plate shown in Fig. 3.

For the purposes of the present disclosure the invention is described as embodied in a preferred form in a sewing machine having an upright standard 15 which carries the overhanging bracket-arm 16 terminating in a hollow head 17. Journaled for endwise movement in the head 17 are the usual reciprocatory needle-bar 18 and presser-bar 19. Suitably mounted upon one end of the bracket-arm is the usual balance-wheel 20 driven from a motor 21 by a belt 22. Disposed within the standard 15 is the usual actuating mechanism comprising the feed-actuating pitmans 23 and 24, and the rotary shaft 25 carrying the bevel gear 26 at its lower end.

For a more detailed description of the actuating mechanism disposed within the standard and the bracket-arm, reference may be had to the U. S. patent to H. J. Goosman, No. 2,063,841, dated Dec. 8, 1936.

Supporting the upright standard 15 is a chambered bed portion comprising a cloth-plate 27 having side-walls 28 and 29 depending therefrom. End-walls 30 and 31, having lips 32, are secured to the end portions of the cloth-plate and the side-walls by welding or suitably fastening the lips 32 to the inner portions of the cloth-plate and side-walls. The depending side-walls 28 and 29 and the depending end-walls 30 and 31 form with the cloth-plate 27 a substantially rectangular shaped receptacle or enclosure.

Tongues 33 are formed on the bottom edges of the side- and end-walls of the cloth-plate; said tongues entering slots 34 provided in a platform member 35. Also formed on the side walls 28 and 29 are vertically apertured brackets 36, of which the apertures 37 are aligned with vertical apertures 38 provided in the platform member 35. Bolts 39 are received in these apertures, and nuts 40 are threaded on the bolts for the purpose of securing the platform member 35 to the chambered bed or receptacle portion comprising the above described cloth-plate.

In the preferred form of this bed portion, the cloth-plate and its depending walls are constructed from a thin sheet-metal, but it is obvious that it could be constructed from divers other materials including a molded plastic substance.

In order to give the bed portion the proper degree of rigidity, a substantially rectangular shaped skeleton-frame member 41 is provided within the chambered bed portion. Upon each of the two end portions of this frame member 41 are formed bearing-elements in the form of bosses 42 which snugly enter apertures 43 provided in the respective end-walls **30** and **31**. The top portion of the frame **41** has a grid structure comprising a plurality of web-elements **44** which are engaged by the bottom surface of the cloth-plate **27** in a plurality of spaced areas thereof, for the purpose of supporting the same against downward deflection.

A raised and substantially circular shaped portion **45** of the frame **41** is provided with apertures **46** and is adapted to enter a raised or flanged boss **47** of the cloth-plate **27**, so that the apertures **46** are vertically aligned with apertures **48** provided in the flanged boss. The arm-standard **15** is adapted to be supported directly upon the flanged boss **47** of the cloth-plate and to be secured to the raised portion **45** of the frame by means of bolts **49** which pass through the aligned apertures **46** and **48**.

As may be best seen in Figs. 4 and 10 respectively, the raised frame portion **45** and the flanged cloth-plate boss **47** are apertured so that the above described rotary shaft **25** and the pitmans **23** and **24** may extend downwardly into the chambered bed.

The bevel-gear **26** is in mesh with a bevel-gear **50** carried by a loop-taker actuating shaft **51** journaled in bearing-lugs **52** which are provided on both ends of the frame **41**. As may be best seen in Fig. 2, the forward end of the looper-actuating shaft **51** extends through and beyond an opening **53** provided in the end-wall **31**. A loop-taker **54** is mounted upon the forward end of the shaft **51**. Rotation of the shaft **25**, through the medium of gears **26** and **50**, actuates the shaft **51** which in turn operates the loop-taker **54**.

Also disposed within the chambered bed are rock-shafts **55** and **56** which impart to a feed-bar **57**, carrying the usual feed-dog, the conventional feed-lift and feed-advance movements. The rock-shafts **55** and **56** are supported on the pivot-pintles **58** carried by the bearing bosses **42** formed in the frame **41**. The rock-shafts **55** and **56** are actuated by the pitmans **24** and **23**, respectively, the pitmans receiving their motion from the usual feed-actuating mechanisms not shown herein. For a better understanding of the looper-actuating and feeding mechanisms, reference may be had to Patent No. 2,063,841, hereinbefore mentioned.

In the forward end portion of the frame **41** is provided a raised segmental throat-plate supporting rib **59** disposed in the throat-plate clearance opening **60** provided in the cloth-plate **27**. A slotted and suitably apertured throat-plate **61** is secured directly to the raised rib **59** by means of screws **62** which may be threaded into apertures **63** provided in the frame.

Depending from one of the grid or web members **44** is a boss **64** which is provided with a threaded aperture **65** entered by a screw **66**. A sheet metal closure-plate **67**, provided with an indented portion **68**, is adapted to be secured to the grid-member **44** by a nut **66'** threaded upon the screw **66**; said screw **66** passing through an aperture **70** in said indented portion **68** and being accessible through an opening **69** in the platform-member **35**. An oil-absorbent pad **71** is provided on the closure-plate **67** for the purpose of functioning as an oil seal and sound-absorbing means disposed between the platform member **35** and the closure-plate **67**.

Projecting upwardly from the frame **41** is an arm **72** formed with a channel **73** in which is slidably disposed a rectangular shaped lug **74** provided upon the frame of the motor **21**. The

lug **74** is adjustably fixed to the arm **72** by means of a screw **75** which extends through a vertically elongated slot **76** in the arm **71** and is threaded into the lug **74**. From the above it will be obvious that the motor **21** may be raised or lowered upon its support.

The end-wall **30** is provided with an opening **77** for receiving an electrical terminal **78**, and the side-wall **29** and the cloth-plate **27** are shaped to form a recess for the reception of the motor **21**.

The throat-plate **61** overhangs a recess **79** in the end-wall **31** so as to support the work above the loop-taker **54**. The end-wall **31** has apertured ears **80** to receive screws **81** which pivotally support a sheet metal extension-plate **82**. As shown in Fig. 3, the extension-plate, when in its lowered position, abuts the edges of the throat-plate **61** and cloth-plate **27**. Fig. 1 shows the extension-plate **82** in a partially raised position.

Having thus set forth the nature of the invention what I claim herein is:

1. In a sewing machine having sewing instrumentalities including a reciprocatory needle and a complemental loop-taker, a loop-taker shaft, work-feeding means including feed-actuating shafts, a bed comprising a cloth-plate, side- and end-walls depending from said cloth-plate and forming therewith a unitary and chambered receptacle; a closure-plate detachably disposed at the underside of said receptacle; and a rigid frame member carried within said receptacle and having bearing portions thereon, said bearing portions being secured to said end-walls, said feed-actuating shafts being mounted in said bearing portions, said loop-taker shaft being carried by said frame member, and a grid carried by said frame member and engaging said cloth-plate in a plurality of spaced areas.

2. In a sewing machine having sewing instrumentalities including a reciprocatory needle and a complemental loop-taker, a loop-taker shaft, work-feeding means, including feed-actuating shafts; a bed comprising a sheet-metal cloth-plate, sheet-metal side- and end-walls depending from said cloth-plate and forming therewith a unitary and chambered receptacle; a sheet-metal platform member to which said side- and end-walls are secured, said platform member having an opening therein; a closure-plate detachably positioned over said opening; and a unitary and rigid frame member carried entirely within said receptacle, bearing elements carried by said frame member and secured to said end-walls, said feed-actuating shafts being mounted within said bearing elements, said loop-taker shaft being carried by said frame member, and a grid carried by said frame member and engaging the lower side of said sheet-metal cloth-plate in a plurality of spaced areas.

3. In a sewing machine having sewing instrumentalities including a reciprocatory needle and a complemental loop-taker, a loop-taker shaft, work-feeding means including a feed shaft, and an electric motor to actuate said shafts; a bed comprising a cloth-plate having a plurality of openings therein, and side- and end-walls depending from said cloth-plate and forming therewith a unitary and chambered receptacle, said end-walls having a plurality of apertures therein; a closure-plate detachably positioned on the underside of said receptacle; a rigid and unitary frame member carried within said receptacle, said frame member including a plurality of bearing bosses which extend into the apertures pro-

vided in said end-walls, said bearing bosses being adapted to carry said feed shaft, a grid element extending from said frame and engaging the bottom portion of said cloth-plate in a plurality of areas, and an arm carried by said frame and supporting said electric motor; and a throat-plate secured directly to said frame and extending through one of said cloth-plate openings; said loop-taker shaft being mounted within said frame and having one of its ends extending through one of the apertures provided in one of said end-walls, said loop-taker being fixed to the end of the shaft extending beyond said end-wall.

4. A sewing machine having an upright standard, a unitary bed-frame consisting of a plurality of interengaging web-elements forming a flat grid, a loop-taker shaft, work-feeding means, said loop-taker shaft and said work-feeding means being carried by and mounted within said bed-frame, a cloth-plate having wall portions depending downwardly therefrom to form a chambered receptacle, said cloth-plate being mounted upon said grid and being clamped between said standard and said bed-frame, and means provided on said bed-frame for securing the same directly to said wall portions at a plurality of spaced areas.

5. A sewing machine having a unitary bed-frame consisting of a plurality of interengaging web-elements forming a flat grid, a loop-taker shaft, work-feeding means, said loop-taker shaft and said work-feeding means being carried by and mounted within said bed-frame, and a cloth-plate having a pair of side-walls depending downwardly therefrom, said cloth-plate being mounted upon said grid, a pair of unitary end-walls each being secured upon an opposite end of said bed-frame, said cloth-plate and said unitary end-walls forming a chambered receptacle containing said bed-frame, and a closure-plate detachably disposed at the under side of said receptacle.

6. A bed for use with a sewing machine, said bed comprising a sheet metal cloth-plate provided with downwardly depending walls forming a unitary and chambered receptacle, a unitary sheet metal platform member to which said walls are secured, said platform member having an opening therein, a closure-plate detachably positioned over the opening provided in said platform member, and a unitary skeleton frame member carried within said chambered receptacle, said skeleton frame member consisting of a plurality of interlocking webs which engage the under side of said depending walls in a plurality of spaced areas.

7. A sewing machine having an upright standard, a unitary bed-frame consisting of a plurality of interengaging web-elements forming a flat grid, a loop-taker shaft, work-feeding means, said loop-taker shaft and work-feeding means being carried by and mounted within said bed-frame, a cloth-plate provided with downwardly depending walls forming a unitary and chambered receptacle, a unitary platform member to which said walls are secured, said platform member having an opening therein, a closure-plate detachably positioned over the opening provided in said platform member, said cloth-plate being mounted upon said flat grid and being clamped between said standard and said bed-frame so that said interengaging webs engage the under side of said cloth-plate, and means provided on said bed-frame for securing the same directly to said walls at a plurality of spaced areas.

8. A sewing machine having a unitary bed-frame consisting of a plurality of interengaging web-elements forming a flat grid, a cloth-plate having a pair of opposed side-walls depending downwardly therefrom, said cloth-plate being mounted upon said grid, a pair of unitary end-walls each being secured upon an opposite end portion of said bed-frame, said cloth-plate and said end-walls forming a chambered receptacle containing said bed-frame, a closure-plate detachably disposed at the under side of said receptacle, one of said end-walls having a portion thereof apertured and inwardly offset to provide an apertured recess, a loop-taker shaft mounted within said bed-frame and having one of its ends extending outwardly through said apertured recess, and a loop-taker positioned within said side-wall recess and being fixed upon the end portion of said shaft extending beyond said end-wall.

DANIEL H. CHASON.

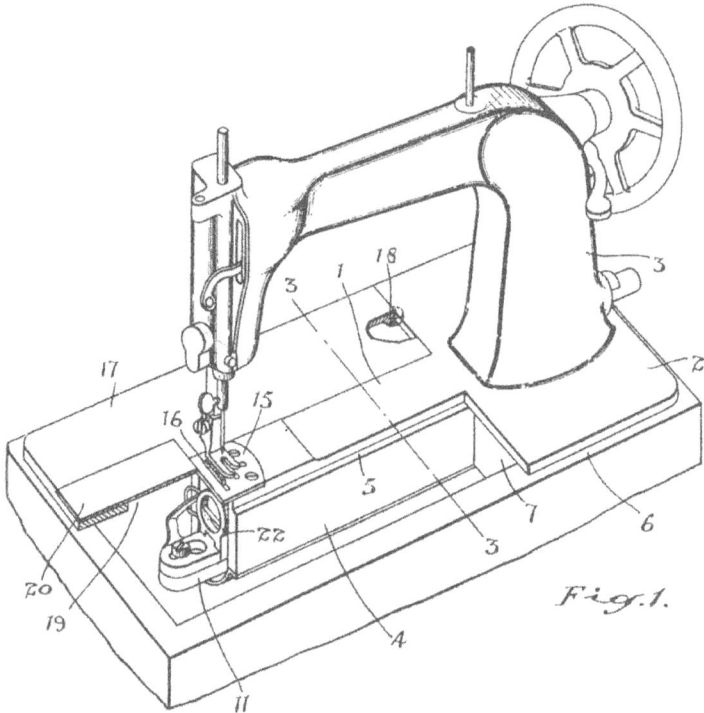

Fig.1.

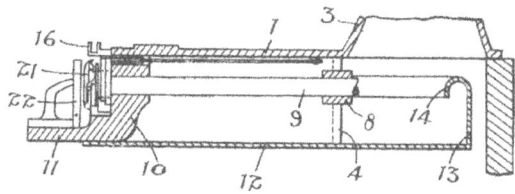

Fig.2.

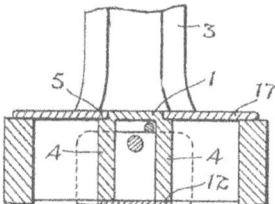

Fig.3.

Inventor.
Bertram Eaton
by H. J. S. Dennison
          atty

118

UNITED STATES PATENT OFFICE

BERTRAM EATON, OF TORONTO, ONTARIO, CANADA, ASSIGNOR TO ARTHUR LATCHAM, OF YORK, ONTARIO, CANADA, AND CLARK TAYLOR PURVIS, OF TORONTO, ONTARIO, CANADA

SEWING MACHINE

Application filed June 7, 1928. Serial No. 283,484.

The principal objects of this invention are, to provide a general utility form of machine which may be used for sewing flat or tubular articles and which may be very quickly changed to suit either purpose.

The principal feature of the invention consists in the novel construction of the bed frame and bed plate, whereby the major portion of the bed plate may be removed presenting an arm containing the bobbin and feed mechanism over which the tubular goods may be inserted.

In the drawings, Figure 1 is a perspective view of the improved machine showing a portion of the bed plate removed, disclosing the arm structure for cylindrical sewing.

Figure 2 is a longitudinal mid-sectional view through the arm structure.

Figure 3 is a cross sectional view taken on the line 3—3 of Figure 1.

In the ordinary types of sewing machines the bed plate is flat allowing only the sewing of flat goods thereon and where the cylindrical or tubular goods are to be machine sewn, special machines are provided wherein the operating mechanism is contained in an arm open at the end to allow the goods to be inserted thereover.

It is very desirable that a sewing machine be produced which will enable the ordinary seamstress to sew tubular goods and this invention has been produced to effect that result.

The bed plate 1 of the machine is of substantial T shape, the back portion 2 of which supports the standard 3 carrying the needle operating mechanism. The forwardly extending portion is preferably centrally arranged and extending downwardly therefrom are the parallel side walls 4. These side walls are formed with a longitudinal ledge 5 level with the under side of the back portion 2.

The back portion 2 is adapted to rest upon a suitable frame 6 and vertical webs 7 extend laterally from the walls 4 beneath the portion 2. Between these lateral webs and arranged centrally between the side walls 4 is a journal bearing 8 supporting one end of the main shaft 9 and the forward end of the shaft 9 is supported in a downwardly extending lug

structure 10 which is provided with a forwardly extending foot 11.

A sheet metal bottom plate 12 is secured to the bottom edges of the side walls 4 and extends underneath the standard 3 having at the rear portion beneath said standard an upward flange 13 provided with an inturned edge 14.

This structure completes the bobbin arm upon the top of which is secured the throat plate 15 through which the feed dog 16 extends.

This structure is complete for the purpose of receiving and operating upon tubular forms of goods but when flat goods are to be sewn it is desirable to have a flat bed plate.

A plate 17 is formed with a longitudinal slot extending inwardly from one end and the said plate rests upon the ledges 5 fitting snugly to the central portion of the bed plate 1 and having the ends abutting the forward edges of the back portion 2.

The plate 17 is preferably provided with lugs 18 adapted to extend under the portion 2 of the main bed plate to hold it firmly in place. The plate 17 extends forward of the throat plate and is provided with an opening 19 closed by a slide plate 20 of the usual form which enables the operator to reach in to manipulate the bobbin which is carried in the holder 21 on the main shaft 9.

The gate 22 is pivotally supported upon the foot 11 and is held in a vertical position against the holder 21 to hold the bobbin in place.

When the plate 17 is in position, a broad flat surface is provided to support the goods being operated upon but when it is desired to sew a tubular member the plate 17 is merely lifted upwardly from the supporting frame 6 and drawn forwardly, thus leaving a projecting arm in the center of the recess of the frame.

A machine as thus described is extremely simple in its construction and may be handled without difficulty by the ordinary user.

What I claim as my invention is:—

1. A sewing machine comprising a frame support having a rectangular opening in the top, a bed frame formed with lateral flanges

resting on the top of said frame support at one end of said opening having the major portion of said opening uncovered and having an extension formed with downwardly extending side walls disposed centrally of said uncovered portion of said opening, a bottom plate secured to said sides and with said sides and top forming an enclosure for the bobbin and feed mechanism, and a unitary bed plate having a slot extending in from one end thereof and adapted to fit snugly to and rest on the side wall extension of the bed frame to complete the closing of the frame opening.

2. A sewing machine, comprising, an open frame, a bed frame resting upon one end of said open frame and having a central extension formed with downwardly extending side walls, said side walls forming longitudinal ledges, transverse walls extending laterally from the side walls beneath the bed frame, a bottom plate closing the arm formed by the extension from the bed frame, a bed plate slotted to fit around the extension and adapted to rest upon the ledges in the sides thereof, the ends of said plate each side of the slot abutting the top of the bed frame and having lug extensions extending under said plate, and a slide plate arranged in the end of the removable bed plate to give access to the bobbin mechanism.

3. In a sewing machine, a frame having a plane top and an opening therein, a bed plate fitting flat on said plane top at one end of said frame opening, said plate having a frame portion, and an extension member extending centrally toward and terminating short of the opposite end of said top opening and carrying the bobbin and feed mechanism, said extension member having a longitudinal recess in each side forming shoulders on the same plane as said top, and a single U-shaped flat plate having its inward marginal portion resting on the longitudinal shoulders of said extension member and having its outer marginal portion resting on said frame top.

4. In a sewing machine, a main frame, a bed frame supported in said main frame and having an extension carrying the shuttle mechanism at the end thereof, a unitary bed plate slotted inwardly from one end to snugly receive said bed frame extension, the slot in said bed plate terminating beyond the end extremity of said frame extension to provide access to the shuttle mechanism carried by the latter, and a removable plate on the unslotted portion of said bed plate adapted to close said bed slot between its terminal end and the end extremity of said frame extension.

BERTRAM EATON.

120

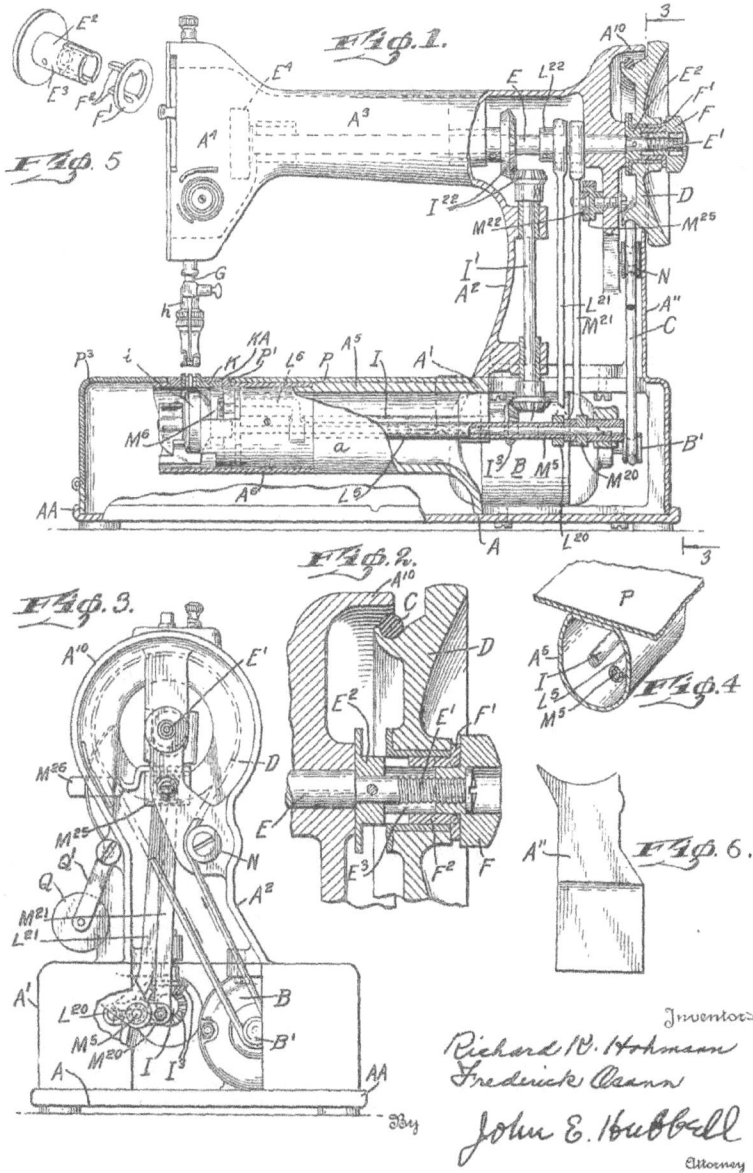

Fig. 1.

Fig. 5

Fig. 2.

Fig. 3.

Fig. 4.

Fig. 6.

Inventors
Richard K. Hohmann
Frederick Osann
By John E. Hubbell
Attorney

121

UNITED STATES PATENT OFFICE

2,247,381

SEWING MACHINE DRIVE MEANS

Richard K. Hohmann, Jamaica, and Frederick
Osann, White Plains, N. Y., assignors to Sears,
Roebuck and Co., Chicago, Ill., a corporation of
New York

Original application December 29, 1939, Serial No.
311,486. Divided and this application August
3, 1940, Serial No. 351,013

4 Claims. (Cl. 112—220)

In our prior application, Serial No. 311,486, filed December 29, 1939, of which this application is a division, we have disclosed a simple and effective sewing machine devised by us especially for interchangeable use as a darning machine and for ordinary sewing operations.

That machine is readily convertible from one to the other of two conditions, in one of which it is adapted for plain sewing and includes a flat work bed, which may be generally similar in form and disposition to the conventional work bed of a plain sewing machine, and in the other of which it is adapted for darning and is adapted to support stockings, or other work to be darned, on a cylinder arm generally like, though preferably somewhat smaller in cross section than, the work supporting cylinder arms of ordinary darning machines. In its preferred form, the machine is adapted, however, for either plain sewing or darning operations, on flat bed and cylinder arm supported work.

The general object of the invention claimed herein is to provide an improved pulley and belt drive connection between a driving pulley mounted on the needle bar shaft and a driving electric motor located in the base of the sewing machine, and including novel provisions by which the portion of the belt above the base of the machine is normally enclosed within the standard and adjacent arm portion of the machine, but may be made readily accessible for belt removal and replacement operations.

The various features of novelty which characterize our novel work feed mechanism are pointed out with particularity in the claims annexed to and forming a part of this specification. For a better understanding of the invention, however, its advantages and specific objects attained with its use, reference should be had to the accompanying drawing and descriptive matter in which we have illustrated and described a preferred form of embodiment of the present invention.

Of the drawing:

Fig. 1 is an elevation, partly in section, of a sewing machine constituting a preferred embodiment of the present invention;

Fig. 2 is an enlarged reproduction of a portion of Fig. 1, showing parts in different relative positions;

Fig. 3 is a section on the line 3—3 of Fig. 1 with parts broken away and removed;

Fig. 4 is a perspective view showing parts of the cylinder arm and flat work bed of Fig. 1 in section;

Fig. 5 is a perspective view illustrating details of the main pulley mounting;

Fig. 6 is a small scale elevation of a removable cover plate at the right hand end of the machine as shown in Fig. 1.

The housing structure, or framework of the sewing machine illustrated in the drawing, comprises a rectangular supporting bottom plate A, and a sewing machine framework proper which is screw connected to the bottom plate and includes a rectangular base or bed portion A', a standard A^2, and a horizontal cylinder arm comprising a portion A^5 and A^6. The portion A^5 is an integral tubular extension of the base portion A' and A^6 is a tubular part detachably secured to the front end of the part A^5 and forming an extension of the latter.

The machine comprises a driving motor B, mounted in the base portion A' and having a pulley B' on its shaft which is operatively connected by a belt C to a driving pulley D mounted on the adjacent end of the needle bar shaft E, which may be journaled in the arm A^3 in any usual or suitable manner. In the preferred construction shown, the rear end E' of the needle bar shaft E is threaded, and supports a nut member F, which may be rotated about the shaft end E' to thereby clamp the hub portion of the pulley D between the head of the nut member F and the radially extending flange of a part E^2 carried by and secured to the shaft E and comprising a tubular hub portion E^3 forming an elongated bearing for the pulley D. When the nut F is backed off, as shown in Fig. 2, the pulley E may be displaced axially of the shaft E, from its normal position, to thereby move the inner, belt groove portion of the pulley out of its normal position within the arm A^3 so as to permit the belt C to be removed from and replaced on said pulley.

As shown, a washer member F' is interposed between the nut F and the hub of the pulley D, said washer member having integral arm extensions F^2 received in longitudinal slots formed for the purpose in the tubular portion E^3 of the part E^2. The member F with its extensions F' and the part E^2 with the slots in its tubular portion E^3, collectively form a split or extensible bearing for the pulley D, which provides a satisfactory support for the latter when in, and when displaced from, the position in which it is normally clamped by the nut F.

At its head end, the machine comprises means including a crank disc E^4, carried by the shaft for actuating a needle bar G, mounted in the head

A⁴ in any usual or suitable manner for vertical reciprocatory movement. At its head end, the machine is also provided with a presser bar h, and in our said prior application, we disclose and claim novel actuating means for lifting said presser bar during each upstroke of the needle bar when the machine is in condition for darning, but as said actuating means form no part of the invention claimed herein, said means need not be illustrated or described. The sewing machine also includes tension and thread take-up provisions which may be of conventional type and hence do not require description herein.

The sewing machine mechanism shown, is of the rotary hook type, and comprises a hook shaft I, which is suitably journalled in the frame part A' and its cylinder arm extension A⁵, and which carries a loop taker or hook element i adjacent the front of the machine. The hook shaft I is rotated by the needle bar shaft E through a vertical shaft I' journalled in the standard A² and having its upper end connected to the shaft E by bevel gears I²² and having its lower end connected to the hook shaft I through bevel gears I³. Desirably, and as shown, the gears are so proportioned that the shaft I will rotate with double the angular velocity of the shaft E.

The sewing machine includes work feeding means comprising a feed dog K adapted to extend up into and to move horizontally in the slot of a throat or needle plate part KA, of conventional flat form and supported by the cylinder arm part A⁶. The work feeding mechanism also comprises mechanism within the hollow cylindrical arm of the sewing machine for giving the feed dog its feeding movements. Said mechanism is fully disclosed in our said prior application, and need not be further referred to herein.

As shown in Fig. 3, the shaft of the motor B is parallel to the needle bar shaft E and hook shaft I, but is laterally displaced from the latter. To accommodate this displacement without requiring the standard A² to have an unconventional and undesirable form, an idler pulley N, normally engaged by the rear run of the belt, is so located as to deflect the lower portion of that belt run into or near parallelism with the belt front run which extends in a direction inclined to the vertical from the pulley B' to the pulley D. The idler pulleys N, arranged as shown, also reduces the risk of belt slippage, by increasing the angular portion of each of the pulleys B' and D engaged by the belt. In the normal operating position, the upper portion of the belt groove in the pulley D is within and closely encircled by a cylindrical portion A¹⁰ of the framework. An opening formed in the standard A² and base member A', at the right hand end of the machine, as seen in Fig. 1, is normally closed by a removable cover plate or member A¹¹, shown in outline in Fig. 6. The removal of the cover member A¹¹ gives access to the portion of the belt and other mechanism within the hollow standard. As will be apparent, the belt may be slackened preparatory to its removal, and tightened up in the course of its replacement, by moving the belt into and out of engagement with the accessible idler pulley N while the belt is in engagement with the less accessible pulleys B' and D.

As shown the sewing machine includes a removable work member P, in the form of a metal box minus its bottom wall and open at its end which, when the part is in use as shown in Fig. 1, is adjacent and bears against the sewing machine frame part A'. The member P is formed with an opening P' in its top wall to receive the throat plate member KA and with an adjacent opening P² partly in the top wall and partly in the closed end of the member P which is normally closed by a hinged cover member P³, which, when moved into its open position, permits access to the bobbin case extending into the loop taker, for insertion and removal of bobbins. As shown, the base plate A is formed with an uprising marginal flange AA in telescopic engagement with the lower portion of the bed plate part P, whereby the latter is anchored in position. With the part P in place, the machine as a whole, has the general appearance and operative capacity of an ordinary flat bed sewing machine. With the bed member P removed, the work support is of the cylinder arm form heretofore used in darning stockings and other work. As shown in Fig. 4, the tubular cylinder arm may advantageously be generally elliptical in cross section but with its top portion flattened to provide a flat seat for the engaging top wall portion of the member P.

As shown, a bobbin winder wheel Q, carried by an arm Q' pivotally connected to the standard A², is adapted to be turned from its idle position, shown in Fig. 3 into the position in which the wheel Q extends through a slot formed for the purpose in the standard A², and frictionally engages the pulley D, which, during the bobbin winding operation is normally free to turn on the needle shaft E.

As previously stated, the machine may be used interchangeably in plain sewing and darning operations, either with the flat bed part P in place, or removed, so that the work may be supported on the cylinder arm. Our improved driving connection between the motor and the needle shaft is relatively simple, and with it the belt removal and replacement operations are simple and of a character to be readily performed by the ordinary housewife. The sewing machine shown is of the portable type, but our improvements disclosed and claimed herein are adapted for use in sewing machines of other types.

While in accordance with the provisions of the statutes, we have illustrated and described the best form of embodiment of the invention now known to us, it will be apparent to those skilled in the art that changes may be made in the form of the apparatus disclosed without departing from the spirit of the invention as set forth in the appended claims and that in some cases certain features of our invention may be used to advantage without a corresponding use of other features.

Having now described our invention, what we claim as new and desire to secure by Letters Patent, is:

1. A motor driven sewing machine comprising a framework including a base portion, a hollow standard, and an arm connected to the upper end of the standard and formed at its rear end with a portion extending about and forming an upper peripheral portion of the wall of a pulley recess, said recess being open at its rear side and open at its lower edge to the interior of the hollow standard, a needle shaft having a body portion within and extending longitudinally of said arm and a rear end portion extending through said recess, a driving motor mounted in said base portion and a driving connection between said motor and shaft, comprising a pulley member mounted on the rear end portion of said shaft and having a pulley groove at its front side,

means for releasably clamping said pulley member to said shaft with said pulley groove received within said recess, said pulley member when not clamped to said shaft being movable longitudinally on the latter to move said pulley groove out of said recess, and a belt extending through said standard and normally having its upper portion received in said pulley groove but being movable into and out of said groove when the latter is out of said recess.

2. A sewing machine as specified in claim 1, in which said standard is formed with an opening in its rear side permitting access to the adjacent portion of the belt, and a detachable cover plate normally closes said opening.

3. A sewing machine as specified in claim 1, in which a split bearing is interposed between said pulley and shaft and comprises portions extending longitudinally of said shaft and overlapping one another and being movable relative to one another in the longitudinal direction of the shaft to accommodate the longitudinal movement of the pulley.

4. A motor driven sewing machine comprising a framework including a base portion, a hollow standard and an arm connected to the upper end of the standard, a needle shaft having a body portion within and extending longitudinally of said arm and a rear end portion extending over the standard, a pulley member mounted on the rear end portion of said shaft, a driving motor mounted in said base portion having a driving pulley revolving about an axis parallel to the needle shaft and displaced to one side of said standard and a belt extending through said standard and about said pulley member and driving pulley, and an idler pulley mounted in said standard and engaging a portion of said belt and deflecting it toward the center of the standard, whereby said belt may be slackened preparatory to its removal and tightened up in the course of its replacement, by moving the belt respectively out of and into engagement with said idler pulley.

RICHARD K. HOHMANN.
FREDERICK OSANN.

124

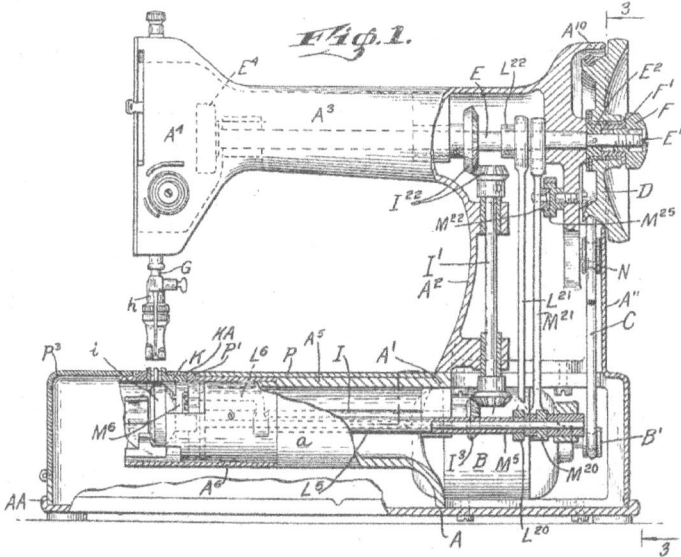

Fig.1.

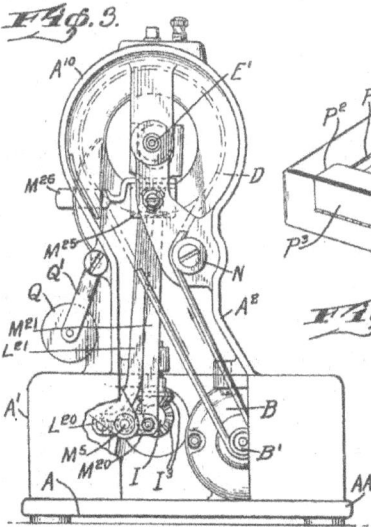

Fig.3.

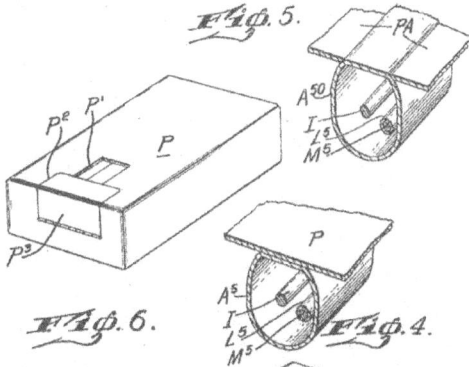

Fig.5.

Fig.6.

Fig.4.

Fig.2.

By
Richard K. Hohmann
Frederick Osann.
John E. Hubbell Attorney

125

UNITED STATES PATENT OFFICE

2,247,383

CONVERTIBLE FLAT-BED CYLINDER ARM SEWING MACHINE

Richard K. Hohmann, Jamaica, and Frederick Osann, White Plains, N. Y., assignors to Sears, Roebuck and Co., Chicago, Ill., a corporation of New York

Original application December 29, 1939, Serial No. 311,486. Divided and this application August 3, 1940, Serial No. 351,014

3 Claims. (Cl. 112—260)

Our prior application Serial No. 311,486, of which this application is a division, discloses a simple and effective sewing machine devised by us for interchangeable use as a darning machine and for ordinary sewing operations.

That machine is readily convertible from one to the other of two conditions, in one of which it is adapted for plain sewing and includes a flat work bed, which may be generally similar in form and disposition to the conventional work bed of 10 a plain sewing machine, and in the other of which it is adapted for darning and is adapted to support stockings or other work to be darned, on a cylinder arm generally like, though preferably somewhat smaller in cross section than, the 15 work supporting cylinder arms of ordinary darning machines. In its preferred form, the machine is adapted, however, for either plain sewing or darning operations, on flat bed and cylinder arm supported work. 20

The general object of the present invention is to provide a sewing machine and a flat work bed part which can be readily put in or removed from the machine, of such character that with the work bed part in place, has the general 25 form and work supporting characteristics of an ordinary flat bed portable sewing machine, and with said part removed, the cylinder arm of the machine is fully exposed, and accessible for the free and unobstructed movements of stockings 30 and other tubular work pieces onto and off said arm.

The various features of novelty which characterize the present invention are pointed out with particularity in the claims annexed to and form- 35 ing a part of this specification. For a better understanding of the invention, however, its advantages and specific objects attained with its use, reference should be had to the accompanying drawing and descriptive matter in which we 40 have illustrated and described preferred forms of embodiment of the present invention.

Of the drawing:

Fig. 1 is an elevation, partly in section, of a sewing machine constituting a preferred em- 45 bodiment of the present invention;

Fig. 2 is a perspective view of the removable flat work bed member shown in Fig. 5;

Fig. 3 is a section on the line 3—3 of Fig. 1 with parts broken away and removed; 50

Fig. 4 is a perspective view showing parts of the cylinder arm and flat work bed of Fig. 1 in section;

Fig. 5 is a view taken similarly to Fig. 4, illus- 55

trating the use of a flat work bed member of modified form; and

Fig. 6 is a perspective view of the removable flat bed part shown in Fig. 1.

The housing structure, or frame of the sewing machine illustrated in the drawing, comprises a rectangular supporting bottom plate A, and a sewing machine body frame member which is screw connected to the bottom plate and includes a rectangular base or bed portion A', a standard A², and a horizontal cylinder arm comprising portions A⁵ and A⁶. The portion A⁵ is an integral tubular extension of the base portion A' and A⁶ is a tubular part detachably secured to the front end of the part A⁵ and forming an extension of the latter.

The machine comprises a driving motor B, mounted in the base portion A' and having a pulley B' on its shaft which is operatively connected by a belt C to a driving pulley D mounted on the adjacent end of the needle bar shaft E, which may be journalled in the arm A³ in any usual or suitable manner. In the preferred construction shown, the rear end E' of the needle bar shaft E is threaded, and supports a nut member F, which may be rotated about the shaft end E' to thereby clamp the hub portion of the pulley D between the head of the nut member F and the radially extending flange of a part E² carried by and secured to the shaft E and comprising a tubular hub portion forming an elongated bearing for the pulley D. When the nut F is backed off, the pulley E may be displaced axially of the shaft E, from its normal position, to thereby move the inner, belt groove portion of the pulley out of its normal position within the arm A³, so as to permit the belt C to be removed from and replaced on said pulley. As shown, a washer member F', specially shaped and disposed as described in said prior application, is interposed between the nut F and the hub of the pulley D.

At its head end, the machine comprises means including a crank disc E⁴ carried by the shaft E for actuating a needle bar G, mounted in the head A⁴ in any usual or suitable manner for vertical reciprocatory movement.

At its head end, the machine is also provided with a presser bar h, and in our said prior application we disclose and claim novel actuating means for lifting said presser bar during each upstroke of the needle bar G, when the machine is in condition for darning use, but said actuating means need not be illustrated or described herein. Our sewing machine also includes tension and thread take-up provisions which may be of conventional type and hence do not require description herein.

The sewing machine mechanism shown, is of the rotary hook type, and comprises a hook shaft I, which is suitably journalled in the frame part A' and its cylinder arm extension A⁵, and which carries a loop taker or hook element i adjacent the front of the machine. The hook shaft I is rotated bythe needle bar shaft E through a vertical shaft I' journalled in the standard A² and having its upper end connected to the shaft E by bevel gears I²² and having its lower end connected to the hook shaft I through bevel gears I³. Desirably, and as shown, the gears are so proportioned that the shaft I will rotate with double the angular velocity of the shaft E.

The sewing machine includes work feeding means comprising a feed dog K adapted to extend up into and to move horizontally in the slot of a throat or needle plate part KA, of conventional flat form and supported by the cylinder arm part A⁶. The work feeding means also comprises mechanism within the hollow cylindrical arm of the sewing machine for giving the feed dog its feeding movements, but the character of said mechanism forms no part of the invention claimed herein and need not be further referred to.

As shown in Fig. 3, the shaft of the motor B is parallel to the needle bar shaft E and hook shaft I, but is laterally displaced from the latter. To accommodate this displacement without requiring the standard A² to have an unconventional and undesirable form, an idler pulley N, normally engaged by the rear run of the belt, is so located as to deflect the lower portion of that belt run into or near parallelism with the belt front run which extends in a direction inclined to the vertical from the pulley B' to the pulley D. In the normal operating position, the upper portion of the belt groove in the pulley D is within and closely encircled by a cylindrical portion A¹⁰ of the framework. An opening formed in the standard A² and base member A', at the right hand end of the machine, as seen in Fig. 1, is normally closed by a removable cover plate or member A¹¹, which is removable to permit access to the portion of the belt and other mechanism within the hollow standard.

In the form shown in Fig. 1, the sewing machine includes a removable flat work bed member P, shown in perspective in Fig. 6. As shown in Figs. 1 and 6, the member P is in the form of a metal box, minus its bottom wall, and open at its end which, when the part is in use as shown in Fig. 1, is adjacent and bears against the sewing machine frame part A'. The part P is formed with an opening P' in its top wall to receive the throat plate member KA and with an adjacent opening P² partly in the top wall and partly in the closed end member. The opening P² is normally closed by a hinged cover member P³ which when moved into open position, permits access to the bobbin case extending into the loop taker, for insertion and removal of bobbins.

As shown, the base plate A is formed with an uprising marginal flange AA in telescopic engagement with the lower portion of the bed plate part P, whereby the latter is anchored in position. With the part P in place, the machine as a whole, has the general appearance and operative capacity of an ordinary flat bed sewing machine. The cylinder arm work support A⁵, A⁶, is substantially above the top of the flange

AA, and with the bed member P removed, no portion of the sewing machine obstructs movements of stockings or other tubular work parts onto and off the cylinder arm. As shown in Fig. 4, the tubular cylinder arm may advantageously be generally elliptical in cross section, but with its top portion flattened to provide a flat seat for the engaging top portion of the member P.

In lieu of the flat work bed part P shown in Figs. 1, 4 and 6, I may make use of the work bed part PA shown in Figs. 2 and 5. The part PA differs from the part P in that it is formed with a longitudinal slot P¹⁰ in its top wall adapted to receive the flattened top wall portion of the cylinder arm A⁵⁰, which to this end may differ in shape from the cylinder arm first described, in that its top wall portion is in the form of a flat rib shaped to fit into the slot P¹⁰.

As shown, a bobbin winder wheel Q, carried by an arm Q' pivotally connected to the standard A², is adapted to be turned from its idle position, shown in Fig. 3 into the position in which the wheel Q extends through a slot formed for the purpose in the standard A², and frictionally engages the pulley D, which, during the bobbin winding operation is normally free to turn on the needle shaft E.

As previously stated, the machine may be used interchangeably in plain sewing and darning operations, either with the flat bed part P or PA in place, or removed so that the work may be supported on the cylinder arm. The flat bed parts P and PA are simple in form and easily put in place and removed. The sewing machine shown is of the portable type, but our improvements disclosed and claimed herein are adapted for use in sewing machines of the cabinet type, or of the convertible cabinet and portable type disclosed in the copending application Ser. No. 313,507, filed January 12, 1940, by Richard K. Hohmann, one of the petitioners herein.

While in accordance with the provisions of the statutes, we have illustrated and described the best form of embodiment of the invention now known to us, it will be apparent to those skilled in the art that changes may be made in the form of the apparatus disclosed without departing from the spirit of the invention as set forth in the appended claims and that in some cases certain features of our invention may be used to advantage without a corresponding use of other features.

Having now described our invention, what we claim and desire to secure by Letters Patent, is:

1. A sewing machine comprising in combination a frame including a base plate, a standard extending upward from the base plate adjacent one end of the latter and a work supporting cylinder arm extending away from said standard toward the opposite end of the base plate and spaced above the latter and a separable flat bed member detachably mounted on and supported by said frame and comprising a flat bed portion adapted to extend over said cylinder arm and a depending marginal portion adapted to engage said base plate adjacent its edge.

2. A sewing machine as specified in claim 1 including an uprising needle plate supported on said cylinder arm, and in which said flat bed portion of the flat bed member is formed with an opening adapted to receive said needle plate and in which said depending marginal portion of the flat bed member comprises side parts at opposite sides of said cylinder arm, and an end part transverse to said arm and at a distance

from said standard greater than the length of said arm.

3. A sewing machine as specified in claim 1 including bobbin-holding means mounted in said cylinder arm and in which said flat bed member is formed with an opening providing access to said bobbin-holding means and including a por- tion in said flat bed portion and another portion in said depending marginal portion, and in which a cover part is hinged to said flat bed member to move into and out of a position in which it closes said opening.

RICHARD K. HOHMANN.
FREDERICK OSANN.

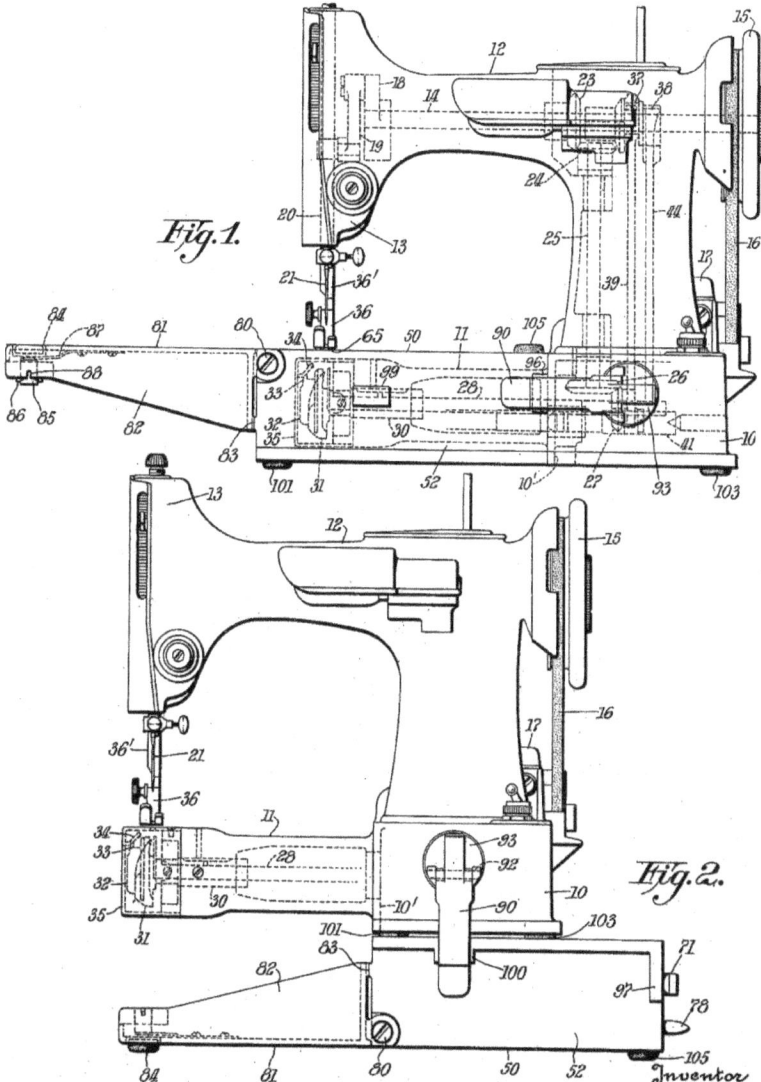

Fig.1.

Fig.2.

129

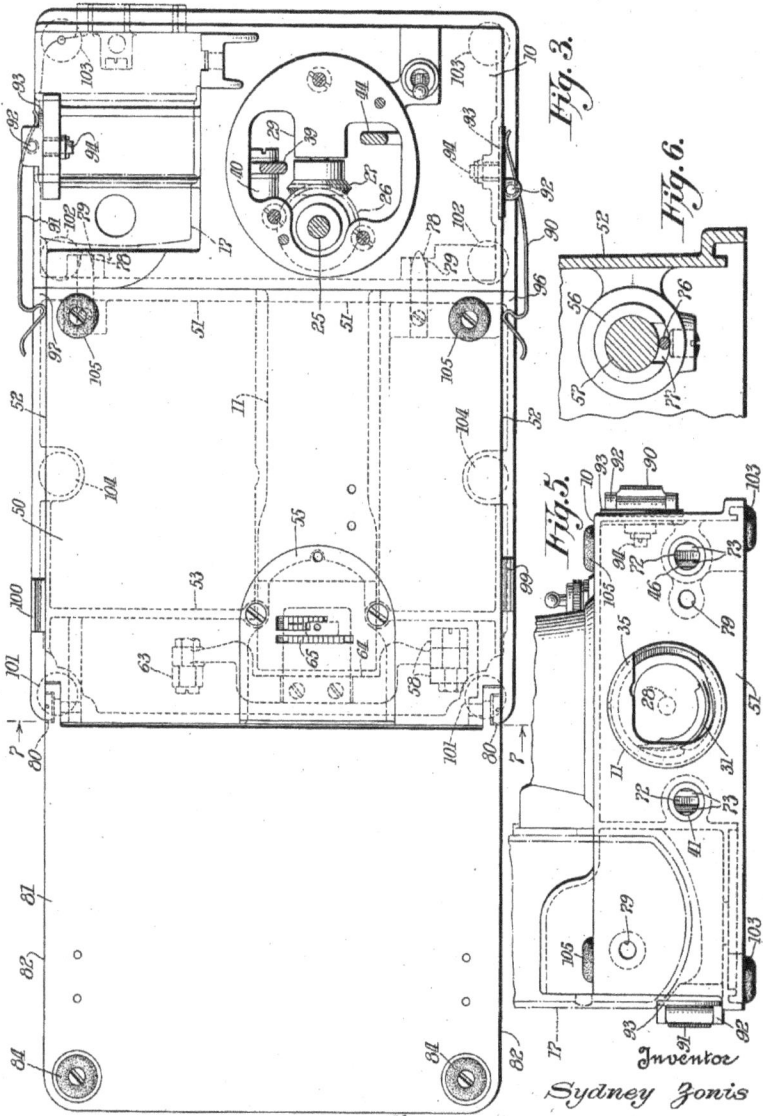

Fig. 3.

Fig. 6.

Fig. 5.

Inventor
Sydney Zonis

By
William P. Stewart
Attorney

Witness:
Godfrey Pecina

130

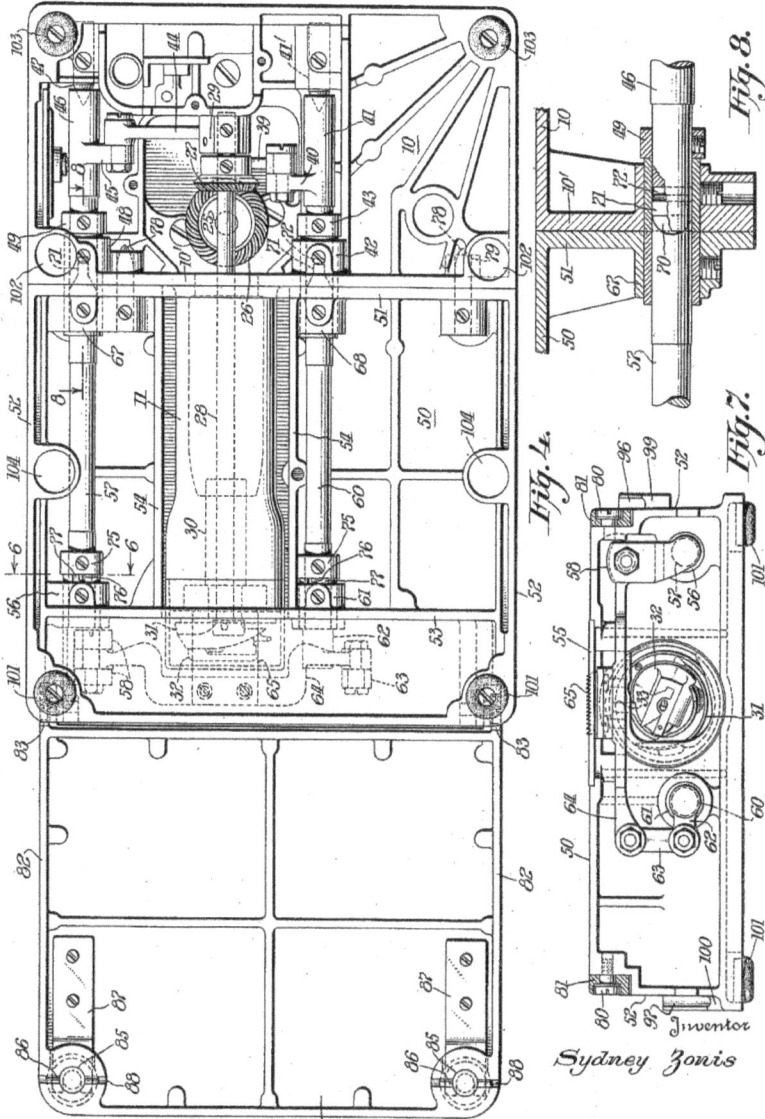

Fig. 8.

Fig. 7.

Fig. 4.

Inventor

Sydney Zonis

Witness·
Godfrey Pecina

By

William F. Stewart

Attorney

131

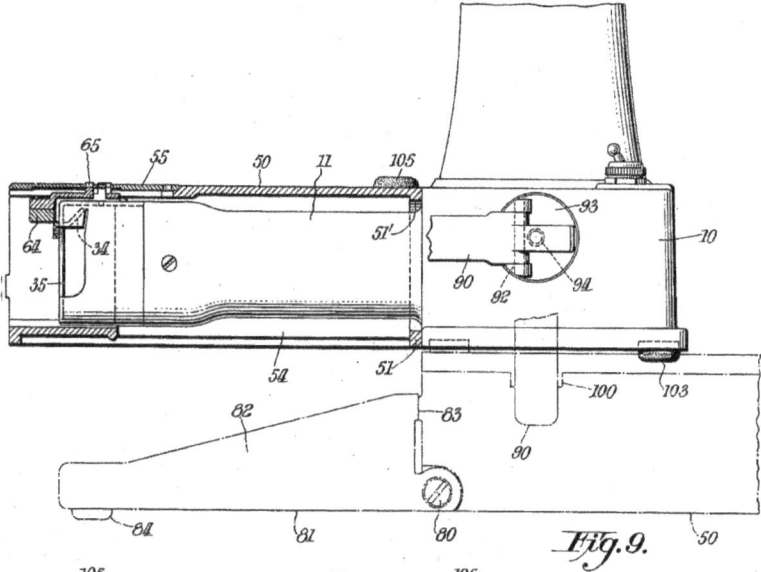

Fig.9.

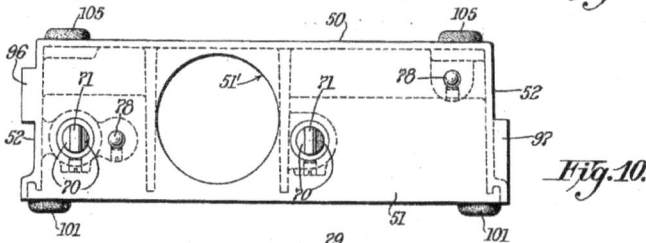

Fig.10.

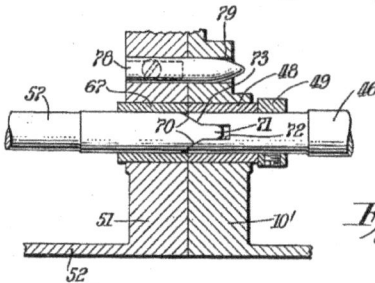

Fig.11.

Inventor
Sydney Zonis

Witness:
Godfrey Peeina

By William P. Stewart
Attorney

132

UNITED STATES PATENT OFFICE

2,424,872

CONVERTIBLE FLAT-BED AND CYLINDER-ARM SEWING MACHINE

Sydney Zonis, Bridgeport, Conn., assignor to The Singer Manufacturing Company, Elizabeth, N. J., a corporation of New Jersey

Application December 16, 1944, Serial No. 568,405

21 Claims. (Cl. 112—260)

1

This invention relates to sewing machines and more particularly to a sewing machine which may be readily changed from a flat-bed machine, used for general sewing purposes, to a cylinder-arm or bed machine.

A primary object of this invention is to provide a sewing machine which is quickly and easily convertible for use either as a flat-bed type sewing machine having work-feeding mechanism of the drop-feed type or as a cylinder work-arm type sewing machine in which the minimum size of the free end portion of the work-arm is limited solely by loop-taker mechanism which is complemental to the sewing machine needle in the formation of stitches.

This invention has also for its object to provide a sewing machine having a detachable flat work-supporting bed underlying the bracket-arm, which bed carries the work-advancing mechanism of the machine and, when removed, exposes a cylindrically shaped arm which carries the loop-taker and its actuating shaft.

Another object of this invention is to provide a sewing machine with a work-support and a feeding mechanism including a feed-dog operating through said work-support, in which sewing machine the work-support and the feeding mechanism in the stitch-forming region are together removable as a unit from the machine.

Another object of the invention is to provide a detachable flat work-supporting bed which may be removed from the machine to expose a cylinder arm, and the detached flat work-supporting bed used as a support for the machine for the purpose of providing substantial clearance beneath the cylinder arm.

Another object of this invention is to provide improved latching means for holding the detachable portion of the flat bed in position when it is used as a work-support and to hold the machine on the detachable flat bed when it is used as a support for the stitch-forming mechanism.

Another object of this invention is to provide the removable portion of the bed with end walls in which are journaled the feed-rock-shafts and to provide a feed-dog offset laterally from the feed-bar so as to overhang the end of the cylinder arm.

With the above and other objects in view, as will hereinafter appear, the invention comprises the devices, combinations and arrangements of parts hereinafter set forth and illustrated in the accompanying drawings of a preferred embodiment of the invention, from which the several features of the invention and the advantages

2

attained thereby will be readily understood by those skilled in the art.

The several features of the present invention will be clearly understood from the following description and accompanying drawings in which:

Fig. 1 is a front elevation of my improved combinational sewing machine showing the flat work-supporting bed in operative position, and the machine ready for use as a flat-bed machine.

Fig. 2 is a front elevation of my improved machine showing the flat bed removed for the purpose of converting the machine into a cylinder bed darning machine and the removable bed used as a support for the machine.

Fig. 3 is a top plan view of the machine shown in Fig. 1 with the bracket-arm removed.

Fig. 4 is a bottom plan view of the machine shown in Fig. 1.

Fig. 5 is a left end elevation of the cylindrical work-arm and base of the machine shown in Fig. 2.

Fig. 6 is a detailed sectional view taken along the line 6—6 of Fig. 4.

Fig. 7 is a view taken along the line 7—7 of Fig. 3.

Fig. 8 is a sectional view taken along the line 8—8 of Fig. 4.

Fig. 9 is a side elevation of the cylindrical arm with a central section through the flat bed and feed-dog, showing the position of the feed-dog and its relation to the cylindrical arm and the flat bed.

Fig. 10 is a right end elevation of the removable flat bed and Fig. 11 is an enlarged detail view showing the detachable connection between the rock-shaft in the bed and the actuating rock-shaft in the base.

In the embodiment of the invention selected for illustration, my improved convertible flat-bed and cylinder-arm machine comprises a base 10 having downturned side and end walls forming a rectangularly shaped enclosure. The bed 10 carries a laterally extending tubular-shaped work-supporting arm 11 and a bracket-arm 12 terminating in a hollow head 13.

Journaled in suitable bearings in the bracket-arm 12 is a shaft 14 having a balance-wheel 15 secured to one of its ends. The balance-wheel 15 is operatively connected by a belt 16 to an electric motor 17 carried by the base 10. A crank 18 is secured to the other end of the shaft 14 and is connected by a link 19 to a needle-bar 20 journaled in the hollow head 13 and carrying an eye-pointed needle 21. The above described mechanism is old and well known and reference

3

may be had to the patent to Goosman No. 2,063,841 of December 8, 1936, for a more detailed description.

Fixed to the shaft 14 is a gear 23 which meshes with a gear 24 fixed to the upper end of a vertical shaft 25, and fixed to the lower end of the shaft 25 is a gear 26 which meshes with a gear 27 secured upon a hook-shaft 28 journaled in a bearing 29 formed on the base 10 (Fig. 4) and a bearing 30 in the work-supporting cylindrically shaped arm 11. To the other end of the shaft 28 there is secured a rotary loop-taker 31 of the rotary hook lock-stitch type which is adapted to cooperate with the eye-pointed needle 21 in the formation of stitches. The loop-taker has journaled therein a bobbin-case 32 restrained against rotation by a finger 33 which extends upwardly from the bobbin-case and engages an inwardly extending portion 34 formed on the end wall of a sheet metal cap 35 which surrounds and houses the hook 32 and is secured to the work-supporting arm 11.

Secured to the shaft 14 are two cams 37, 38 which are adapted to impart rising and falling and feed and return movements to the feeding mechanism. The cam 37 is connected by a pitman 39 to an arm 40 (Fig. 4) formed on a rock-shaft 41. The rock-shaft 41 is journaled in the base 10, one of its ends being supported by the pintle bearing 41' and its other end extending into a sleeve bearing 42 formed in the downturned side wall 10' of the base 10. A collar 43 is secured to the rock-shaft 41 to prevent endwise movement thereof. The cam 38 is connected by a pitman 44 to an arm 45 on the rock-shaft 46, one end of which is pivotally supported by the pintle bearing 47 in the base 10, and the other end journaled in a bearing 48 formed in the end wall 10'. A collar 49 is secured to the rock-shaft 46 to restrain the shaft against endwise movement relative to its bearings. The shape of the ends of the rock-shafts 41 and 46, proximate to the side wall 10; and their functions will be hereinafter described.

Fitted over the work-supporting arm 11 is a rectangularly shaped bed 50 having downturned side walls 52 and a downturned end wall 51 formed with a work-arm clearance aperture 51'. The bed 50 is also formed with a downwardly extending wall 53, arranged parallel to the end-wall 51, and centrally arranged walls 54 located on opposite sides of the work-supporting arm 11.

Journaled beneath the bed 50 in the bearing 56, at one side of the work-supporting arm 11, is a feed-advance and return rock-shaft 57 which extends through the bearing 56 and has secured to its free end an upstanding arm 58. Also journaled beneath the bed 50 and located on the opposite side of the work-supporting arm 11 from the rock-shaft 57, is a second rock-shaft 60 which is adapted to impart a rising and falling movement to the feed-dog. The shaft 60 extends through the bearing 61 and fixed to its end is an arm 62 which is connected by means of a vertically arranged link 63 to one end of a feed-bar 64 laterally offset as shown in Fig. 4 to provide clearance for the end of the work-supporting arm 11. A feed-dog 65 is secured to the feed-bar 64 and extends laterally from the feed-bar 64 to a point overlying the loop-taker 31 and into a position in which it extends through suitable slots in the throat-plate 55 and cooperates with a presser-foot 36 carried by a presser-bar 36'. The other end of the feed-bar 64 is pivotally secured to the arm 58 on the rock-shaft 57. It will be

4

understood that with these connections when the rock-shafts 57 and 60 are oscillated about their longitudinal axis in the proper timed relation a four-motion feeding movement is imparted to the feed-dog 65.

The other ends of the rock-shafts 57 and 60 are journaled in and extend through the bearings 67, 68 in the wall 51 of the bed 50. The end portion of each of the shafts 57 and 60 which extends through its respective bearing is formed with convergently inclined sides 70 terminating in an axially extending tongue 71 (Fig. 11) which is adapted to enter a slot 72 having divergent side walls 73 and formed in the end of the rock-shafts 46 or 41. In order to limit turning movement of the rock-shafts 57 and 60 about their longitudinal axis when the bed 50 is removed, each of the rock-shafts 57 and 60 has secured thereto a collar 75 carrying a laterally extending pin 76 which enters a notch 77 formed in their respective bearings 56 and 61 (Figs. 4 and 6). With this arrangement when the bed 50 is replaced to cover the arm 11 after having been removed, the rock-shafts 57 and 60 will be retained in a position in which the free end of their extending tongues 71 will engage the divergent side walls 73 and cam the rock-shafts 57 and 60 into positions in which the tongues 71 will enter the slots 72. To guide the bed 50 to the correct position relative to the base 10 the end wall 51 of the bed 50 is provided with two laterally extending dowel pins 78 each having a bullet shaped nose adapted to enter one of the apertures 79 in the base 10.

To the corners of the bed 50 located to the left of the stitch-forming mechanism there is pivotally secured by the screws 80 an extension plate 81 formed with depending side walls 82 which are inclined downwardly from the free end toward the machine. To limit the downward movement of the extension plate 81, the lower ends of the side walls 82 are arranged to abut the ends of the side walls 52 of the bed 50 at the points 83. The extension plate 81 enlarges the area of the work-support when the extension is in its horizontal position and the pivotal support permits the extension plate to be raised to a vertical position to decrease the overall length of the machine when it is not in use.

Located at the corners on the left end of the extension plate 81 are foot-pads 84 each of which is carried by a post 85 having a transverse pin 86 extending therethrough. Each of the foot-pads is located in a depression in the extension plate 81 and is urged upwardly by a flat spring 87. It will be obvious from Fig. 1 that, by turning the foot-pad 84 and post 85, the ends of the lateral pins 86 will enter slots 88 and the foot-pad 84 will be raised above the level of the surface of the extension plate 81 and resiliently held in that position by the spring 87.

In order to hold the bed 50 in the correct position relative to the base 10 I have provided latches 90 and 91 made of spring strips and located on the front and back of the base 10. Each of the latches is pivotally secured at 92 to a disk 93 which is adapted to turn about a horizontal pivot-pin 94 journaled in a suitable bearing in the base 10. Each of the latches 90 and 91 has its free end bent back upon itself to form a hook and the ends of these latches are adapted to extend over the lugs 96 and 97 formed on the bed 50 to hold the bed 50 firmly on the base 10.

When desirable, the flat-bed machine shown in Fig. 1 may be converted to the cylinder-arm machine shown in Fig. 2 by first releasing the

5

latches 90, 91 from the lugs 96 and 97, then moving the bed 50 and the portion of the feeding mechanism carried thereby to the left as a unit until the bed is clear of the arm 11. The foot-pads 84 are now released and assume the position shown in Fig. 2. The bed 50 is provided on the work-supporting side thereof and in the region of the base 10 with upstanding rubber-feet 105. When the bed is inverted, it rests upon the foot-pads 84 and the rubber-feet 105 as illustrated in Fig. 2.

The bed has front and rear feet 101 and the base 10 has front and rear feet 103 which are complemental to the feet 101 as a support for the machine as illustrated in Fig. 1. When the bed is detached and inverted as above described, the base 10 is placed thereupon so that the feet 101 of the bed enter circular apertures 102 provided in the base 10, and the feet 103 of the base 10 enter apertures 104 formed in lugs provided on the side walls 52 of the bed 50. The arrangement produces an interlock between the bed 50 and the machine and prevents the machine from shifting laterally relative to the bed when it is operated. The latches 90 and 91, as previously described, are pivotally supported and may be swung to a depending position in which they cooperate with lugs 99 and 100 formed on the side walls of the bed 50 to securely hold the machine on the bed.

As shown in Fig. 9, the throat-plate 55 on the bed 50 is spaced above the cap 35 on the arm 11, the presser-foot 36 being adapted to rest on the throat-plate 55, and responding to upward movement of the feed-dog 65. When the bed 50 is removed, the presser-foot 36 is held slightly above the upper surface of the cap 35 by the presser-bar 36' which is limited in its downward movement by any suitable means. This construction provides clearance between the presser-foot and the work-supporting arm for the shifting of the material during darning or other stitching operations.

From the above description, it will be understood that my improved machine may be readily converted from a flat bed general purpose machine to a cylinder-bed machine. It will be observed that the flat bed may be quickly removed to expose the cylinder-arm and that as the flat-bed carries the feed-advancing mechanism it is removed from the machine with the bed. When the machine is converted to a work-arm type machine, the extension plate 81 forms a support against tilting of the machine when pressure or weight is applied at the free end of the cylinder-arm; ample work space being provided beneath the arm 11 due to the inclined sides 82 of the extension plate.

Having thus set forth the nature of the invention, what I claim herein is:

1. A sewing machine having in combination, a base, a work-supporting arm extending therefrom, a bracket-arm carried by said base and located above said work-supporting arm, feed-actuating mechanism within said base, a rectangularly shaped bed adapted to fit over said work-supporting arm to provide a flat work-supporting surface, said bed carrying feeding mechanism for advancing the material, and means for operatively connecting the feeding mechanism in the bed with the feed-actuating mechanism in the base when said bed is fitted over said arm.

2. A sewing machine having in combination, a base, a cylindrically shaped arm extending from said base and having loop-taking mechanism at

6

its free end, feed-actuating mechanism located within said base, a bed removably fitted over said arm and having a flat work-supporting surface, a feed-bar and feed-dog carried by said bed, and means for operatively connecting said feed-bar with the feed-actuating mechanism within the base.

3. A sewing machine having in combination, a bracket-arm terminating in a hollow head, a work-supporting arm underlying said bracket-arm and having a free end terminating beneath said hollow-head, sewing instrumentalities including a needle carried by said head, a loop-taker carried by said work-supporting arm and cooperating with said needle, a bed overlying said work-supporting arm, said bed being provided with work-feeding mechanism, and means for detachably securing said bed to said machine whereby the bed and feeding mechanism may be removed as a unit.

4. A sewing machine having in combination a laterally extending work-supporting arm, a loop-taker carried by said arm, a flat work-supporting bed overlying said arm, four-motion feeding mechanism carried by said bed and arranged exteriorly of said arm, and means for detachably securing said bed to the machine.

5. A sewing machine convertible from a flat-bed machine to a darning machine and having a base carrying an overhanging bracket-arm, a work-supporting arm carried by said base and located beneath said bracket-arm, feed-actuating mechanism within the base including a feed-lift and a feed-advance rock-shaft, a removable flat bed embracing said work-supporting arm, a feed-lift and a feed-advance rock-shaft carried by said bed, a feed-bar and feed-dog actuated by said last mentioned rock-shaft, and separable operative connections between the rock-shafts in said base and the rock-shafts carried by said bed.

6. A sewing machine convertible from a flat-bed machine to a cylinder arm machine comprising, a sewing machine having actuating mechanism and a tubular work-support in which a shaft carrying a loop-taker is journaled, a flat bed adapted to fit over said arm, said bed carrying work-advancing mechanism, means for detachably securing said bed to said machine, and means for operatively connecting the work-advancing mechanism in the bed with the actuating mechanism of the machine when the bed is fitted over the tubular work-support of the machine.

7. In a sewing machine having a frame comprising a base, a cylindrical work-arm extending from said base and having a free end, and a bracket-arm rising from said base and terminating in a head overhanging the free end portion of said work-arm, in combination, a reciprocatory needle-bar journaled in said head and carrying an eye-pointed needle, means for reciprocating said needle, a rotary loop-taker housed within the free end portion of said work-arm and complemental to said needle in the formation of stitches, means for rotating said loop-taker, a flat-bed work-support detachably secured upon said base, a feed-dog disposed externally of said work-arm and operating through said work-support, and feed-dog actuating mechanism including separable connections in part journaled in said base and in part journaled in said flat-bed work-support.

8. A sewing machine having in combination, a base, a bracket-arm carried by said base and terminating in a head, a reciprocatory eye-pointed needle carried by said head, loop-seizing means

135

7

located below said head and cooperating with said needle in the formation of stitches, a removable flat bed secured to said base, and disposed between said head and loop-seizing means, and feeding mechanism carried by said base whereby said bed and feeding mechanism can be removed from said bed as a unit.

9. A sewing machine having in combination, a base, a bracket-arm carried by said base and terminating in a head, a reciprocatory eye-pointed needle carried by said head, loop-seizing means located below said head and cooperating with said needle in the formation of stitches, a removable flat bed overlying said loop-seizing means, feed rock-shafts and a feed-bar and feed-dog carried by said bed, and latch means for releasably securing said bed to said base.

10. A sewing machine having in combination, a base, a work-supporting arm extending therefrom, a bracket-arm carried by said base and located above said work-supporting arm, actuating mechanism within said base including rock-shafts, a detachable rectangularly shaped bed having depending walls and adapted to fit over said work-supporting arm to provide a flat work-supporting surface, rock-shafts journaled in said bed and having their ends extending through one of said walls, and means connecting the ends of said rock-shafts with the rock-shafts in the base.

11. A sewing machine having in combination, a base, a work-supporting arm extending therefrom, a bracket-arm carried by said base and located above said work-supporting arm, actuating mechanism within said base including rock-shafts, a detachable rectangularly shaped bed having depending walls and adapted to fit over said work-supporting arm to provide a flat work-supporting surface, rock-shafts journaled in said bed, means detachably connecting the ends of said rock-shafts with the rock-shafts in the base, and means for limiting the movement of the rock-shafts in the bed about their longitudinal axes, whereby the rock-shafts in the bed are maintained in a position so that they may be connected to the rock-shafts in the base in their correct radial position.

12. A sewing machine having in combination, a base member, a work-supporting arm extending therefrom, a bracket-arm carried by said base member and located above said work-supporting arm, actuating mechanism within said base member, a detachable rectangularly shaped bed member having depending walls and adapted to fit over said work-supporting arm to provide a flat work-supporting surface, rock-shafts journaled in said bed member and having their ends extending through one of said walls, means connecting the ends of said rock-shafts with the actuating mechanism in said base member, and a dowel pin carried by one of said members and entering an aperture in the other of said members for guiding and holding said members in their correct position relative to each other.

13. A sewing machine having in combination, a base, a work-supporting arm extending therefrom, a bracket-arm carried by said base and located above said work-supporting arm, actuating mechanism within said base including rock-shafts, a detachable rectangularly shaped bed having depending walls and adapted to fit over said work-supporting arm to provide a flat work-supporting surface, rock-shafts journaled in the walls of said bed, and detachable mechanical connections be-

8

tween the rock-shafts in the base and the rock-shafts carried by said bed.

14. A sewing machine having in combination, a base, a work-supporting arm extending therefrom, a bracket-arm carried by said base and located above said work-supporting arm, actuating mechanism within said base including rock-shafts, a detachable rectangularly shaped bed having depending walls and adapted to fit over said work-supporting arm to provide a flat work-supporting surface, rock-shafts journaled in the walls of said bed and detachably connected to the rock-shafts in said base, and a feed-bar having its ends operatively connected to the rock-shafts in the bed, said feed-bar being formed with an offset portion to provide clearance for the free end of the work-supporting arm.

15. A sewing machine having in combination, a base, a work-supporting arm extending therefrom, a bracket-arm carried by said base and located above said work-supporting arm, actuating mechanism within said base, a rectangularly shaped bed having depending walls and adapted to fit over said work-supporting arm to provide a flat work-supporting surface, said flat bed being spaced slightly above the work-supporting arm, feed-actuating mechanism carried by said flat bed and detachably connected to the actuating mechanism in the base, and a feed-dog located in the space between the flat-bed and work-supporting arm, said feed-dog being given a four-motion movement by said actuating mechanism.

16. A sewing machine having in combination, a base, a work-supporting arm extending therefrom, a bracket-arm carried by said base and located above said work-supporting arm, actuating mechanism within said base, a rectangularly shaped bed having depending side and end-walls forming an enclosure, said bed being adapted to fit over said work-supporting arm and to be detachably secured to said base to provide a flat work-supporting surface, rock-shafts journaled in said bed and having their ends extending through one of said walls, means detachably connecting the ends of said rock-shafts with the actuating mechanism in the base, a feed-bar actuated by said rock-shafts, and a feed-dog carried by said feed-bar.

17. A sewing machine having in combination, a base, a work-supporting arm extending therefrom, a bracket-arm carried by said base and located above said work-supporting arm, actuating mechanism within said base, a rectangularly shaped bed having depending side and end-walls forming an enclosure, said bed being detachably secured to said base and spaced above said work-supporting arm, rock-shafts journaled in said bed and having their ends extending through one of said walls, means detachably connecting the ends of said rock-shafts with the actuating mechanism in the base, a feed-bar actuated by said shafts and having an offset portion to provide clearance for the free end of the work-supporting arm, and a feed-dog carried by said feed-bar and extending into the space between the bed and the work-supporting arm.

18. A sewing machine adapted to be converted from a flat-bed machine to a darning machine and having in combination, a base, a work-supporting arm extending therefrom, a bracket-arm carried by said base and located above said work-supporting arm, a rectangularly shaped bed having depending side and end-walls forming an enclosure, said bed being removably fitted over said work-supporting arm and detachably secured

9

thereto to provide a readily removable flat work-supporting surface, and supporting means located on the bottom of said bed and adapted to cooperate with the base of said machine whereby the flat bed may be removed from the machine and used in an inverted form as a pedestal to support the darning machine.

19. A sewing machine adapted to be converted from a flat-bed machine to a cylinder bed darning machine and having in combination, a base, a work-supporting arm extending therefrom, a bracket-arm carried by said base and located above said work-supporting arm, a rectangularly shaped bed having depending side and end-walls and adapted to fit over said work-supporting arm to provide a flat work-supporting surface, said bed being removably secured to said base, an extension plate pivotally secured to said bed, and means carried at an edge of the side and end walls of said bed for supporting said base, whereby the flat bed may be removed from the machine and used in an inverted form as a pedestal for the darning machine with the extension plate on the base located beneath the work-supporting arm.

20. A sewing machine having in combination a bracket-arm terminating in a hollow head, a work-supporting arm underlying said bracket-arm and having a free end terminating beneath said hollow head, stitch forming devices including loop-taker actuating mechanism disposed within and extending lengthwise of said work-supporting arm, a bed removably fitted over said

10

work-supporting arm, work feeding mechanism for advancing work crosswise of said arm, said work feeding mechanism including a four-motion feed-dog disposed externally of said arm and operating through said bed, and feed-dog actuating connections extending lengthwise of said work-supporting arm.

21. A convertible sewing machine having in combination a laterally extending work-supporting arm, a loop-taker carried by said arm, a removable flat work-supporting bed adapted to fit over said arm to form a flat work supporting surface, a work-advancing feed-dog disposed externally of said arm and operating through said bed, substantially parallel feed-advance and feed-lift rock-shafts each comprising endwise separable shaft sections, means for actuating said rock-shafts, and operable connections with sections of said rock-shafts remote from said means for actuating said feed-dog.

SYDNEY ZONIS.

REFERENCES CITED

The following references are of record in the file of this patent:

UNITED STATES PATENTS

Number	Name	Date
2,247,383	Hohmann et al.	July 1, 1941
2,360,048	Christensen	Oct. 10, 1944
2,325,510	Heggie	July 27, 1943
2,350,807	Parry	June 6, 1944

Summary

Summary

As you read in the previous pages, the SINGER Model 221 and 222 designs were not the accomplishment of one or two designers. Pratt, Chason, Goosman, Fleckenstein, Marsac, Graesser, Eaton, Hohmann, Osann, and Zonis were only the ones that I was able to identify. Many more that remain unknown also contributed.

I hope you enjoyed this book and that it answered most of your questions. I am sure it also raised some new questions.

Copies of all the patent applications in this book are available thru the United States Patent Office, or the British Patent Office.

Digitally restored larger copies suitable for framing with higher clarity and resolution are also available from the author. Contact author by email at Dar-bet@att.net for information on ordering, price and shipping. For more about these copies, and for more about the Featherweight sewing machine, visit my websites and see my book

"the Featherweight Ads"

www.DarrelKaiserBooks.com
www.SewingMachineTech.com

Books by Darrel P. Kaiser
www.DarrelKaiserBooks.com

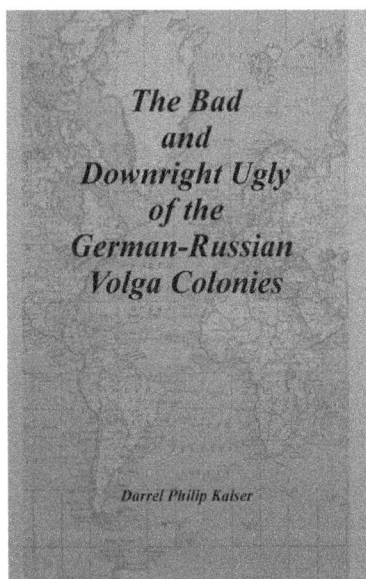

Origin & Ancestors
Families
Karle & Kaiser
of the
German-Russian Volga Colonies

Adolf	Heylmann	Roth
Andreas	Hieronimus	Rudolph
App	Horn	Schaeffer
Arnst	Ikdadi	Scherer
Becker	Kaiser	Schiller
Bapp	Kurz	Schmiedt
Barbach	Köhler	Schneider
Degenhien	Krämer	Schütz
Fohl	Lieders	Simon
Freund	Maurer	Stolz
Geringer	Michel	Trieber
Grün	Neff	Trippel
Hart	Neumann	Vogt
Helbod	Nicolausen	Werner
Hermann	Nillmayer	Will
Hess	Popp	Zelchmann

Darrel Philip Kaiser

Moscow's
Final Solution:
The Genocide
of the
German-Russian
Volga Colonies

Darrel Philip Kaiser

Religions
of Germany
and the
German-Russian
Volga Colonies

Darrel Philip Kaiser

The Bad
and
Downright Ugly
of the
German-Russian
Volga Colonies

Darrel Philip Kaiser

Books by Darrel P. Kaiser
www.DarrelKaiserBooks.com

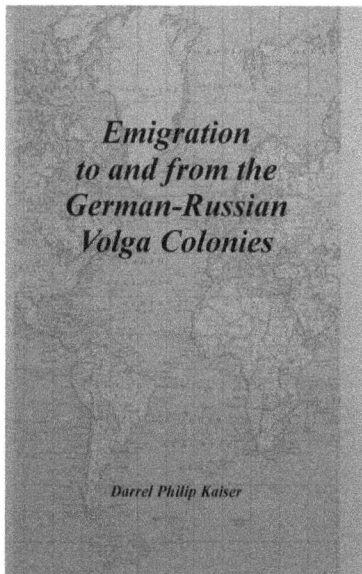

Emigration to and from the German-Russian Volga Colonies

Darrel Philip Kaiser

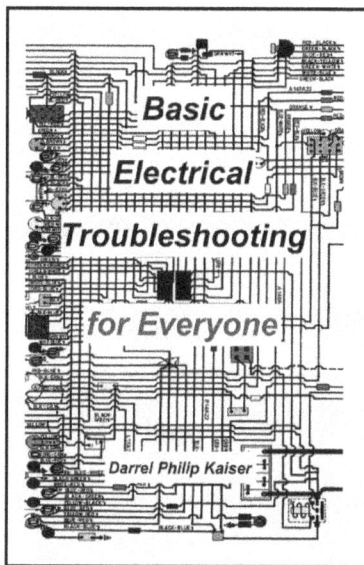

Basic Electrical Troubleshooting for Everyone

Darrel Philip Kaiser

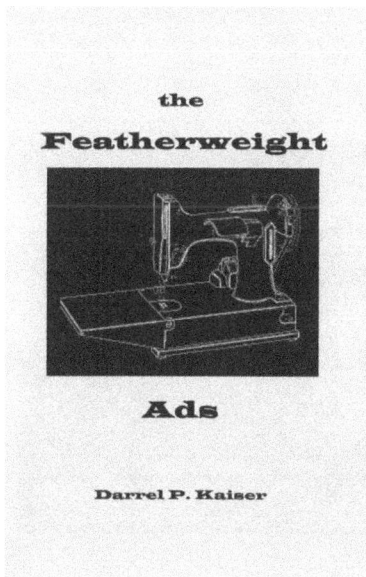

the Featherweight

Ads

Darrel P. Kaiser

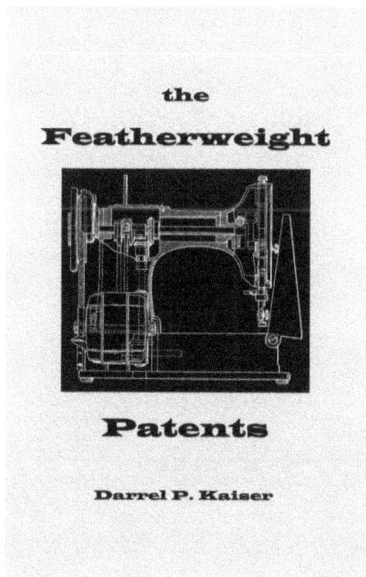

the Featherweight

Patents

Darrel P. Kaiser

Books by Darrel P. Kaiser
www.DarrelKaiserBooks.com

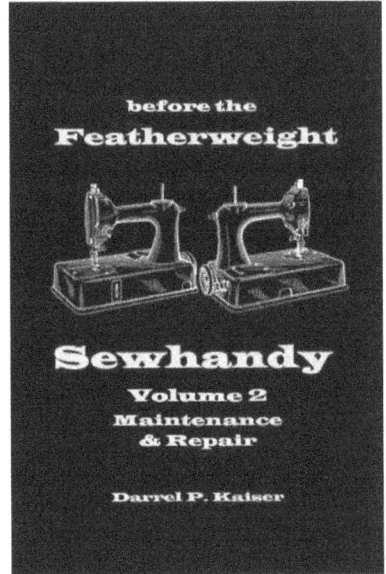

before the
Featherweight

Sewhandy
Volume 1
History

Darrel P. Kaiser

before the
Featherweight

Sewhandy
Volume 2
Maintenance
& Repair

Darrel P. Kaiser

**Logical
Sewing Machine
Troubleshooting**

ALL BRANDS

ANTIQUE - COMPUTER

for Everyone

Darrel Philip Kaiser

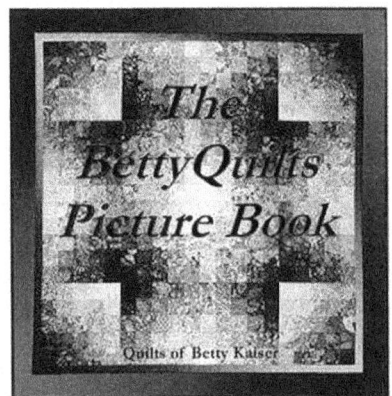

*The
BettyQuilts
Picture Book*

Quilts of Betty Kaiser

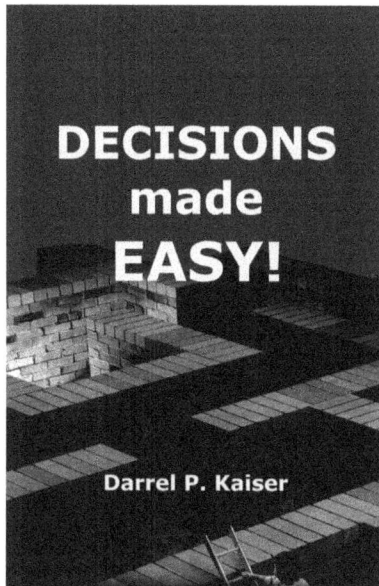

www.ingramcontent.com/pod-product-compliance
Lightning Source LLC
La Vergne TN
LVHW011239080426
835509LV00005B/550